CW00747616

Rethinking the Western Understanding of the Self

In this book, Ulrich Steinvorth offers a fresh analysis and critique of rational-ity as a defining element in Western thinking. Criticizing revelation, tradition, and collectivism, Western thinking champions rationality, human rights, and individualism, and culminates in a unique understanding of the self. The pre-vailing understanding of the self was formed by the Lockean conception and utilitarianism. Compatible with classical physics, it does not, however, explain the cataclysms that occurred in the twentieth century. Steinvorth argues that Descartes's understanding of the self offers a more plausible and realistic alter-native. When freed from the dualism in which Descartes conceived it, such a conceptualization enables us to distinguish between self and subject. Moreover, it enables us to understand why individual rights – one of the hallmarks of modernity and the West – became a universal ideal to be granted to every mem-ber of society; how acceptance of this notion could peak in the seventeenth cen-tury; and why it is now in decline, though not irreversibly so. Most importantly, as Steinvorth demonstrates, the Cartesian concept of the self presents a way of saving modernity from the dangers that it now encounters.

Ulrich Steinvorth is professor of philosophy at Bilkent University in Ankara. He has taught at Hamburg and other German universities and as a guest pro-fessor at French and American universities. He is editor of *Rechtsphilosophische Hefte*, is on the Advisory Board of *Wittgenstein Studies*, and has published a dozen books on topics in political philosophy, ethics, and metaphysics.

Rethinking the Western Understanding of the Self

Ulrich Steinvorth

CAMBRIDGE
UNIVERSITY PRESS

CAMBRIDGE UNIVERSITY PRESS
Cambridge, New York, Melbourne, Madrid, Cape Town, Singapore, São Paulo, Delhi

Cambridge University Press
32 Avenue of the Americas, New York, NY 10013–2473, USA

www.cambridge.org
Information on this title: www.cambridge.org/9780521757072

© Ulrich Steinvorth 2009

This publication is in copyright. Subject to statutory exception
and to the provisions of relevant collective licensing agreements,
no reproduction of any part may take place without the written
permission of Cambridge University Press.

First published 2009

Printed in the United States of America

A catalog record for this publication is available from the British Library.

Library of Congress Cataloging in Publication data
Steinvorth, Ulrich.
  Rethinking the Western understanding of the self / Ulrich Steinvorth.
    p.   cm.
  Includes bibliographical references and index.
  ISBN 978-0-521-76274-8 (hardback) – ISBN 978-0-521-75707-2 (pbk.)
    1. Self (Philosophy) – Europe.   2. Descartes, René, 1596–1650.   I. Title.
  BD438.5.S74 2009
  126.09–dc22   2008050508

ISBN 978-0-521-76274-8 hardback
ISBN 978-0-521-75707-2 paperback

Cambridge University Press has no responsibility for the persistence or
accuracy of URLS for external or third-party Internet Web sites referred to in
this publication and does not guarantee that any content on such Web sites is,
or will remain, accurate or appropriate. Information regarding prices, travel
timetables, and other factual information given in this work are correct at
the time of first printing, but Cambridge University Press does not guarantee
the accuracy of such information thereafter.

Contents

Preface

Though I have tried to give every chapter a unity, this book is no collection of papers. It is the exposition and defense of a thesis on the self, rationality, and the social world in the order I found most convincing. I think it is best to follow it, though I do not want to exclude that a reader who follows another order can come to a better understanding.

In writing the book I found most agreeable and useful help for which I want to express my gratitude: to Sabine Jentsch for her discussion of many topics, in particular that of perfectionism, for asking so many intelligent questions, so few of which I was able to answer, and for pointing out a lot of mistakes; to Thomas Besch for confirming my intention to write the book; to Radu Bogdan for practical advice; to Robin Turner for correcting my English and commenting on my views; and to Ed Dunkley for the interest he showed in my book. Of course, neither they nor anyone else can be blamed for the mistakes that have survived. I also found it agreeable to think that the book might be of use for my children and grandchildren, to whom I dedicate it.

Important though I think my reflections are, I am fully aware how far they are from exhausting our understanding of the self, rationality, and the social world. They cannot be but the continuation of reflections that have been started by theorists, some of whom I have exploited, and badly need correction and continuation by other authors.

Bilkent/Ankara
September 2008

Part I

Introduction

You are not thinking. You are merely being logical.
Niels Bohr to Albert Einstein

Chapter 1

The West and the Self

THIS BOOK ATTEMPTS TO RETHINK THE RATIONALITY THAT DEVELOPED in the West. The West has its origins in ancient Greece, Rome, and Christianity, but it is guided by ideas propagated and pursued by the Enlightenment. These ideas replaced or enriched traditional religion with belief in the value of the individual and her rational powers and inalienable rights, and with trust in science and technology, production, and trade. Openness to these ideas constitutes modernity,[1] with which the West can be identified. It constitutes a specific rationality, a way of justifying and explaining actions, that is oriented to utility, happiness, and individuality. The West can be defined neither geographically nor historically but only by its ideas and its superior rationality. This at least is the self-understanding of the West.

In a formal sense, there can be only one rationality. In this sense rationality is a way of thinking that follows the rules of logic. Though different logics have been developed, they are different interpretations of logical thinking rather than different rationalities. All civilizations have standards of how to judge, and hence possibly change, their habits and traditions. Such standards allow for detecting logical inconsistencies in one's intentions. Yet they may also allow for

---

[1] Huntington, "The West: Unique, Not Universal," argues that modernization does not imply Westernization; Inglehart, *Culture and Democracy*, musters empirical evidence that in the long run it implies democratization. Similarly, Roy, *Globalized Islam*, 14. Fukuyama, *The End of History and the Last Man*, 126, argues that "Modern natural science has provided us with a Mechanism whose progressive unfolding gives both a directionality and a coherence to human history over the past several centuries," yet 234–44 comes closer to Huntington. I understand modernity as an attitude that favors individuality in a sense to be explored in this book, and civilization in a sense explained by Braudel, *A History of Civilizations*: Civilization in the singular means "broadly the opposite of barbarism" (4); in the plural it refers to different ways to oppose barbarism and to solve basic social problems. Huntington, "The Clash of Civilizations?," 30, approvingly quotes Braudel on civilization, yet from another work.

detection of what Max Weber called value rationality. There are as many value rationalities as there are ultimate values by which practical rightness of thought and action are judged, not logical truth. It is in this broader sense of rationality that the West has produced a rationality that claims superiority to alternatives.

Its claim is based on the idea that value rationality is measured by a general value that eschews the arbitrariness of using one rather than another specific value for a standard. This standard is most often understood as utility or happiness. Yet since Rousseau has opposed liberty to happiness, critics, implicitly or explicitly, oppose liberty, authenticity, or even the superhuman to the value of happiness and accuse Western or modern thinking of having degenerated into a logic that enslaves man, ruins nature, and produces world wars and extermination camps.[2] I agree with this critique of utility but reject the premise that it is identical to Western rationality. Rather, the West has produced two competing versions of the idea of an orientation to a general value; one for which happiness is the highest value and another for which it is the constructive enactment of one's capabilities. This book will defend the second conception.

The two conceptions share the immensely important property of enabling a society to reject traditions that do not stand up to its rational judgment. They liberate it from culture dependency.[3] A society that develops a conception of rationality, whether it orients to utility or capabilities, becomes forward looking and cannot but believe in progress,[4] as its rationality delivers a criterion of rightness. So despite all the differences of the two rationalities that I'll indicate, they agree in their commitment to the rejection of all traditions that do not stand up to rational judgment. Rethinking rationality is not abandoning it. Yet it makes a difference whether rationality is measured by utility or capability enactment, and a lot of criticism that is leveled against the West in fact can be leveled only against its utilitarian rationality.

Rationality and the concept of the self are closely interwoven. It was Europe's seventeenth century that developed two incompatible conceptions of the

---

[2] The criticism starts with Rousseau, was continued by Nietzsche, and in the twentieth century found its most prominent advocates in Heidegger, Horkheimer, Adorno, and Hannah Arendt. On Muslim critics, cp. Chapter 22.

[3] I mean by *culture dependency* dependence on a culture that excludes its adaptation to nonrelativistic standards of rightness. Belief in it implies cultural relativism. For its criticism, cp. Robert Edgerton, "Traditional Beliefs and Practices," in Harrison and Huntington, *Culture and Criticism*, loc. cit. 126–40. The role of culture is well described by Daniel Patrick Moynihan: "The central conservative truth is that it is culture, not politics, that determines the success of a society. The central liberal truth is that politics can change a culture and save it from itself." (cited by Huntington in his Foreword to ibid., xiv.)

[4] As pointed out, among others, by Lawrence Harrison (in his Introduction to ibid., xxvi), the idea of progress, "of a longer, healthier, less burdensome, more fulfilling life – is not confined to the West; it is also explicit in Confucianism and in the creeds of a number of non-Western, non-Confucian high-achieving minorities – India's Sikhs, for example." It is an aim of this book to explicate what capability enactment is. Provisionally, I may explain it as talent development.

self: a Cartesian conception and a Lockean one that later merged with utilitarian rationality. Though the utilitarian approach has prevailed, it is the Cartesian conception that best preserves the values of the West, is most adequate to history and human nature, and inspires to envision a form of association that enables us to respond to the specific challenges of the present by allowing everyone to enact their capabilities. This is what this book aspires to convince its readers of. It defends the West by rejecting its prevailing Lockean understanding of both the self and itself (for a conception of the self implies a self-understanding as well). It aims at "promoting the coherence of the West" and of its "precious and unique civilization" by using its capacity to be self-correcting,[5] and recognizes that we "risk destabilizing the entire world, including the declared enemies of the United States," if we do not rewrite rationality.[6]

This book is addressed to the general public, both within and outside academia, that is interested in contemporary social and political development and the reasons and causes that have produced the present and restrict and open up the future. Though it has an eye on practice, it is a contribution to theory and tries to meet the standards of theory. It is to these standards that I subject the interpretation of the authors I examine: Descartes, Weber, Heidegger, Hannah Arendt, and Freud among them. Pointing out their contributions to a conception of the self that is adequate to human capabilities shows them in unexplored perspectives that will deepen our understanding of them. This is why the book is also addressed to university classes in political philosophy and theory, ethics, and the history of ideas that discuss those thinkers.

To introduce you to my venture, consider that until the seventeenth century, the West followed a conception of the self that was stamped by Aristotle and the Stoa. Though it never lost influence, in the eighteenth century it was eclipsed by Locke's conception of the self that in the nineteenth century combined with utilitarian psychology and action theory. The self has a central position in Western thought because the way it is conceived commits us to a conception

---

5   Huntington, "The West," 46. Former European Community President Jacques Delors urged that the "West needs to develop a deeper understanding of ... other civilizations" (quoted by Huntington, "If Not Civilizations, What?," 194). True, but still more it needs to understand its own civilization, else it sees itself too fast as the victim of other civilizations' (Islam's) plots or vices. The need for self-analysis and self-correction is pointed out by Alex Inkeles, *One World Emerging*, Boulder, CO (Westview) 1998, 83, and Michael Fairbanks, "Changing the Mind of a Nation," in Harrison and Huntington, loc. cit., 268–81, 273. Belief in civilizations does not imply that what are clashing today are civilizations. There probably are very different causes of today's violent conflicts. Nor does it imply what (in analogy to what Pogge, *World Poverty and Human Rights*, 139ff, calls *explanatory nationalism*) may be called justificatory culturalism, the view that economic underdevelopment can be blamed on domestic cultures.

6   Jacques Derrida in Giovanna Borradori, *Philosophy in a Time of Terror*, Chicago University Press, 2003, 93. Derrida, ibid, describes (value) rationality as "the system of interpretation, the axiomatic, logic, rhetoric, concepts, and evaluations that are supposed to allow one to *comprehend*."

of rationality and action, science and religion, and, most momentously, to a distinction of rational and individualist societies from less rational and more collectivist societies. Many Westerners felt that it was by this distinction that they differed from the rest of the world.[7] In philosophy the distinction appears in the development of the concept of mind.

The development starts when Plato distinguishes the "part of the soul with which it calculates" as its rational part and says it is "fighting a civil war" with another part of the soul, the seat of desires.[8] Thus, what has been called the higher faculties of the mind was distinguished from desire. The next step is Aristotle's distinction of active and passive reason and his exclusive ascription of the former to male Greeks. He declares "the male (to be) ruler and the female subject," and everyone "who participates in reason so far as to apprehend it but not to possess it" – that is, participates in passive reason only – to be "by nature slaves."[9] What rules the individual is active reason; it is by it that those who possess it are to rule the rest of mankind. Modern Europe will follow this idea, modifying it by the assertion that the faculty Aristotle ascribes only to male Greeks is given to everyone, though often tacitly, assuming that in fact it is used only by Europeans.

But Aristotle also ascribed to the ruling part of the soul an element that adds to its impersonal power of godlike reason a quality that will prove it to belong to an individual human self. This element is the power of deciding after deliberation "both to do and not to do" a possible action.[10] What we decide after deliberation depends not only on the reasons deliberated but also on our arbitrary will. Hence, reason as the faculty of deliberating reasons is inseparable from arbitrary will that decides differently in different individuals. The scholastics called the will enacted after deliberation free will and distinguished it from the power of free action, just as Aristotle had distinguished deliberate and voluntary action.[11] Descartes, as I'll explain, distinguished it as the self from the subject. I'll show that reason and the power of saying both *yes* and *no* to a proposition (that is, a possible action or a thought) can indeed rule both individuals and societies but is unfit for supporting any privilege for ruling.

---

[7] An example of this feeling is Rudyard Kipling's poem "The White Man's Burden"; cp. Chapter 6.

[8] Plato, *Republic*, bk. IV, 439d, 440b.

[9] Aristotle, *Politics* I, 1254b13–24. Aristotle distinguishes active and passive reason in *De anima*, 429b26–30a25.

[10] Aristotle, *Nicomachean Ethics* III, 1110a18. He discusses here voluntary actions, but decisions that spring from a capacity both to do and not to do a possible action presuppose that the action is "choosable," Haireton (ibid., a12), hence presupposes deliberation. H. Rackham and Grube mistranslate the "and" as "or."

[11] In *Nicomachean Ethics* III, ch. 1–3. The Stoics developed a similar view about the power of *synkatathesis*, of assenting to propositions. Via Cicero, it was no less if not even more influential than Aristotle. On its influence on Descartes, see Hiram Caton, *The Origin of Subjectivity: An Essay on Descartes*, Yale University Press, 1973.

However, the Cartesian conception of a *self* was rejected by most post-Cartesian philosophers primarily for its commitment to free will. With Locke, they blunted its specificity by identifying the self with an individual's consciousness; with Hume, they abandoned the concept of a self; with Kant, they faded it to a transcendental idea that no empirical data can ever correspond to. Or they continued talking of the self in a Cartesian way, leaving its properties in the darkness of contradictory explanations. In such muddy conceptual waters, no clarification of the concept of the self might seem possible. Yet it was provided as a result of ideas developed by sociologists and psychologists in an attempt to solve problems of social and individual development.

The sociologists' problem concerned the analysis of premodern clan societies, called Asian form of production in the Marxist tradition and closed society by Popper. Such societies proved amazingly resistant to change until the twentieth century, in particular in their ancient Chinese and Indian form. How was this possible? Hegel was explicit in asking this question;[12] Marx tried an answer, yet only Max Weber was fully aware of the difficulties of overcoming the bonds of premodern society and the significance that breaking them had for the development of the individual self and man's rationality. He laid the ground for assigning a collectivist and authoritarian rationality and self to premodern societies and an individualist and fallibilist one to modern societies.

The psychologists' problem concerned the passage from childhood to adulthood. Weber had pointed out the difficulty and improbability of passing from collectivist to individualist societies that had not been fully recognized before him. Freud did so for the passage from a stage in which we trust in the infallible authority of parents to one in which we accept responsibility and fallibility. Freud's reflections led to a similarly radical distinction of an adult self and rationality from childhood ones. Though the conceptual status of the self remained obscure, Weber and Freud rendered any conception of the self obsolete that would not integrate their distinctions of an individualist form of a self and rationality from a preceding authoritarian form.

In fact, when Heidegger restarted reflection on the self, he took account of this distinction. Like Wittgenstein a decade later, Heidegger rejected the Lockean conception that defines the self as continuous consciousness. Yet unlike Wittgenstein, Heidegger, though perhaps he did not think of his predecessors Weber and Freud, distinguished two forms of a self: an inauthentic self, the self of *das Man* or *them*, that in the beginning, and ordinarily guides, the person; and an authentic self that extraordinarily, in rarer and special cases, directs her but is difficult to attain. Due to Weber, Freud, and Heidegger and in spite of its schism between the majority Lockean and the minority Cartesian conception of the self, the West has produced a concept of a two-phased self in which a collectivist and authoritarian self precedes an individualist and fallible one. The latter is

---

[12] In his *Philosophy of History*, when he analyzed what he calls the Persian empire.

considered preferable because it uses faculties that the former self does not. It is the self that Westerners have ascribed to themselves and denied non-Westerners. This distinction of two phases has found less attention than the schism on free will. Yet it is no less important. It raises the prevailing Western understanding of the Western self and its difference from that of other civilizations onto a conceptual level and, still more importantly, implies another distinction.

This is the distinction of an *ordinary* life, self and rationality dependent on the first stage, from the *extraordinary* actions an autonomous self performs by a rationality that is fallible but instigates extraordinariness. Weber even found in the necessary liaison of the autonomous self with extraordinariness the reason for the extraordinary achievements he ascribed to the West. Like the distinction between a rational individualist and an only imperfectly rational collectivist self, the commitment, or condemnation, of the autonomous self to extraordinariness is not necessarily felt by everyone who feels they are a member of the West, though (as we'll see) it was expressed in Kipling's, "The White Man's Burden" and other documents of imperialism. But it can be reconstructed from the Cartesian conception, and not from the Lockean one, and thus allows testing the superiority of the Cartesian conception by looking at historical facts, as I'll do in Chapters 6–9. Let me present a first explanation.

Descartes's great discovery is that we cannot enact our faculty of judgment without enacting our self. It results from his distinction between having experiences, including desires, beliefs, and doubts, and judging whether we should do what desires and beliefs suggest. The deliberate judgment is what I cannot distance myself from; hence, it is myself. It is something that does not happen to me; I can even arbitrarily judge against evidence; therefore, my self is not an impersonal reason but an individual power. This Cartesian argument, to be explicated later,[13] is darkened by its often dualistic dressing. But we can present it without recurring to any kind of dualism.[14]

What we desire and believe is something that happens to us. Though it happens to *us*, it *happens* to us; we can decide that we do not want it to happen. What happens to us constitutes only, as I'll use the terms, our *subject*, not our *self*. We also can distance ourselves from anything that we do and judge without deliberation. We can say that we could not resist it and thus can refuse to accept it as something that might constitute our *self*. Even if we have to judge a proposition that seems to offer no way to say *no* – if, for instance, we agree that $2 + 2 = 4$ – we

---

[13] In Chapters 2–5.

[14] In the twentieth century, Descartes was everyone's punching bag. Heidegger, Wittgenstein, the analytic philosophers, among others, tried proving their novelty by criticizing him. Belatedly, the fashion overtook leftists like Hardt and Negri, *Empire*, judging him "counterrevolutionary" and "cunning" in "effectively reaffirm(ing) dualism as the defining feature of experience and thought" (78–80) and basing the judgment on a defense of "immanence" that rejects an ontological difference of men from "simians and cyborgs" (91f). We need not be dualists to think such an immanence is just silly.

may say that it is not we who judge, as we do not decide but rather cannot resist agreeing. We can distance ourselves from our consent by stating that even the "peculiarly coercion-free coercive power of the better argument"[15] does not make our consent *our* consent. Only our deliberate decisions that we have been free to make and might have not made are what constitute our selves. From them we cannot distance ourselves without implying that our judgment has not been deliberate enough. Hence, we find our self in the power of judgment by which we can say *no* to any reason, also to moral ones. In this and only this quality, we remain identical over time. The self is what we are left with when we distance ourselves from anything that only happens to us, just as Descartes's *cogito* is what we cannot doubt after having doubted anything else. As we'll see, it is not only what renders reason, the power to weigh or deliberate arguments or reasons, an individual power, but also what makes us morally ambivalent and dangerous.

Deliberate decisions are at the same time acts of reason, of free will and of selves. They are acts of reason as we have to deliberate reasons for deciding deliberately. They are acts of free will as we may reject even the most evident reason (as Descartes argues) for the special reason that we want to demonstrate our independence of all predetermining factors. They are acts of selves, as we cannot distance ourselves from them. Our selves form a trinity with free will and reason.

Nevertheless, we are individuals who not only act (as a self), but also suffer (as a subject). As we are a unity of self and subject, we are creatures characterized by a specific dynamic and imbalance; for self and subject stand in a changing relation. Though necessarily we are led by the self, it is not the self but the subject that originally provides our existence with content and will always do so, though not exclusively. We start our existence as subjects that are free from any intervention of a self. We respond to our desires and other stimuli by following any impulse. Yet we can only avoid disaster if we develop controls for our spontaneous responses and initiatives. We learn most of such controls from our parents or other close persons. They represent to the pure subject the authority that controls the motions of the subject. We become adult when we take over the role of the control instance. This is only possible if, to the subject, the new instance of the self is added. To use Freud's terminology, when becoming adult we as the ego take over from the superego control of the id that represents our desires and constitutes the original subject. Yet once the self is added to the subject, conflicts between subject and self are bound to arise. As subjects we desire satisfaction of our desires; as selves we strive for the enactment of reason and free will.

Originally, the self, like the control authority of the parents, is only a means for attaining the aims set by the desires. But when we become selves, the

---

[15] This is how Habermas describes the power of argument on several occasions, e.g., *Theorie des kommunikativen Handelns* I, 28, 48, 552f; *Erkenntnis und Interesse*, 224 and 226.

enactment of this means becomes an end we pursue for its own sake, as the enactment of any capability is a delight for the agent. The self becomes master of the subject and is felt to be so. We cannot but be dissatisfied with restricting the self to satisfying the subject. What we demand is self-assertion. Desire satisfaction is what our life starts with; it is the ordinary. What we oppose to it, self-assertion, is the extraordinary. So the subject is necessarily associated with the ordinary and the self with the extraordinary. As what we deliberately decide is decided by our self and we aim at self-assertion, deliberate decisions follow the idea of the extraordinary, of something that denies any given desire or expectation, which are the ordinary. The self is inseparable from an ambition that pits it against the subject. As we'll see, this ambition can even survive the self.

If we can cull the story of the subject, the self and the ambition of extraordinariness, from an ideal-typical biography of modern man, we should also be able to cull it from a universal history of mankind; for there must have been a time in history when individuals started following their self rather than the social authority represented in the early individual as the superego. No society was ever able to survive without instances that control the spontaneous actions of individuals. In early human societies, control instances probably represented the authority of the strongest individuals, who may often have understood their judgments as revelations that were sent to them from divine powers. Already in such authoritarian societies some men have developed a self, and hence, craved for extraordinariness, as becomes plain in the conquests and adventures undertaken in many premodern societies. Yet they did not develop ideas that made it a duty for everyone to choose their life and develop a self, hence, to assert their self and to act extraordinarily. If we follow Weber, such ideas have been developed only by a special kind of salvation religion. Only by them could mankind take the step from childhood to adulthood. I'll examine how far history can confirm this Weberian reading of the Cartesian conception.

Once we understand the connection of judgment and extraordinariness, we can no longer explain action and history in terms of utilitarian rationality. Utilitarian rationality explains any action A as the conclusion from two premises: a premise P_1, understood to be either normative or descriptive, that agents strive for maximizing their happiness, and a descriptive premise P_2 that A will produce more happiness than any alternative to it. In contrast, Cartesian rationality explains an action as the agent's decision for the best way to enact her specific capabilities, including her capability to aim at extraordinariness. It does not enable us to predict an action, because the choice for how best to enact one's capabilities is never without arbitrariness. But it allows an understanding of actions that for utilitarian rationality are irrational or unexplainable.

An example is the set of decisions for what became World War One. These decisions were compatible with the intention to increase happiness only if we consider glory, even the glory of suffering, a form of happiness. If we do so, the idea of happiness becomes inflated and loses its meaning. The decisions for war are better understandable as decisions for the best way to enact the capabilities of those who had to decide. They are understandable as choices for extraordinariness. Utilitarian rationality led nineteenth-century liberals and socialists to expect peace and progress for the twentieth century. It blinded them to facts that might have warned them.[16] History is full of examples showing that the powerful preferred enacting their ambition of extraordinariness in war rather than in peaceful activities, if peace does not offer opportunity for extraordinariness, and that under the same condition the powerless preferred extraordinariness in the dissolution of their selves in supraindividual selves of tribes and ideologies.

If we are Cartesian rather than Lockean selves, we can expect history to show our ambition of extraordinariness not only in wars but also in constructive forms. In fact, even though utilitarian rationality did not allow Europeans to think of extraordinariness, they excelled in scientific, artistic, political, and economic activities. Such activities set positive values as objects to the indefinite and infinite craving for extraordinariness and transformed ambivalent ambition into the excellence of a discipline. Moreover, the spheres of science and art offered opportunities for escaping the restriction of extraordinariness to politics and the economy, the traditional fields of extraordinariness that sought political and economic power. However, to harness our ambition of extraordinariness today, we need to conceive and institute value spheres in a more comprehensive way than Weber did. We have to understand them as the core institutions of autonomous and even stateless societies that respond to a change in life conditions that is as deep as that to which the modern society of the past was the historical response.

To summarize the book, its idea is that we cannot understand the current complex problems of the West and the rest of the world, unless we understand how the West conceived of itself and the self. This idea is not new. It conforms to the everyday experience that to understand someone we must know her self-understanding and the way she reasons. Charles Taylor explicitly applied it to modernity. He attempted "to articulate and write a history of the modern identity," considered his attempt "the starting point for a renewed understanding of modernity," pointed out that "selfhood and morality" are "inextricably intertwined themes" and that in this relation morality is to be understood in a broad

---

[16] True, as Hannah Arendt, *The Origins of Totalitarianism*, 147, remarked, "the answer to the fateful question: why did the European comity of nations allow this evil" (of a war that she also compares to "some unredeemably stupid fatality," 267) to happen is that "the body politic was being destroyed from within." Yet one reason for this destruction was lacking understanding of extraordinariness. Herfried Münkler, *Empires*, 18–34, shows how little economic utilitarian theories of imperialism held by both social democrats (Sombart, Schumpeter, Hobson) and socialists (Luxemburg, Lenin) explain World War One. His insistence that recourse to "the striving for prestige" is unavoidable and cannot be consigned "to the realm of the irrational *tout court*." (31) agrees with the thesis of this book.

sense that includes "questions about what makes our lives meaningful or fulfill-ing." Though this book agrees on the aim, it differs from Taylor's approach by its different conception of the self.

Taylor describes "modern identity" as the "notion of what it is to be a human agent, a person, or a self," and as designating "the ensemble of (largely unartic-ulated) understandings of what it is to be a human agent: the senses of inward-ness, freedom, individuality, and being embedded in nature which are at home in the modern West." Though he gives agency a prominent place in his concep-tion of the self, it is only one element among others. He does not distinguish self and subject.[17] Yet, if we restrict the concept of the self to the element of agency, rather than exploring with Taylor the many facets of modernity and its devel-opment, we need to concentrate on the aspect of how individuals can and did detect their self and satisfy their ambition of extraordinariness. Concentrating on it has at least the pragmatic virtue of enabling me to be briefer than Taylor.

A last remark before I start my investigations. I have associated the ambi-tion of extraordinariness with the second phase of the self that Heidegger called authentic. So we have to conclude that no individual can be authentic without the ambition of extraordinariness. Isn't this plainly false? Are we not to deny anyone authenticity who is ambitious of extraordinariness? Such objection, however, would not be raised if we used the term *excellence* for *extraordinariness*. Striving after extraordinariness reeks of vulgarity; striving after excellence is the ambition of extraordinariness under a name that escapes the reproach. But talk of extraordinariness has the advantage of marking out that, first, extraordi-nariness is meaningful only in its contrast to something ordinary or vulgar and, second, we can be both extraordinarily good and extraordinarily evil. We can excel in crime and cannot be hindered from doing so by reason alone, as reason, even though it is the only means to distinguish right and wrong and true and false, is inseparable from self-assertion.

[17] Charles Taylor, *Sources of the Self: The Making of Modern Identity*, ix, and 3f.

Part II

Basics of Philosophical Psychology

*Man is a free agent; but he is not free if he does not believe it, for the
more power he attributes to Destiny, the more he deprives himself of
the power which God granted him when he gave him reason.*
Giacomo Casanova[1]

In this part, I examine Western understanding of the self. I start by expounding the two-phase conception in Heidegger and the basic role of judgment in Descartes, but point out their flaws in order to discount them right from the beginning. Heidegger succeeds in showing a radical difference between the childhood and the adult form of the self but fails to identify their crucial difference. Analysis of the difference will lead us to the Cartesian conception of the self, but also to his dualism that I want to show is not necessary for his conception of the self at all. The result of my argument is what I call the basics of philosophical psychology. It claims to present not the factual Western understanding of the self, but a reformulated form freed from its misconceptions.

[1]   Giacomo Casanova, *History of My Life*, Johns Hopkins University Press, 1966, Vol. 1, 26.

Part I

Basics of Philosophical Psychology

Chapter 2

Heideggerian and Cartesian Self

L IKE WITTGENSTEIN A DECADE LATER, HEIDEGGER REJECTED THE undifferentiated conception of the subject-self developed by empiricists in the seventeenth century. Yet unlike Wittgenstein, Heidegger replaced the subject-self by an unequal couple: an inauthentic self, the self of *das Man* or *them* (or the *man selbst*) that *ordinarily* guides the person; and an authentic self that does so *extraordinarily*, in special cases and times. Both his rejection of the traditional conception of the subject and his distinction of an inauthentic and an authentic self are momentous philosophical achievements. His conception of the authentic self, though, is burdened with problems. He starts his *Being and Time* by analyzing how we know or have access to our world, the world all men share and know they share. We do so by social interaction that precedes what according to empiricism is the first step in knowing the world, namely, its construction out of sense impressions by a subject-self.

To mark out the importance of this thesis, let me explicate it by Wittgensteinian ideas. The sense impressions that empiricists say the world is constructed from are given to the subject-self independently of its interaction with other individuals. They are private in the sense that others can never know what they are. So the world is as private and unrelated to other people as the sense impressions it is constructed from. Hence, empiricism suggests solipsism, the view that the only thing I know exists is my mind. Yet solipsism is too absurd to be accepted. This is why Kant called it a "scandal of philosophy and of rational common sense to be coerced to assume the existence of the things outside of us only as a belief."[1] Actually, most empiricists reject it. They interpret our sense impressions as evidence that the world is independent of

---

[1] Immanuel Kant, *Kritik der reinen Vernunft* B, xxxix fn.: "Skandal der Philosophie und allgemeinen Menschenvernunft." He refers to "psychological idealism," which I think can be identified with solipsism. Translation mine (as are all the following if a translator is not mentioned).

our consciousness, relying on the arguments of analogy ("some phenomena behave like me, hence they are selves like me") or best explanation ("phenomena are best predicted by conjecturing some of them exist independently of me"). Such arguments, though, accept that the common world is epistemologically dependent on a private one, so they cannot stop empiricism from inclining to solipsism. Heidegger and Wittgenstein, in contrast, claim that what we may call our private or subjective worlds are epistemologically dependent on the common world.[2]

There is probably sufficient evidence that our subjective worlds are epistemologically dependent on the common world indeed rather than the other way round. But we need not yet decide who is right in this controversy. What now is crucial to see is how different the model of the self is that Heidegger and Wittgenstein oppose to the empiricist model. The empiricists find its importance in its role as the epistemological world constructor. This seems to be a role comparable to a divine world creator that cannot be topped in importance. However, as we shall see, this role goes along with complete impotence in affecting the world. In contrast, the self Heidegger and Wittgenstein oppose to the empiricist one is distinguished by its capacity to act on the world, just because it is not its epistemological constructor. On this point they follow Descartes.

Now, Heidegger and Wittgenstein owe part of their reputation to their critique of Cartesianism; how can they contribute to the Cartesian conception of the self? What they rejected was Descartes's view that there can be a self without a body; hence, a solipsistic self. But they also implied that this view is a superfluous and distorting form Descartes gave to a conception that shows its virtues only when liberated from it. Heidegger even agreed with Descartes that the fact that we can *think* that nothing but our self exists tells us something of extreme philosophical importance.

Let us look at this match, for it will show that not only can Heidegger improve Descartes, but also Descartes Heidegger. Heidegger called the question "why there is anything at all rather than nothing"[3] – a question analytical philosophers argued is meaningless[4] – the "basic question of all ontology," "the question about the meaning of Being in general."[5] Whatever this question means,

---

2   Cp. my *Wittgenstein über den Willen* in *Wittgenstein Studies* 16, 2008, 185–212.

3   Martin Heidegger, *Was ist Metaphysik?* in the last sentence: "Warum ist überhaupt Seiendes und nicht vielmehr Nichts?" "(Why is there anything at all rather than Nothing?)."

4   Paradigmatically Rudolf Carnap, "Überwindung der Metaphysik durch logische Analyse der Sprache," *Erkenntnis* 2, 1931, 219–41. Carnap declares the "senselessness of all metaphysics," and cites as examples of senseless metaphysical assertions Descartes (cp. fn. 8) on the *cogito* and Hegel and Heidegger on Being. By contrast, Wittgenstein, "Lecture on Ethics" (1929), *Philosophical Review* 75, 1965, 3–12, remarked that his "experience *par excellence*" is that "*I wonder at the existence of the world*," implying sympathy with Heidegger's question.

5   Heidegger, *Being and Time*, 274. In Chapter 6, I consider two interpretations of Heidegger's *Being*.

it presumes we can think that nothing exists, not even our self asking the question. Heidegger probably had two somehow opposed reasons for considering the question so important. First, if the world were our construct, we would not wonder at its existence, as we do not wonder at the existence (though maybe at the quality) of our products. So the fact that we do confirms that the world is not our construct and solipsism is false. Second, in thinking that there is nothing at all we abstract from the existence of the world. I thus place myself outside the world, supposing that even my self might not exist. This supposition may have confirmed Descartes in his solipsistic view of the self. But Heidegger thinks we can acknowledge both the importance of the ontological question and the epistemological dependence of the self on other objects. We have only to distinguish the ordinary self, the *man selbst* that results from the social relations constituting the world, from an extraordinary one. The extraordinary self is a development out of the ordinary self; therefore, it is not a world-constructing self either. Nonetheless, it detects itself only in the ontological wonder. When it wonders at the existence of the world it wonders at its own existence as well, at its existence in its extraordinariness, and constitutes itself, though never abandoning its origin in *das Man*.

Heidegger demonstrated the self-detection of the self in its wonder at the existence of the world in a specific context: when people consider their death. Probably he did so to prove that the ontological question is rooted in the ordinary world and that philosophers who formulate it only redetect it. Indeed, like the ontological question, consideration of death confronts us with *"the possibility of the impossibility of any existence at all."* In its "anticipatory revealing of this potentiality-for-Being," *"Dasein,"* as Heidegger calls the self, "discloses itself to itself as regards its uttermost possibility." Becoming aware that there might be nothing at all, even not me, makes clear to me how much depends on me. "Anticipation turns out to be the possibility of understanding one's *ownmost* and uttermost potentiality-for-Being – that is to say, the possibility of *authentic existence*." What "turns out to be" such extraordinary possibility is the transubstantiation of an ordinary self into the extraordinary self that knows how much depends on its very existence.[6]

By pointing to both the ontological wonder at the existence of the world and the anticipation of death as "the possibility of the impossibility of any existence at all," Heidegger marks out an important difference between the first and the second stage of the self: Only the second one is capable of such wondering and anticipating. But he does not show that it is the quality of wondering or anticipating that transubstantiates the self. The transubstantiation might have another reason. In fact, there is a strong candidate for such a reason that moreover is thoroughly rooted in the ordinary world: that of judging after deliberation.

---

[6]   Heidegger, *Being and Time*, loc. cit. 307. Heidegger's italics.

Deliberation is learned from adults. Like the anticipation of one's death, it presupposes the ordinary self. Yet it radically changes when the youth no longer relies on adults for her judgment, but decides herself. Moreover, like ontological wondering and anticipating death, it implies that its object might not exist. It presupposes the "possibility of the impossibility" of what is deliberated on, as it presumes that what is deliberated is only possible and might not exist. It proves my capacity of placing myself outside the world and presuming its nonexistence. Finally, it is more basic than ontological wonder and anticipating death, as we can judge without wondering and anticipating, but cannot wonder or anticipate without judging. Hence, deliberation is the crucial activity that turns an ordinary into an extraordinary self and changes qualitatively itself, when we start judging ourselves.

Replacing Heidegger's baroque drama of anticipating death with deliberate judgment as the birthplace of the authentic self saves his distinction of an ordinary and an authentic self but changes its character. Heidegger describes the birth of the authentic self as a kind of devout attention to possibilities that are "uttermost" and not checked by judgment. Such possibilities even include the renunciation of one's own judgment; they allow the individual to stop judging and to dissolve her self in the uttermost possibilities of a totalitarian movement. But if the authentic self is born by deliberation, we can take account of the fact that its birth rarely goes without self-assertion and a hard fight for one's self that can be won only by deliberate judgment.

If we speculate on the reasons for Heidegger's conspicuous eschewal of conceiving the formation of the authentic self in terms of judgment and its activity, it is unlikely that he was influenced by an inclination to the Nazi movement. Such influence would rather have led him to give prominence to active elements in the "disclosure" of the authentic self. More probably, he wanted to take account of our dependence on an experience of being provoked to (or "called into") becoming an authentic self. Yet though such an experience necessarily precedes any self-assertion, it is not by *listening* to the "uttermost potentiality-for-Being" but by responding to it in asserting our selfs in deliberate judgment that we become authentic selfs.

Whatever Heidegger's reason may have been; had he described the passage to the authentic self as an active process in which the youth dares her own judgment, he would have been led to ascribing to deliberate judgment the due role. Perhaps that might also have led him to a better deliberation and judgment on the question of whether to support Hitler.[7]

---

[7]   Some of Heidegger's colleagues, although with a similar or even more conservative background, showed better judgment. An example is Max Scheler, no less a phenomenologist and a conservative than Heidegger. Already in the early 1920s he incisively criticized the fascist movements in Europe. Unfortunately he died in 1928.

It is just this insufficiency of Heidegger's conception of the authentic self that we find remedied in Descartes. In his *Meditations,* Descartes argued that there is an insurmountable difference between the world on one side and the self on the other, because we are capable of doubting the existence of everything but the entity that doubts. His opposition of an indubitable self and a dubitable world neatly corresponds to Heidegger's opposition of metaphysician and world in his ontological question. His argument presents an informal implication together with an interpretation of the implication. The *implication* is that when I doubt something or even only think I doubt, then as long as I think, I exist. Descartes tried to formulate this implication by the famous words *cogito ergo sum.*[8] A lot of authors (such as Lichtenberg,[9] Nietzsche,[10] Carnap,[11] and Popper[12]) have objected that when I doubt, only a doubt and no doubting entity exists. But thoughts without thinkers are as impossible as cats' grins without cats. True, it would be rash to identify the doubting self with the

---

[8]   René Descartes, *Discourse on Method* (1637) pt. 4. The French original is "*Je pense, donc je suis.*" The Latin version reads "*Ego cogito, ego sum,*" hence, does not suggest an implication. Nor do the *Principles of Philosophy* (1644) pt. I §7, which read: "*Ego cogito, ergo sum.*" In the *Meditations*, the decisive passage, in the translation by John Veitch (1901) reads: "Doubtless, then, I exist, since I am deceived; and, let him deceive me as he may, he can never bring it about that I am nothing, so long as I shall be conscious that I am something. So that it must, in fine, be maintained, all things being maturely and carefully considered, that this proposition (*pronunciatum*) *I am, I exist*, is necessarily true each time it is expressed by me, or conceived in my mind." It does not formulate an implication either. Yet as the French translation and the *Discourse* show, an informal implication is presumed.

[9]   Georg Christoph Lichtenberg, *Schriften und Briefe*, 2 Bde. (ed. W. Promies). Darmstadt (Wiss. Buchges.) 1968/ 1971, K 76: "Es *denkt*, sollte man sagen, so wie man sagt: es blitzt. Zu sagen cogito, ist schon zu viel, sobald man es durch Ich denke übersetzt. Das Ich anzunehmen, zu postulieren, ist praktisches Bedürfnis."

[10]   Friedrich Nietzsche, in *On the Genealogy of Morals and Ecce Homo*, ed. Walter Kaufman, New York (Vintage) 1989, 45: "A quantum of force ... is nothing other than precisely this very driving ..., and only owing to the seduction of language ... can it appear otherwise ... there is no 'being' behind doing ...; 'the doer' is merely a fiction added to the deed – the deed is everything." Cf. Nietzsche in a posthumous fragment, *Sämtliche Werke*, vol. 11, 639f: "Seien wir vorsichtiger als Cartesius, welcher in dem Fallstrick der Worte hängen blieb. ... In jenem berühmten cogito steckt 1) es denkt 2) und ich glaube, das ich es bin, der da denkt, 3) aber auch angenommen, daß dieser zweite Punkt in der Schwebe bliebe, als Sache des Glaubens, so enthält auch jenes erste, es denkt' noch einen Glauben: nämlich, dass, denken' eine Thätigkeit sei, zu der ein Subjekt, zum mindesten ein, es' gedacht werden müsse ...! Aber das ist der Glaube an die Grammatik ... Lassen wir also auch jenes problematische, es' weg."

[11]   Rudolf Carnap, loc. cit.: "Aus, ich denke' folgt nicht, ich bin', sondern, es gibt etwas Denkendes."

[12]   Popper, *Objective Knowledge*, 35f, argues that the fact that one can believe he is dead, not only in dream, but also after being struck by lightning, as he was himself, "throws doubt on that directness and indubitability which Descartes was claiming." Yet if Popper claims Descartes's *cogito sum* is dubitable, he should accept that it might be true that I do not exist when I think I am dead, which I doubt Popper would accept.

bodily individual René Descartes, but this was just what Descartes was very eager to reject.[13] So the objection suits only the Wonderland where Alice meets grins without cats.

The *interpretation* is that the implication shows that what is indubitable in me can exist without a physical world. It interprets the opposition of doubting agent and dubitable object as the ontological independence of the mental from the physical and, hence, as proof that there are two independent realms in the world, the mental and the physical. This assumption is untenable if doubting and any other mental activity are impossible without a bodily activity.

This is what Wittgenstein maintained, for the following reason.[14] When I doubt, I must know that I doubt and not, for example, judge. I need a concept of doubt. Such a concept is what I have learned from other people. I learned it when I showed signs of insecurity or saw others doing so and was instructed that I or they have doubts (or, correspondingly, are judging). Such learning is impossible without bodily movements by me and the other that show to the other my or their mental activity. Once I have learned to silently doubt or judge, it may seem that we can refer to mental activities without referring to bodily movements. Yet this semblance is only lack of memory.

Yet so far, Wittgenstein shows only that mental activities are *conceptually* dependent on physical ones. Rather than showing their ontological dependence on physical movements, he only shows what distinguishes them from physical ones, namely, that we do not identify them with the bodily movements by which we recognize them. But if so, he does not disprove their ontological difference; hence, Descartes's dualism stands unrefuted. Dualism may still be defended along the following lines.

Even though I lack the common concepts of what I am doing and feeling, whether, say, I am doubting rather than judging and feeling something that is soft rather than hard, I learn what judgments and sensations are without the help of others. It is only because I already know what judging and feeling are that I can understand the explanations of the others about the difference between judging and doubting and the other mental activities and sensations. Suppose as an infant I lie in the grass and suck a blade of grass and remember it is the taste of sourness I tasted when yesterday I lay in the grass. I lack the ordinary language concept of sour taste, but don't I know what a sour taste is in perfect independence of any physical movements of other people? Similarly, I may look at the sky and see a cloud that looks like my mother. Can't I then judge what we would express in the sentence "This is mum"? When the cloud changes form, can't I then experience doubt as we would express in the sentence "Is this

---

[13] Descartes, *Meditations* II, ed. Adam and Tannery, p. 21.

[14] Ludwig Wittgenstein, *Philosophical Investigations*, pt.1, §§ 243ff, et al. Cp. also my *Wittgenstein über den Willen*.

really mum"?[15] Again, I would have learned without the help of others what something mental is; this time not a sensation but a judgment and a doubt.

If this is how I come to know what sensations and mental activities are, learning my native language would consist of coordinating the concepts of my own original private language that I acquired by experiences of the kind described with the concepts of my native language. This implies that the meaning of concepts of mental activities and sensations is not something the speakers of a public language agree on but those private and in principle incommunicable experiences that we learn in those early experiences. The implication conforms to the empiricism Heidegger and Wittgenstein tried refuting. It commits to the view that we can never be absolutely certain that what we feel as, say, a burning pain, is not felt by the other as a piercing one or even a pleasure or as something absolutely different from a feeling. If this is true, our sentiments and mental activities would constitute private worlds. We could assume the existence of other persons and a world that is independent of what we think about it only by inference from analogy or by arguing to the best explanation or, as did Descartes, by trying to prove the existence of a nondeceiving god who makes us believe in the existence of a common world.

Wittgenstein seems to have thought his arguments disproved both empiricism and solipsism. If so, he was wrong. He cannot disprove them. But he proves how to understand that we are not living in private worlds. Empiricism is a theory we incline to, but it also inclines to solipsism, hence, entangles us in incongruities and incoherencies. Wittgenstein offers an alternative to escape them. He shows that we can recognize that thinking and feeling are mental activities and still are not committed to empiricism or Descartes's dualism. This is just what we need.

Moreover, he allows us to conceive of the self as a communicative agent. The bodily movements by which alone both the other and I can share a concept of mental activity and sensations relate one judging agent to another. I can never judge without presupposing other judging agents that might contradict or correct me. Any judgment is potentially addressed to other judging agents, so if we follow Wittgenstein's argument, it is conceptually necessary that the self is communicating with other selves.

So there is a double conceptual dependence of the self on its body and on the other, in its being known to the other by its body and its motions and movements, and in its addressing its judgment to the other. Remarkably, there are signs, difficult to understand by dualists (and curiously not considered by Wittgenstein), that there is such a dependence that is felt by us. We feel it in shame. As recognizing one's dependence hurts one's pride, we can expect such feeling to be humiliating or embarrassing, and that's what shame is. We feel

---

[15] Contemporary idealists argue this way. Cp., e.g., Howard Robinson, *Perception*, London (Routledge), 1994.

embarrassed by the fact that we are judged by our body, in particular, if it is bare of anything veiling and in a way dephysicalizing it. Shame is not felt by small children and persons who are debased in a literal sense, as they lack a self, hence, are without the base of autonomy. It starts when I become conscious of my self as something observed by other selves in my body, which to some extent is identified with me even though they and I know that it is not identical with me. Yet I also know that it represents me to the others, because they can know me only by my body. Similarly, much as I dislike to, I must refer my judgments to their judgment.

Shame indicates the dependence of the self on its own body and on the existence of other selfs, yet also its nonidentity with its body and with its relations to other selfs. It proves that the self is neither a mental substance unrelated to living bodies nor reducible to a living body nor the "ensemble of its social relations," as Marx said of the individual.[16] The others necessarily judge me by the movements and state of my body, yet also judge me as something different from my body, as, like me, they know that we can distance ourselves from our body and what happens to it.

My judgment, a mental act that necessarily is expressed in bodily movements, is also bound to bodily movements by the language I use for my judgment. This property of judgments is a more specific form of their being necessarily expressed in bodily movements, as language is the development of nonverbal expressions to verbal ones. As they are bound to language, judgments can become more than mere decisions on whether to say *yes* or *no* to a proposition, though this remains always the core of judgments. They can become differentiated by the mode of expression and by stating conditions and provisos, modal operators and, what is most important, by time relations. I can refer to my past and future and bind me to performing specified actions at future times. Thus, the self becomes a flexible and stretchable agent with a scale of expressions that brings into its character all the differentiations that a propositional language allows for judgments.[17]

That it becomes a self that continues over time, remaining the same despite the changes of its subject and its body means that I, an individual of body and mind, become a person identifiable over time and responsible for all deliberate decisions. The body by which the others identify me becomes the criterion of my identity, although I am not identical with it. Also for me, if after amnesia I do not know who I am, there is no other way to know than by checking whether the body that embodies my self now is the same as the one that embodied it before.

There is no unambiguous moment in which the self starts to exist. The capability that makes me a self comes in parts; to become a full-fledged self, I need to

---

16   Karl Marx, *Thesen über Feuerbach*; Marx, Engels, *Werke*, vol. 3, 6.
17   I'll explain what defines a propositional language in Chapter 6.

meet different conditions: At least, I must use a propositional language, become aware of my dependence on others that shows in shame and pass judgments without depending on others. As we'll see in the next chapters, even before meeting these conditions, I must be capable of initiating actions. These conditions are met at different ages: The capability of initiating actions is given already with birth; use of propositional language comes next, awareness of dependence on others comes before the age of youth; capability of independent judgment comes late; some never attain it. The self develops in steps, starting from what I'll call the proto-self and advancing by degrees to a full-fledged self.

The constitutive property of the Cartesian self is its capacity of judging after deliberation. Once we understand judging as an activity that is necessarily connected with bodily movement, the self's constitutive property can be seen in a clear light no longer darkened by its dualistic presentation. It is even an error to think it is necessarily conscious; often, we are not conscious of our judgments. What is necessary for a self is that it can become conscious of its judgments.[18] But if we can *become* conscious that we are judging, we have not been conscious of judging before. Hence, the self cannot be consciousness, as Locke claimed. Unfortunately, Descartes's dualistic presentation of the self has confirmed the Lockean error. It blurred the sharp difference of the Cartesian self that is the power of judgment from the Lockean self and made Descartes's revolutionary achievement unrecognizable.

Like Heidegger, Descartes detects the self in an opposition of the thinking, philosophizing individual to the whole of the world. But unlike Heidegger, he finds the essential property of the self in its action of deliberate judgment. Hence, it is impossible for Descartes to ascribe an authentic self to an individual who has renounced her own judgment and with it self-assertion and the pursuit of her self-interest (and might find its extraordinariness in a totalitarian movement).

Descartes did not content himself with asserting that the self is a judging agent. He, rather, pointed out that judging is a necessarily free action and judgment is the place of freedom of the will. I'll expound this point in the next chapter. Only then will it become clear why in spite of the prevalence of the Lockean conception the Cartesian conception of the self is more suitable to modernity.

---

[18] Cp. Chapter 5.

Chapter 3

Free Will

THERE IS NO DOUBT THAT WE CAN ACT *voluntarily*. EVEN ANIMALS have a power of originating actions, which enables them to act spontaneously, without a stimulus that causes them to act in the very way they act.[1] Yet there is doubt as to whether we have *free will*, a will, that is, that makes our decisions independent of any predetermining factor and yet requires ascribing them to us as the agents responsible of them. It is important to distinguish the capability of acting voluntarily, the *freedom of action*, and the capability of acting by free will, the *freedom of the will*. Though Aristotle had already distinguished them,[2] today quite a few theorists confound them. In particular, compatibilists, who argue that we can both accept determinism and free will, do so, relying on the trivial truth that freedom of action and determinism are compatible.[3] Unlike Descartes and Leibniz, they neglect that the answer to the question of whether we have freedom of will or only freedom of action depends on our understanding of what happens in our deliberation of reasons before and when we judge.[4]

Let us look at the arguments of Descartes and Leibniz. In a letter to Mesland, who had asked for clarification of contradictory assertions on free

---

[1] This has been shown by B. F. Skinner who, despite his radical determinism, proved against the mechanistic view made famous by Ivan Pavlov that to explain animals' actions we need to presuppose that they start with spontaneous actions. They are comparable to the uncaused behavior of quantum particles and can be predicted only with a certain probability but are formed by "patterns of reinforcement" imposed on them by life conditions or the human experimenter.

[2] Aristotle, *Nicomachean Ethics* III, i–iii, 1109b30–1113a14.

[3] Contemporary compatibilists are Daniel Dennett, Harry Frankfurt, and Peter Bieri. It is interesting to note that most neuroscientists, whether they ascribe free will to men or not, stick to the incompatibilist and libertarian conception of free will, as do most lawyers and laymen. Unfortunately they do not distinguish between the Kantian and the Cartesian version of the libertarian conception, as little as most compatibilist philosophers do.

[4] I have treated this subject in my *Freiheitstheorien der Philosophie der Neuzeit*.

will in the 4th Meditation, Descartes argued that in deliberating reasons before passing a judgment, no reason can ever absolutely determine our judgment, however convincing or strong the reason may be. True, he said, "morally speaking," that is, if we look at what happens ordinarily, "we are hardly able to move ourselves to the contrary" of a convincing reason; "but considered absolutely," that is if we look at our capability, "we are. For we are always capable of revoking a good or a truth we have clearly recognized, if only we judge it to be good for proving the freedom of our will."[5]

We can revoke a *good* we have clearly recognized, because we can reject any reason for a *practical* judgment, that is, for *doing* something, even though it seemed evident to us that we should. This is not implausible, because in our judgments on an *action*, we can overturn a reason that showed us its goodness, if we think we rather should prove by our action our independence of any preceding determinant. But can we therefore also overturn an evident reason for the *truth* of a proposition (or possible *fact*) if we judge it "good for proving the freedom of our will"? This is not plausible. True, we can reject even the most evident theoretical reason for the *practical* reason that we want to prove our free will. But we will not recognize the resulting judgment as true. For theoretical judgments, we admit only *truth* reasons, and such are theoretical reasons only.

Science, in particular, lives on the distinction of theoretical and practical reasons. We might define it as the effort to exclude practical reasons from slipping into the deliberation of the truth of its propositions. Descartes's claim that we can revoke "a truth we have clearly recognized" by appealing to the (practical) reason of proving our free will seems incompatible with belief in science. But Descartes believed in science. So, isn't this claim a rhetorical exaggeration he would not have maintained if pressed? Not necessarily. He probably would have argued that in the end all reasons are practical, because in the end we have to *judge*, and judging is an *action*. Though in scientific judgments we ought to exclude practical reasons from the deliberation of their truth, they still are judgments, hence actions, for which practical considerations can always slip in. We can, for instance, always ask if we are not victim to an illusion fed by practical interest when we consider a reason to be most convincing. As we'll see more clearly in the next chapter, there are no infallible judgments. Therefore, Descartes can admit that scientific propositions ought not to be revoked for proving the freedom of the will and yet maintain that because no judgment is infallible, we actually are capable of revoking them for proving our free will.

Anyway, as determinism claims that we are determined in *any* decision, for asserting free will it is sufficient to claim that in judging on a "good," that is, a possible *action,* we can reject any reason, evident though the reason may seem, if we judge it better to reject it for proving our free will. By thus rejecting evident reasons

5 Descartes to Father Mesland, Feb. 9, 1645; *Œuvres complètes de Descartes*, ed. Adam et Tannery, vol. IV, p. 173.

we do not fall back on an animal state of lacking the power of following reasons, because we still follow the special reason that we want to prove the freedom of our will. What Descartes has to presuppose is that we know the idea of free will when we judge on a possible action. He does not tell Mesland where we come by this idea, but he would have reckoned it among the inborn ideas we have of a perfect being. It belongs to the powers of a perfect being to have free will, and such a "power," as Descartes says in his 4th Meditation, "consists only in this, that we are able to do or not to do the same thing (that is, to affirm or deny, to pursue or shun it),"[6]

To accept his claim, we need not follow his belief in inborn ideas. We may just assume that we prefer originating actions to suffering coercion and often even resent being necessitated by the evidence of reasons. Such preference is sufficient for the rise of an ideal of freedom also from the force of reasons. This ideal is attractive enough to become a new reason in the range of reasons among which we can choose when we judge. This is why, by rejecting evidence, we do not relapse onto the reasonless state of animals and still act for a reason, which makes us responsible. We even enhance the power of judgment by shaking off even predetermination by reasons.

Leibniz disliked Descartes's argument: "... they say people even after knowing and deliberating everything have still the power of not only willing what pleases them most but also willing the contrary, just for proving their liberty. But you have to consider that this spleen or spite or at least this reason that prevents us from following the other reasons is no less a factor in the deliberation that makes us to be pleased with what otherwise we would not be pleased with."[7]

So far Leibniz is right. The Cartesians' reason of proving "their liberty" is a factor that determines judgment. But Descartes's point is that it is a codetermination of a special sort: It invalidates the power of all other reasons and makes the choice of the reason for judging unpredictable, although the judgment is based on the choice of a reason. Hume rejected free will by arguing, rightly, that if an action has not been chosen for some reason then it cannot be ascribed to the agent.[8] Yet he overlooked the possibility Descartes exploits of choosing an action for a reason that excludes any form of predestination or predeterminism, namely, the reason that one wants to prove her liberty.

Still, Leibniz insisted: "A spirit that would have the peculiarity of willing and being capable of doing or willing the contrary of what can be predicted about him ... belongs to the range of beings that are incompatible with the existence of the being that knows everything, i.e., with the harmony of the things and therefore neither have been nor are nor will be."[9]

---

6   Descartes, *Meditation* IV, 8, transl. John Veitch.
7   G. W. Leibniz, *Nouveaux Essais*, in Locke, *An Essay Concerning Human Understanding*, bk 2, ch 21, § 25, p. 168. My translation.
8   David Hume, *A Treatise of Human Nature*, 404.
9   Leibniz, 84f.

Leibniz is right in insisting that even when we follow the reason to prove our free will we are *determined*. But he is wrong in concluding that therefore we are *pre*determined; we are determined by a reason that decouples us from any predetermination.[10] His idea is that even when we think we are arbitrarily deciding to say *yes* rather than *no* to a proposition, we are chosen by a reason rather than choosing one. Descartes's idea is that our experience that we are choosing a reason is reliable.

Is there a way to decide who is right? I think there is a way by the following thought experiment. Imagine a future brain scientist who knows all the laws of brain processes and everything about your past. He is picturing the present state of your brain by functional magnetic resonance and similar techniques onto the screen of a computer. He has sufficient knowledge to predict what you will do. All his predictions prove correct as long as he does not tell *you* his predictions.

Now, what happens if he predicts to you that, say, you will take a drink of water in the next moment? If you are a bit mischievous and like proving your independence of predetermining influences, you will not take the drink. Even if you feel very thirsty, it is not difficult to delay a drink. So you will falsify the scientist's prediction. Yet the determinist will argue, as did Leibniz, that given your spite it was *necessary* for you to refuse drinking the water. You believed you were freely choosing the reason to falsify the prediction but were chosen by your spite. But if the determinist is right, he should be capable of predicting which reason will choose you. If the idea of being chosen by a reason has any sense at all it must imply the possibility of such predictions. If the determinist says he cannot predict which reason you will follow, as you will always follow the reason that is contrary to his prediction, this just means you are choosing the reason rather than being chosen by it.

Now the determinist may argue that the talk of being chosen by a reason is a metaphor and cannot be used as an argument to refute him. So the question is what can be meant by the idea that it is *necessary* that you decide however you will decide. It is meaningful to say that however the weather will develop, its development is necessary, even though for lack of empirical data we cannot

---

[10] Leibniz was probably led to his view by his physics that, as David Papineau, *The Rise of Physicalism*, 14f, explains, taught "both the conservation of linear *momentum* and the conservation of kinetic *energy*." By contrast, Descartes's mechanics incorporated only the conservation of what he called "'quantity of motion,' by which he meant mass times speed," and did not "require that, if a physical body changes direction, this need result from any other physical body changing direction. Even if the change of direction results from an irreducibly mental cause, the quantity of motion of the moving body remains constant." But though Leibniz's conservation laws were "a great improvement" on Descartes's, it does not apply to the Cartesian conception of "free will." It is interesting to see that Hannah Arendt, *The Promise of Politics*, 127, correctly describes free will as "opposition to all possible predetermination." Cp. Chapter 9.

forecast it for the next year. But the prediction made about you is not impossible for lack of empirical data. We have presupposed that whatever contributes to your future behavior is known and that only by your knowledge of the prediction will you opt for an action that has not been predicted. The problem with weather forecasts is lack of empirical data or perhaps the existence of an indeterminacy principle that excludes causal necessity. The problem with action predictions is that the prediction becomes itself a factor in the chain of causes that has the peculiar property of excluding predictions.

This point is perhaps still more obvious if we imagine that the brain scientist pictures *his* brain on the computer screen and predicts *he* will take a drink of water in the next moment. He cannot avoid knowing his prediction, but as a brave determinist he will verify his prediction by taking a drink. Yet if taking the drink was necessary or predetermined, he might lean back and wait to see what will happen to him. This of course is impossible. He has to make up his mind.

Now the determinist, if he is a bit sophisticated, will concede that it is we who decide, that it is up to us to decide, and that we do not suffer a fate if we deliberate our decision. He may even grant free will to men by following a compatibilist conception of free will. So he can insist that the decision was necessitated by the past. Determinism, he will argue, is a causality that acts through our decisions. Therefore, determinism is different from fatalism. Fatalism is myth; determinism is science. Brain science can never show that determinism is wrong. It must rather presuppose determinism, for else there would be no laws of our behavior to explore.

This defense, like Leibniz on Descartes, presupposes there *are* laws that determine our actions, whether we know them or not. The determinist insists on our being predetermined anyway but must concede that because of our capacity of using a prediction for falsifying it, it is impossible in principle to predict our action if we know the alleged prediction. Yet this impossibility, as we have seen, is radically different from the impossibility of predicting the result of complex processes, like the weather in a month. Here the impossibility results from too little knowledge, there from too much.

Insisting on determinism when prediction is impossible turns determinism into a myth. It is an affirmation that cannot be falsified. Hence, according to the generally recognized Popperian criterion of scientificity, according to which a scientific theory needs to be falsifiable, it is not scientific. Nor is it a necessary presupposition for doing science, because it does not change anything in scientific descriptions, explanations, and predictions. It is a decorative key that we press without moving anything else, a mere ideological relic that suits prejudice. By contrast, if we say that in specifiable conditions we decide freely, we risk falsification, because how we decide might be predicted even if we know the prediction, and we stick to the important scientific principle to describe events with as little prejudice as possible.

But I have to qualify my assertion that free will violates only *pre*determinism, not determinism.[11] Actions that are chosen by free will are determined as well, namely, by our will. That is why they are not actions of Hume's lunatic. Yet the choice of the reason after deliberation for which we act is not determined. Hence, by this assertion we contradict determinism. If so, don't we violate scientific conservation principles by rejecting determinism? At least in some of their interpretations, we do. But conservation principles can be and have been reinterpreted in order to avoid incoherence.[12] Yet it is incoherent to concede impossibility of prediction of action told to the agent and to stick to determinism for such action.

Now Descartes says that, "considered absolutely," we are "always" capable of rejecting the most evident reason, "if only we judge it to be good for proving the freedom of our will." This implies that we can reject the most evident practical reason not only *if* we judge it right for proving our free will, but that we are always capable of judging so; not only if the decision is about whether to take a drink, but also if it is about whether to kill one's children. Such decision, he even says, is a "greater use" of liberty than one that would conform to morality since it proves the "positive capacity we have of following the bad even though we see the good."[13] With these words Descartes alludes to a description of the mythological heroine Medea by Ovid in his *Metamorphoses*. Medea, who eloped with Jason from the Caucasus but was betrayed by him, kills her children by Jason, though she says she knows what would be good, but still is "following the bad." Descartes deviates from the traditional understanding of Medea as driven by passion that was expressed by Euripides.[14] He says that she thus makes a "greater use" of liberty. He asserts that freeing oneself even from the fetters of morality is a greater use of liberty than staying in them, and that Medea did so. It even "makes us in a certain way equal to God and seems to exempt us from being his subjects."[15] Creatures with free will cannot be mere subjects of their

---

[11] As beomes clear in Lucretius, *De rerum natura*, II 251–7, determinism has been understood as predeterminism.

[12] Cp. again Papineau's paper cited in footnote 10.

[13] *Adam et Tannery* IV, 174. "Maior enim libertas consistit vel in maiori facilitate se determinandi, vel in maiori usu positivae illius potestatis quam habemus, sequendi deteriora, quamvis meliora videamus."

[14] Descartes alludes to *Metamorphoses* VII, 20f, where Medea says: "Video meliora proboque Deteriora sequor: I see what is better, approve it, yet follow what is worse." Unlike Descartes, Euripides, *Medea* 1078–80, probably a source for Ovid, presents Medea as determined by her passion, having her say: "I know indeed what evil I intend to do. But my resolutions yield to my fury (*thumos*), Fury that brings upon mortals the greatest evils." (trans. Rex Warner). Romilly, 1992, 151, convincingly argues that Euripides, in his view that "nature forces" people, was influenced by the sophists.

[15] Descartes to Christina of Sweden, Nov. 20, 1647; *Adam et Tannery* V, 85. Also in the 4th *Meditation,* Descartes says that it is particularly by free will that "I understand myself to be a certain image and resemblance of God"; *Adam et Tannery* VII, 57.

creator because they are capable of rejecting his command. This makes us capable of rebelling against God and gives us the very same arbitrariness of judging even against the most evident reason that Descartes ascribes to God.

Probably Descartes did not want to assert that everyone is capable of acting like Medea, because also for him she was a heroine; few parents will be capable of killing their children to prove their liberty. He does assert that there is the capacity in men of acting like her, though "morally speaking" only few will be able to use it. He implies that free will does not, as Kant assumed, coincide with moral reason, understood as the power that detects and makes us follow the rules of morality. *Pace* Kant, this is plausible. There are many situations that prove our capacity of doing the worse though we know the better. Think of a party when you take another drink when you are still in complete control of yourself, but favor the ideal to be free to decide even against what you know and morally approve, namely, that you must not take another drink as it makes you a greater risk when you'll drive home. Like Medea, you then know the better but choose the worse. Like her (in Descartes's interpretation), you do what you know is bad not because you are in the grip of a passion or addiction, but because you want to prove your independence.

Leibniz might still argue that Medea and the party guest are determined by the intended good, as they delight in proving their free will. But this delight is not the cause but the effect of their choice. The cause is their will to prove their independence of any predetermining cause. The effect of such choice can, but need not be, delight. Medea certainly felt pain at the death of her children, and this pain can have deleted any delight in having proven her independence of predetermining conditions.

Three consequences of our capacity of judging at least sometimes against the most evident moral reason merit noticing. First, it makes conspicuous the element of arbitrariness contained in any judgment. Because judgment does not necessarily follow the most evident reason, it is by its very nature arbitrary in the choice of the reason to follow. Nevertheless, judgment is the vehicle of reason. It is not a vehicle that necessarily follows the principles of morality, not only because it is always liable to error but also because of its arbitrariness. Still, it is the only vehicle by which reason can enter human affairs. Rationality is necessarily bound to the arbitrariness of individuals or their collectives.

Second, the use of reason is always self-assertion. As individuals and their collectives are arbitrary judgers, they are different vehicles driving reason in different directions. Hence, even if we could assume that people always act deliberately and, therefore, rationally, we could not predict our future.

Third, Kant's idea that free will is identical with morality follows a model of reason, judgment and the self that is taken from the childhood stage of the self and rationality. In this stage, we can be called rational only if we follow the rules of morality. Before we can reject evident reasons for the specific reason of proving our independence of any predetermining factor, we have to learn the rules of morality and acting on reasons. Only when we have learned this have we acquired the adult stage of rationality, a stage that condemns us to judging without reliance on models, and hence, to including arbitrariness. It also excludes that man has a fixed nature, because we can always arbitrarily choose when we deliberate on reasons.[16]

Descartes did not yet distinguish two stages of rationality but implied a model of rationality that suits the second stage. Most philosophers, even if they argue for free will, reject this model. Though Kant agrees with Descartes that free will makes men independent of any predetermination, he blocks the consequence that free will enables us to opt for the evil by explaining bad actions as a consequence of our *failing* to use free will. So he has to understand evil actions as a relapse into the state of animals that lack free will, which puts him in the mess of explaining good actions as the product of free will but bad actions as the product of a nature that we cannot be responsible for. He sincerely admits that "experience proves often enough" that "the rational subject is capable of making a choice that contradicts his law-giving reason." Yet he insists that freedom of the will can "by no means consist in this, that the rational subject is capable of making a choice that contradicts his law-giving reason."[17] Though he clearly sees that full rationality implies that people have to rationally choose their own laws, he still conceived of rationality as something that excludes arbitrariness.

Kant's conception of rationality is supported by Socrates, Aristotle, later Enlightenment thinkers, and many contemporaries. They all agree that men only do what they think is good for them and, like Leibniz, overlook that sticking to this idea implies an inflation of the concept of the good that robs it of meaning. In contrast, the Cartesian view accords with the myth of Lucifer who, just because he is the angel with the most powerful judgment, rejects obedience to his creator.[18] Here, rationality, far from implying morality, is understood to be a seduction to immorality. This understanding is also expressed in languages that (like Turkish) use the word for devil (*sheytan*) also for someone particularly clever. We need not be religious to recognize the truth of the myth. So we should abandon conceptions of rationality that cannot take account of Lucifer's, Medea's,[19] or common party decisions. Yet we also need to be aware that we can only *learn* what rationality and morality are

---

[16] Pico della Mirandola has nicely expressed this conclusion in his *Oratio de dignitate hominis* by praising "nostrum chamaeleonta" (§7).

[17] Kant, *Metaphysik der Sitten*, 30 (*Rechtslehre, Einleitung in die Metaphysik der Sitten* IV).

[18] It took some time for Lucifer to become the paradigm of disobedience to God, if we believe Henry Ansgar Kelly, *Satan*, Cambridge University Press, 2006. On efforts to ascribe to Lucifer a deeper form of obedience in spite of his rebellion, see Peter Awn, *Satan's Tragedy and Redemption: Iblis in Sufi Psychology*, Leyden 1983.

[19] Is it an accident that one of the first persons to be recognized for the capability of doing bad despite knowing the good is a woman and a barbarian?

if we follow a model that excludes arbitrariness. We have to accept a two-stage concept of rationality and the self.

For a better survey, let us mark out the important properties of the Cartesian conception of free will.

First, free will is a power of *blocking* an impulse to action. It is not *creative*, but *reactive* and *critical*. It responds to an offer of what might be done or believed, either by consenting to or rejecting it, but never by replacing it with a new idea. When we deliberate on an action, we may of course have a new idea, but it springs from our imagination, hence, our subject. By our self, which is our power of judgment or free will, we can only decide to say *yes* or *no* to a thought. It is by saying *no* that we start feeling our free will, because consent is what we give to our impulses before we come to develop free will. But saying *no* is not constructive. Of course the power to say *yes* doesn't make free will a creative power either. Only by becoming aware that we can do nothing; hence, that there is non-action, "nothing," or "emptiness," can we detect our selves. Perhaps this is why Heidegger and other thinkers assume nothingness at the core of being.[20]

Some decades ago, a couple of philosophers, Ernst Tugendhat and Jürgen Habermas, considered free will a chimera but did not deny that men have the power of negation.[21] They interpreted the freedom of negation as a freedom of action. This is a mistake. Negation is at the core of free will. If we veto an action impulse or an inclination to a belief we are breaking any predetermination. We do not originate an action that may again be determined by preceding causes, as we do when we exercise freedom of action. Rather, we decouple the action deliberated from all preceding influences. The power of negation that we exercise in deliberating practical reasons enables us to both affirm and deny the action we deliberate. It is for this property of the deliberation process that freedom of the will was defined in scholastic philosophy as "that which, if conditions are met, is capable of both acting and not acting or of doing something such as to be capable of doing the contrary as well."[22] This definition marks out that freedom of the will conforms to what philosophers call the principle of alternative possibilities: For an act A to be an act of free will, it is necessary that the agent is capable of doing non-A as well as A. If an agent has the power of negation, she meets this condition.

For this property free will was called a liberty of *indifference*. If you are capable of doing both A and non-A, you are indifferent to them in the sense

---

[20] Cp. Fred Dallmayr, *Sunyata*, 175–99.

[21] Cf. E. Tugendhat, *Vorlesungen*, 110; and Jürgen Habermas, *Theorie des kommunikativen Handelns*, I 370 and II 113f.

[22] Ludovicus de Molina, *Liberi Arbitrii*, quaestio 14, art. 13, disput. 2, p. 8, column 1: "illud agens liberum dicitur, quod positis omnibus requisitis ad agendum, potest agere et non agere, aut ita agere unum, ut contrarium etiam agere possit." Molina adds to this definition this fine description: "potest voluntas sua innata libertate velle, aut nolle, vel neutrum elicere actum": will by its innate liberty can decide for or against a choice or not choose at all (ibid., p. 9, column 1). My translation.

not of lacking preference for one side but of being capable of doing A as well as non-A and, if need be, of *making* yourself indifferent against the preference. Critics of free will argued that indifference will make us incapable of any action and pointed to the example of an ass (discussed by Buridan) that has to choose between two equally attractive and close haystacks and will starve for having no reason to prefer either. Yet the same example has been used as proof that even though we are indifferent we can act, because even an ass will not starve between his haystacks. This confirms that in the end we need to decide arbitrarily, according to the motto *Sit pro ratione voluntas*; will has to take over from reason.[23] Thinking this is a lack of rationality betrays lack of understanding the difference between authoritarian and authentic reason.

Recognizing that free will is a power of negation that responds to an impulse is important for the contemporary discussion among brain scientists. Some have taken the fact that brain processes precede the utterance of a decision for proof that the decision is determined by them. A scientist concluded: "We do not do what we will but will what we do."[24] Fortunately there are also thinking neuroscientists. Benjamin Libet has argued that if we conceive free will as a veto power, we have to expect brain processes that correspond to deliberation acts and necessarily precede decision utterances without predetermining them.[25] Far from being refuted by modern brain science, the Cartesian conception can guide brain research by formulating testable predictions on neuronal processes that embody our decisions. It might be informative to observe the effect of a prediction on brain processes.

For some philosophers of the twentieth century, the paradigm of acts of free will has been artistic inspiration.[26] Yet though artistic inspiration may be unpredictable or even undetermined, it is not an act of free will. It is not an act at all, it is something that happens. An individual can be responsible for using or not using her inspirations, for being attentive to or even stimulating them by drugs or meditation, and she can morally praise herself for doing so, but not for having an inspiration.

Second, although free will is not a creative but a reactive power, it is a power of *action*, just as the freedom of action, the power of originating action, is. In deliberate judgment on a possible action, we initiate an action by saying *yes* to it and start something new. We thus allow the action impulse that we have considered to become effective. We may also judge in the abstract that a possible action is right, yet still withhold our judgment that we should realize it now. If

[23] The example can be traced back to Aristotle, *De caelo* 295b32. Jean Buridan discusses the example in his commentary *Expositio textus* to *De caelo*. Buridan was indebted to Ghazali (1058–1111); see Nicholas Rescher on *Buridan, Encyclopedia of Philosophy*, ed. Paul Edwards, New York (Macmillan), 1967.
[24] W. Prinz, "Freiheit oder Wissenschaft," 87.
[25] B. Libet, "Do We Have Free Will?," 47.
[26] Cp. Popper, "*Objective Knowledge*," 223 and 254.

we act and not only react to a stimulus, there are only two ways for doing so. We either act spontaneously without deliberation (in this case we follow a motive or a whim and are caused by them to act) or we decide after deliberation for some reason. Such decision is the initiation of an action; nothing is required but the choice of a reason and the decision to act now.

Free will is sometimes considered a freedom of thinking that does not imply acting. Yet there is no free will without the choice of a reason for doing or believing something. The freedom to both believe and not believe something is inseparable from the freedom to both do and not do something. It is true that there has been political suppression that suppressed action but not thought. But suppression can also succeed in suppressing thought, as we know by unfortunately rich experience; it can even destroy the power of judgment. So free will is not indestructible, though it can be destroyed only along with reason.

Third, the Cartesian conception of free will does not imply Descartes's dualism. It presumes that mental activities and sensations cannot exist without physical processes, but physical processes can exist without mental ones. As free will is choice after deliberation – and we cannot deliberate if we cannot become conscious of the reasons we weigh – it may seem that individuals act by their consciousness when they freely choose an action. Yet for a choice to be free, it is completely irrelevant whether we deliberate silently or publicly; we may even deliberate unconsciously. What is necessary for a will to be free is only that we discuss reasons, can reject any one and still act for a reason, and *can* become conscious of them. An act is free willed, not because it is enacted by consciousness, but because it is deliberately chosen. Assuming people have free will commits to Descartes's dualism as little as assuming people can decide after discussion does.

Fourth, free will is an *empirically* detectable capacity. Kant declared it to be a "pure transcendental idea that, first, contains nothing that is taken from experience and whose object, second, cannot be met in any experience."[27] It is true that no capacity can be *observed*. What we observe is always an event or fact; we need interpretation to understand it as something that springs from a power. But we have empirically applicable criteria for deciding if an event springs from a power – and from which power. Solubility in water is a (passive) power we cannot observe directly, but if we observe that a piece of sugar dissolves in water, we take this empirical fact for a criterion of its solubility in water. Similarly, though we cannot directly observe free will, if we observe that someone who has been told she will take a drink of water does not take the drink, saying that she wants to demonstrate that she is free to both drink and not drink, we would take this as proof of her free will if we were not impressed by deterministic arguments. If such arguments are understood as fatalistic, they can be easily refuted. If they are understood as compatibilist, they exclude an empirical refutation, but cannot belong to a scientific theory. This does not exclude their truth. But if they

[27] Kant, *Kritik der reinen Vernunft* B, 561.

are unscientific, they cannot back the thesis that science excludes that free will can be empirically detected, as Kant and others believed.

Moreover, there are empirical criteria to distinguish the power of free will from the power of free action. We recognize that an entity has the power of originating action if it starts a movement without being forced against its desires, while we recognize that its action springs from free will only if it follows on a deliberation of reasons for acting. This distinction has already been pointed out by Aristotle.[28] Once we recognize that its rejection by the determinists is like the turning of a knob that does not move anything in science, we have no reason not to use it.

By contrast, if we follow Kant in his thesis that free will cannot be found in experience, we get in extreme trouble when we try to understand what a judge is doing who considers if a defendant can be declared culpable for an action. In such cases, the question is not if the defendant has committed the action voluntarily but whether he had the capacity of deliberating reasons for and against the action, including the capacity of taking account of the consequences of the action. If the judge denies him such competency, he will assign him no (or diminished) responsibility and either not punish him or reduce punishment. Kant's conception demands of us to say that the judge's efforts to find out the defendant's degree of competency cannot have anything to do with his freedom of will, because this is a pure, transcendental idea never met in experience. If we do not want to call this consequence a *demonstratio ad absurdum,* it is at least a demonstration that philosophy can develop ideas so far away from ordinary concepts that it is no longer fit for enlightening the world.

What motivated Kant and many other theorists to consider free will a non-empirical capacity was the idea that the agent of free will cannot be the empirical individual of bones, blood, and brain. Such an individual was thought to be subject to the natural laws that either predetermine any movement in the world or permit only chance movements. Both predetermined and chance movements exclude free will, the first because they make the individual a wheel in the giant mechanism of the universe; the second because they do not allow her to determine her actions. As despite these presuppositions Kant wants to ascribe free will to men, he had to postulate a supernatural realm in which free will is possible. So he says of the intention of his critical enterprise that he wanted to "abolish knowledge to clear a space for faith."[29] He wanted to abolish the competence of science in questions of morality and make room for faith in a transcendent sphere where freely willed action is possible.

But the Cartesian conception of the self rejects the idea that any movement in the world is either predetermined or a chance happening. Rather, it maintains that by considering reasons in deliberation, an organism becomes capable of both decoupling her decisions from any former determining factor

---

[28] Aristotle, *Nicomachean Ethics* III, i–iii.
[29] Kant, *Kritik der reinen Vernunft*, Vorrede B, XXX.

and determining her action by the free choice of a reason she performs the action for.

Fifth, free will is *not autonomy*. Everyone who is capable of judgment has free will, but not everyone capable of judgment is autonomous. The concept of autonomy is vague but usually refers to qualities that are not implied by free will. Such qualities are both subjective and objective, that is, qualities of an agent and of the social context she acts in. To the subjective qualities belongs the capacity of not only choosing freely but also choosing an option that suits her character. We need a self if we are not to dissolve in the sea of changes we cannot escape from. But we would shrink to bores if we were nothing but agents without the rich content that is given by the subject's passions. The self can suppress the subject, and the subject may overwhelm the self. To be autonomous, the individual must be in harmony with her subject and use the subject's qualities for her extraordinariness.

To the objective qualities belongs the existence of a society that offers options the agent can choose from so that she can acquire a specific character. People cannot be autonomous in societies where they have no choice between meaningful options, that is, options whose choice allows them to become extraordinary. This is why, as we'll see, there is no autonomy without a social system of value spheres. Free will, in contrast, is independent of social conditions. Free will is necessary but not sufficient for autonomy.

As autonomous people choose their actions after deliberation that includes deliberation of their own subjects, their choices are less arbitrary and hence better predictable than those of nonautonomous people who nonetheless have free will. For this reason Aristotle implies that "the free (*hoi eleutheroi*)," meaning those who are not slaves, are "less free" than the slaves,[30] presuming that a socially free man is more autonomous, and hence more reliable, than a slave.

Sixth, free will is neither reason nor the self. Reason is the power to detect and evaluate reasons; free will is the power to reject even the most evident reason for the reason to prove one's independence of predetermining factors; and the self is the power of deliberate judgment from which we cannot distance ourselves. Yet deliberate judgment uses both reason and free will; reason cannot be used without free will, and free will presupposes reason. The self, free will, and reason form a trinity united in judgment, as the three divine persons of Western theology are united in divinity.

So far we have discussed only one characteristic of the Cartesian self, though an extremely important one, its free will. There are more worth considering. Their importance becomes more conspicuous by comparing the Cartesian with the Lockean and the Kantian conceptions.

---

[30] Aristotle, *Metaphysics* Λ, 1075a19. Aristotle does not say they are "less free" (this is how David Ross, in his commentary to the text, translates the passage) but that they act less accidentally.

Chapter 4

Cartesian, Lockean, and Kantian Self

LIBERATED FROM DESCARTES'S DUALISM, THE CARTESIAN CONCEPTION of the self has the virtue of identifying the self with a capability. The Cartesian self is the capability of deliberate *judgment*; it is the individual considered in her capacity of judging, more exactly of *acting by judging* and *preparing* judgment. By definition, it, or we considered in this capacity, do not suffer or feel, as far as feeling is a passion without judgment (sometimes it includes judgment). What we suffer is something *happening* to us and therefore not part of the self. The self is constituted only by judging and by examining thoughts and feelings to determine whether they are to be accepted or rejected. Such examining is thinking. Thoughts in the sense of inspirations or ideas are different from the action of examining them; it is only such examination that I call thinking. Like passions and (nonjudging) feelings, thoughts (in distinction from thinking) are *objects* of the self, not its constituents. They belong to the subject. The self experiences them; or else it could not judge them. Nevertheless, it is not the experiencing of the subject that defines the self, but only our capacity of judging. Let's never forget that it is only the individual, the whole of self and subject, who acts and feels, not the self and the subject, although I often say so to mark out that the individual acts by her self and not her subject.

Yet modern philosophy followed a conception of the self that Locke introduced in this definition:

> Self is that conscious thinking thing (whatever Substance made up of, whether Spiritual, or Material, Simple, or Compounded, it matters not) which is sensible, or conscious of Pleasure and Pain, capable of Happiness or Misery, and so concern'd for it self, as far as that consciousness extends. Thus every one finds,

that whilst comprehended under that consciousness, the little Finger is as much
a part of it self, as what is most so.[1]

Though Locke calls the self a *thinking thing*, his conception differs from the
Cartesian one, as he does not distinguish *thinking* from *thought*. He subsumes
both under *consciousness*, which is not an activity. One of his reasons for doing
so probably was that, if we define the self by the capacity of judging, we still
cannot assume that it is deaf to what we are conscious of. But this looks like a
problem to the Cartesian conception only if we forget that the self is the property of the individual by which we distinguish what defines her identity. Strictly
speaking, the self neither acts nor feels; the individual does. Still, not any property defines her identity; which one does? If it is her consciousness, we run into a
fatal difficulty. Actions we have forgotten having done cannot be actions we are
responsible for, because what we are not conscious of does not belong to our self,
and what does not belong to it, we are not responsible for. This consequence has
rightly been taken for a refutation.[2]

In contrast, a self that is defined by deliberate judgment includes as actions it
is responsible for all deliberate judgments and the resulting actions it has performed. What it includes is not determined by what it is conscious of, but by
which actions it has deliberated and chosen.

Interestingly, in his political philosophy Locke uses a concept of a person that
conforms to the Cartesian conception. The person is what we can dispose of as a
possession[3] and what makes individuals responsible and objects of punishment
or reward.[4] It is something God cannot be responsible for. While people's bodies
are "his Property, whose Workmanship they are," that of the "one Omnipotent,
and infinitely wise Maker," the *person* is something "every Man has a *Property*
in."[5] Locke's *person* is the faculty of deliberate judgment by which we even can
decide to stop judging and allow a guardian to judge in our place. The same is
true of the Cartesian self.

---

[1]   John Locke, *An Essay Concerning Human Understanding*, bk.2, ch. 27, §17; ed. Nidditch, 341. I
     have put the second comma three words after the place it stands in this edition. By substance
     Locke does not understand the Aristotelian substance, but material or stuff. By describing the
     self as something "concern'd for it *self*," Locke comes close to the famous definition of the self as
     a relation I have to myself by Kierkegaard, Heidegger, and existentialists.
[2]   Joseph Butler, Dissertation I, "Of Personal Identity," appended to *The Analogy of Religion,
     Natural and Revealed, to the Constitution and Course of Nature*, 2nd ed. (London 1736), and
     Thomas Reid, *Essays on the Intellectual Powers of Man* (Edinburgh 1785), essay III, ch. 4, "Of
     Personal Identity," belongs to the first critics to use this argument.
[3]   Cp. Locke, *Two Treatises of Government* II, §§ 6, 27, 44, 173; Hobbes, *Leviathan* ch. 16, also uses
     this concept.
[4]   Ibid., §28: "... the Turfs my servant has cut ... become my *Property* because I am responsible for
     cutting the turf."
[5]   Ibid., §§ 6, 27. Laslett, in his Intro., ibid., 101, missing the meaning of *person,* says § 27 "almost
     contradicts" § 6.

We are not necessarily conscious of the activities of the self, but only capable of becoming aware of them. We become aware of them in the special operation of doubting and judging that Descartes produces in his first two Meditations. Kant has clearly seen this particularity of the self. He says of the "original-synthetic unity of apperception" that it is "the: *I think*" that "must *be able* to accompany all my ideas."[6] Kant thus takes account of three facts. First, very often we are not aware that it is us who think or do something, yet, second, we can nonetheless make sure that it is us, and, third, if we could not, we would not ascribe a self to ourselves. We have to include the same three characters into the Cartesian conception of the self.

But we have to replace the Kantian *I think* with the Cartesian *I judge*. Like the Kantian *I think*, the Cartesian *I judge* does not always express a thought that exists before it is expressed in a judgment. Rather, when we *first* detect our ability to accompany all our ideas by thinking *I think*, we "produce," as Kant says,[7] the idea "I think," and hence, ourselves as selfs. Similarly, by detecting that it is I who judges, as Descartes presents himself doing in his first two Meditations, we produce our selfs as a power of accompanying our judgments and any action we are judging on.

Yet this power of accompanying our thoughts is differently conceived by Kant and Descartes. In Descartes, it is a power not only to accompany but to control the actions we are judging on, to both prevent and allow them. In Kant it is but a power to get aware of them; it is the power of a consciousness that Locke conceived as the self. What is accompanied by Kant's *I think* happens anyway, so what is the importance of our *producing* ourselves by adding a thought to what happens anyway? Is our self really a powerless observer of events that become ours just because we become aware of them? In contrast, the Cartesian *I judge* implies the power to both admit and reject the action judged on. Accompanying my activities by an *I judge* produces my self as an active power, not as a passive observer. It is the act by which I become aware of my capacity of choosing either to go on doing what I did or not to go on. My power of selecting among my action possibilities can be overlooked in Descartes's demonstration of the self-disclosure in his first two Meditations, because in becoming aware of our indubitable existence as doubting agents we have no choice but to recognize, and identify with, the doubting by which we detect our self. Yet once we are constituted as such selfs, we have acquired the power of selecting among our action possibilities. This power enables me (my self) to form my individual self

---

6 Kant, *Kritik der reinen Vernunft* B, 131. ("Von der ursprünglich-synthetischen Einheit der Apperzeption. Das: *Ich denke*, muß alle meine Vorstellungen begleiten *können*").

7 Ibid., B, 132 ("Diese Vorstellung," i.e., the *I think*, "aber ist ein Aktus der *Spontaneität* ... weil sie dasjenige Selbstbewußtsein ist, was, indem es die Vorstellung *Ich denke* hervorbringt ... von keiner weiter abgeleitet werden kann." I follow Goldschmidt and Paton in substituting *abgeleitet* for *begleitet*.

(the way I choose actions) by models that I can arbitrarily choose, though often enough will choose under the influence of current fashions. Nonetheless, by this power I can even reject using it, preferring subjection to an authority.

So considering the virtues of the Cartesian conception, why did the Lockean conception prevail? Perhaps the most important reason is related to the one mentioned previously. Locke does not distinguish thinking from thought, the self from the subject; the active from the passive side of individuals. By this non-distinction he escaped a problem that burdened the Cartesian conception, as long as it seemed committed to Descartes's dualism: that of interaction between the mental and the physical. If we blur the difference of acting and experiencing under the cover of the concept of consciousness, we need not understand how we can act on the world and our own consciousness. The Cartesian conception, in contrast, as long as it was understood by the dualism Descartes defended, implied the idea that the self, rather than being an individual's capacity to judge after deliberation, is a ghost in the machine of our bodies, a homunculus some-where in our body pressing the knobs that moves it.[8]

However, because Descartes' dualism is not necessary at all for his conception of the self, we can see that the nondistinction of acting and experiencing in the Lockean conception is its basic failure rather than a virtue. We are organisms that can act on the world and our own consciousness; hence, there is something that was called "interaction" between the mental and the physical, although it is better called "an act of ourselves on the world and the subject." Locke's nondis-tinction does not even allow asking how such acting is possible.

The nondistinction of acting and experiencing favored and was favored by utilitarianism. This theory assumes that everyone is seeking to maximize their pleasure and minimize their pain. It was attractive because it seemed to agree with both Greek philosophy that taught that everyone pursues what seems good to them, and with Christian morality that teaches that we are to help oth-ers as much as possible. In fact, they differ, because neither the good the Greeks thought everyone pursues nor the good Christians are to do is a pleasure that can be maximized.[9] Yet theorists liked utilitarianism because it seemed scien-tific, ascribing to humans the natural tendency of pursuing the apparent good that was understood to be as irresistible as the tendency of birds to fly and fish to swim.[10] By it one might both predict human action and test traditions.[11] Perhaps

---

[8] This reproach became popular by Gilbert Ryle, *The Concept of Mind*, London (Hutchinson), 1949.

[9] Cp. Aristotle, *Nicomachean Ethics*, bk. I. What he calls happiness (*eudaimonia*) cannot be max-imized. Nor can Christian happiness.

[10] As Lichtenberg said, "Everyone seeks his happiness, even he who goes for hanging himself (Ein jeder sucht sein Glück, auch der, der geht, um sich aufzuhängen)." I was not able to find a source.

[11] As Jeremy Bentham formulated in the very beginning of his *Introduction to the Principles of Morals and Legislation* (1789): "Nature has placed mankind under the governance of two

most important is that, like the Lockean self-conception, it leaves no place for the distinction of acting and experiencing. To the utilitarian, even my judgments happen to me. As Hobbes had already claimed, "In *Deliberation*, the last Appetite, or Aversion, immediately adhering to the action, or to the omission thereof, is what we call the *Will*."[12] Hence, there is no way to distinguish self and subject, not to mention to conceive of free will.[13]

By the merging of the Lockean self-conception with utilitarianism, its opposition to the Cartesian conception became a deep, general opposition of two world views. It is an opposition that in the first place concerns questions of fact, namely whether men have a self, that is, the power of saying both *yes* and *no* to a proposition and whether they always strive after happiness. Only by implication is it also a normative question, namely if we ought to act according to the Cartesian or the Lockean-utilitarian conception. What we already can see is that the Lockean-utilitarian conception, though as a matter of historical fact prevalent in the West, can only insufficiently express the significance individualism has in modernity.

By its belief in human rights and equal liberty, the West ascribes to individuals moral priority over the claims of collectives. In the Lockean conception, this priority finds an expression in the epistemological priority that individuals have by their individual and private construction of the world from their sense impressions. (I have described it in Chapter 2.) Yet it is only in this construction, which is not physical but a special sort of mental activity or even nonactive process, that individuals are given priority. For the rest, they are completely passive, the objects of exterior forces. In contrast, the Cartesian conception denies individuals epistemological priority, as it claims that the subjective worlds are formed by the interaction of individuals in a shared physical world. It considers individuals to be epistemologically and conceptually dependent on each other. But it ascribes to them the power to act on and change the world and their subjects. This is a capacity that, better than the epistemological priority, fits the respect the individual is thought to be owed. For we certainly think that individuals merit the specific respect we grant them but deny animals for the capacities by which they differ from animals, and such are the capacities by which we can act on the world and our subjects. In contrast, the Lockean epistemological priority is bound to a privacy and determinism in individuals that gives little reason for respecting them, not to mention the problems that privacy and determinism raise for any kind of moral action.

---

sovereign masters, *pain* and *pleasure*. It is for them alone to point out what we ought to do, as well as to determine what we shall do. On the one hand the standard of right and wrong, on the other the chain of causes and effects are fastened to their throne."

12 Thomas Hobbes, *Leviathan*, ch. 6; ed. Macpherson, Penguin 1968, 127.

13 Another disadvantage of the Lockean conception is that it excludes collective selves, as consciousness can only be individual. Yet deliberation, the crucial property of the Cartesian conception, can be collective. Cp. Chapter 5.

Hoping for more evidence in favor of the Cartesian conception, let us consider how we decide on the identity of persons not at different times but at nearly identical places. When do we say that two human bodies, grown together by birth, are identical persons? Think of Siamese twins who share the head. We consider them to be one person; conversely, if they have the same body and two heads with separate brains, we shall consider them two persons. The reason is that we think of the brain as the seat of judgment and consciousness, at least one of which decides on the identity of persons. Now imagine two pairs of Siamese twins with two complete bodies and two heads but, *first*, they share some parts of the brain, *second*, brain science has proved that certain brain areas are responsible for judgment and others for consciousness, and *third*, one pair of the twins is grown together in the brain areas necessary for consciousness and the other in the brain areas necessary for judgment. Will we then consider the individuals of *both* pairs to be different persons?

I think we will not. We'll consider the pair having different judgments to be two persons, whether they have the same consciousness or not, and the "pair" having the same judgments as one person only, even if she suffers from a double consciousness. It is certainly improbable that the brains of two organisms grow together just in an area that is necessary for judgments and stay separate in the area necessary for consciousness, if local separation of these two functions in the brain is possible at all. But as far as we know, it is not conceptually impossible, because consciousness and judgment are different functions. There may be a person who has two different bodies and faces grown together at a certain point of her two heads, but in addition to that has also two different chains of pains and pleasures, sentiments and moods that she feels in her different bodies and expresses in her two different faces and bodies. But if this pair is governed by only one chain of judgments, deliberate intentions and decisions, we'll consider it only one person. Yet, if there are two different chains of judgments commanding the different bodies and their surroundings, we have to consider the pair two different persons.

How can we be sure that we shall thus decide? It belongs to the concept of an organism that we distinguish it from other organisms by the criterion of whether its movements start from it. If they don't we do not ascribe them to the organism, as Aristotle said when he analyzed the concept of the voluntary.[14] Yet what happens to an organism – feelings, thoughts, moods – is no movement that starts from an organism; they cannot constitute its identity, while the reactions to them can. Such responses are judgments and actions and what makes them possible and prepares them, as thinking and deliberating do.

But we have to take into account that most of our actions are not done after deliberation. Most of them are more or less spontaneous responses to desires, interests, or habitudes. How is this compatible with the Cartesian conception

[14] Aristotle, *Nicomachean Ethics* III, 1110a16.

of the self as the power of judgment? Actions without judgment cannot be governed by the Cartesian self indeed. Yet even animals and children coordinate their desires and initiate actions in a way that they become aim-directed and intentional. To use Freud's term, they have an ego that can act on the world and their desires and can be deranged by illness and other kinds of disorders. This ego is not yet a self, but we can call it a *proto-self*, because when children grow up under favorable conditions, it will become a self. It is what the self develops from. Even after developing a self from the proto-self, we initiate most of our actions by our proto-self. For being responsible for our actions, it is sufficient that we are *capable* of deliberating our actions and of replacing the proto-self with the self in controlling what we do. Now, just as we consider the brain or some part of it the crucial embodiment of the self, as it is the necessary and sufficient neural condition for agents to initiate their actions, we have to consider it the embodiment of the proto-self. Just like the self, the proto-self enables an organism to have numerical identity over time that lasts as long as the brain part does that embodies it.

So I conclude, with the proviso of judgment revision in case new evidence shows up, that the identity of an individual, animal or human, over a certain time depends on whether, over this time, it uses the same faculty of *originating action*, whether by judgment or without judgment. The criterion of whether it uses the same faculty is whether it exclusively possesses and uses the same brain or brain area that is a necessary neural condition for originating actions. This identity criterion is compatible with the Cartesian conception, but not with the Lockean one.

Let me point out the different kinds of personal identity that we ascribe to individuals when we attribute to them a proto-self or a self. As long as our identity is constituted only by our capacity of *originating* actions, a response to a stimulus or constellation of stimuli is processed by our nervous system in conformity with the laws of nature or by chance accidents. It is *my* response because it has been processed by *my* organism or the organism I am identified by. This does not imply that it is not nature that, by its laws or accidents, originates the action ascribed to me. On the contrary, it implies just that. It implies that the last and decisive origin, cause, or author of my action is nature or some power whose dependent product I am. This situation changes only when our identity passes over from our capacity of originating actions to our capacity of judgment.

What happens then? We can presume that the thought we judge on is an impulse to some action or belief. Before developing the new capacity this impulse is processed but not judged on. For being judged on it must become present to the organism in a way that the organism reflects whether what it expects of the impulse will materialize. It stops the impulse if the reflection results in a *no*. We do not know *how* this new control of impulses arises, but we know it does, since we are capable of it. The control is revolutionary, but not because the new self is a spiritual or mental entity. It is revolutionary because the power of judgment makes the individual capable of (in public or private) saying as well *no* as *yes* to the impulse so that, for the reasons discussed, her actions can become free from any predetermination. Though her power of judgment is a product of nature, it makes her judgments independent of it.

Natural evolution looped a strange loop with us. In deliberate judgments we, products of nature, decouple our selfs from nature, as we become independent of any natural predetermination. This decoupling has a remarkable effect on some of our ideas. We can oppose them to the natural conditions we decouple us from in deliberate judgment. Originally, the ideas of goodness, justice, and truth are standards that indicate what is good, just, and true for us, the language community we happen to be born into. Once we know we can be independent of any natural predetermination, we can conceive them as universal ideas that indicate what is good, just, and true for everyone. Conceiving them thus forbids us to form our ideas of truth and justice after self-interest. We can act against self-interest because we then enact our capacity to reject any predetermination, which at the same time is an enactment of extraordinariness. Those ideas seem to be supernatural and to refer to a realm beyond nature. They are supernatural indeed, as they spring from our capacity to decouple us from nature. But they refer not to a supernatural realm but to a capacity of ours that is a product of natural evolution.

The decoupling, though, occurs only in judgments. In thousands of other respects, we remain dependent on nature. We can sometimes become masters of nature, but never its creators. One of our indelible dependencies on nature is that the self always remains fallible. Traditionally, philosophers agreed that judgment is fallible but they distinguished reason and understanding from judgment. Following this tradition, Kant lists three higher cognitive faculties: reason, understanding, and judgment. Unfortunately, this is not only a terminological difference from the Cartesian conception, because it implies the idea that, while judgment is fallible, reason and understanding are not.

In his distinction, Kant presupposes that judgment is always more or less subjective and arbitrary, hence fallible, just as the decision of one judge can differ from that of another one. At the same time, he exempts reason from subjectivity, following tradition in defining *reason* as the "faculty of mediated inferences."[15] Such inferences are infallible indeed. When we deduce, from the premises that all men are mortal and Socrates is a man, the conclusion that Socrates is mortal, there is no latitude for subjectivity. Similarly, the faculty of *understanding* was thought to deal with conceptual relations outside of logical

---

[15] Kant, *Kritik der reinen Vernunft* B, 355f. He adds that outside of logic, i.e., in philosophical investigations like his own, reason is better called the "faculty of principles," because he considers it the faculty by which we recognize the principles of theoretical and practical reason that he claims to formulate.

syllogisms. Kant called understanding "the faculty of rules" or "of concepts"[16] and excluded subjectivity and fallibility from it, as he considered understanding the finding of a concept (e.g., that of an animal) under which to subsume a given concept (e.g., that of a lion). Although he sometimes calls the understanding a faculty of judgment,[17] the distinction is as important for him as that between fallible and infallible knowledge.

To the faculty of *judgment* Kant ascribes the function "of discerning whether something" – that is, an individual or particular case, not a concept – "falls under a given rule," that is, a concept.[18] Such discerning, he says, cannot follow a rule, because rules by definition can only be formulated for general cases. Therefore, all knowledge that refers to the particular (as does all empirical knowledge) is delivered by the faculty of judgment. Because this faculty cannot rely on rules, and it is only rules that Kant thinks can be taught, judgment cannot be taught. It is "a special talent that requires not teaching but use. For this reason, judgment is the specific property of wits, lack of which no school can repair."[19] In his *Critique of Judgment*, Kant distinguishes two cases of judgment: that of finding a concept for a particular case and that of finding a particular for a concept, marking the latter out as aesthetic judgment (as he considers the task of the artist is to give concrete intuition to abstract thought).[20] In either case, we cannot avoid subjectivity and fallibility.

However, according to the Cartesian conception of judgment, the difference Kant finds between judgment on one hand and reason and understanding on the other is not a difference of faculties but that between knowledge acquisition and tools for knowledge acquisition. The logical relations that Kant and the tradition he followed consider an object of infallible knowledge acquired by reason and understanding are not knowledge at all, but rules for the use of concepts and statements by which we can acquire knowledge. There is only one way to come by knowledge. It consists, first, in grasping a problem or a question; second, in finding possible answers; third, in considering and weighing reasons for and against the truth or rightness of the answer; fourth, in deciding on which reason to follow. Such a decision, as we have seen, is never free of arbitrariness. Because it raises a validity claim that demands consent of any other agent of judgment, to some extent, the judgment community can correct individual arbitrariness. Yet because its judgments are again only the result of

---

[16] Ibid., A, 126.

[17] E.g., ibid., A, 126; A, 69; B, 94.

[18] Ibid., A, 132; B, 171.

[19] Ibid., A, 133; B, 172. By "wits," I translate "Mutterwitz." According to Wittgenstein, *Philosophical Investigations* I §§ 143–242, the problem, meanwhile known as that of "following a rule," is solved by assuming that subsumption of an individual under a concept rests on "training" to respond to a stimulus with the correct verbal response.

[20] Kant, *Critique of Judgment*, Introduction IV; transl. J.H. Bernard, London, Macmillan, 1914.

individual judgments, they cannot escape arbitrariness, fallibility, and subjectivity either.

Hence, Kant and the tradition he follows mistake logical and conceptual rules for knowledge. *If* I accept that all men are mortal and that Socrates is a man and *if* I use the tool for knowledge acquisition that consists in the rules of syllogism, *then* I do not judge but deduce that Socrates is mortal. Unlike the judgment, the deduction can be performed by a computer as well. But it is not necessary that I deduce (only the computer needs to, if it is thus programmed). I may reject the premises, or erroneously judge them insufficient, or reject the rules of syllogism. Moreover, if the premises state only conceptual relations, also the conclusion only states conceptual relations and cannot acquire knowledge. If they do not state conceptual relations but refer to particulars, then, according also to Kant, they are judgments, hence, fallible. Then, of course, the conclusion is fallible as well. So there is no other way to come by new knowledge than by deliberating reasons and deciding on them, hence, by judgments that necessarily are both fallible and more or less arbitrary.

Ironically, in his *Critique of Judgment*, the faculty he admits is fallible, Kant points to a kind of knowledge that is neither acquired by deliberation nor fallible. He gives the examples of "the joy of a needy but well-meaning man at becoming the heir of an affectionate but penurious father" that the heir disapproves of, and "the sorrow of a widow at the death of her excellent husband" that the widow approves.[21] The heir's joy and the widow's sorrow present them with feelings they censure; what they censure is necessarily known to them, hence, a kind of knowledge. But it is a knowledge that cannot be reasonably called fallible, as there are no means to disprove it.

So, there is infallible knowledge of sorts. It consists in *veridical* feelings:[22] If we feel them, we can like and dislike and ignore, misunderstand, and adulterate them, but as far as we feel them we can only state them. Joy and sorrow belong to a wide class of infallible knowledge that on the one hand we state and on the

---

[21] Ibid., § 54.

[22] Arendt, *Lectures on Kant's Political Philosophy*, 68f, refers to Kant's analyses of judgment in his *Critique of Judgment* to support her theory, according to which judgment is a specific quality of decision in politics. Though unfortunately she accepts Kant's distinction of reason, understanding and judgment, in her use the distinction often makes perfect sense. So when, in her comments on the Pentagon Papers, she says: "The problem-solvers did not *judge*; they calculated ... If, for instance, it can be calculated that the outcome of a certain action is 'less likely to be a general war than more likely,' it does not follow that we can choose it even if the proportion were eighty to twenty, because of the enormity and *incalculable quality* of the risk" ("Lying in Politics," in *Crises of the Republic*, 37; italics Arendt's). Yet the calculation she rightly opposes to a *fallible* judgment in the end is a judgment as well; the problem solvers only *purported*, and in the end believed, that it was an objective calculation without a subjective element. As she said, "This categorizing ... in which nothing is decided except whether we have gone about our task in a demonstrably correct or incorrect way, has more to do with thinking as deductive reasoning than with thinking as an act of judgment." (*The Promise of Politics*, 104).

other can take an attitude to: physical pains and pleasures, sentiments, emotions and passions, thoughts and ideas of all sorts. Stating them is uttering them, and utterances are as little judgments as cries are. They are what are presupposed by judgment; for judging, we need something we can judge on that is not a judgment. It is not only feelings that may be called infallible knowledge but also ideas and reasons that we deliberate before judging.

It is in a special sense that we can call the wide class of sentiments and thoughts knowledge. Ideas, thoughts, and sentiments are known to us in the sense that they are given to us; they present us with something we have to take as given for deciding on their truth or rightness. It is not the world nor morality that we learn by them but whatever belongs to our subjectivity, including how the world seems to us. It gives knowledge of our subjects, but it is subjective knowledge. It is infallible because it is what seems to us. We can call it acquaintance with our subjects.

Isn't there also infallible knowledge of the self? Do I not infallibly know that I judge when I judge, think when I think, doubt when I doubt? No; I may believe that, for instance, I judge that Peter is a good man when in fact I do not judge but doubt he is; I may believe that I think about how to go to Boston when I think about whether it is good to go to Boston or do not think at all. I can distinguish between what it seems to me that I do, judge or think, and what I really do, judge or think; therefore, my assertions concerning my self, unlike my acquaintance with my subject, must be backed, and can be attacked, by reasons. Knowledge of my self implies knowledge of the objective world, because the self is an agent that acts in and on the world, and all knowledge of the objective world is dependent on decisions on which reason to follow, hence, fallible.

To sum up, Kant's diverging view on the infallibility of some kinds of knowledge acquisition and even of judgment does not disconfirm the Cartesian view on knowledge acquisition. But it reminds us that there is a particular source of knowledge, sentiments, and thoughts that gives us infallible acquaintance with the subject and the matter we judge on. A conclusion we might draw has the air of a paradox: As soon as knowledge can be called true it can be false, as it necessarily is fallible; and as long as we do not judge, our knowledge is infallible. But though theorists may have been misled by this paradox, it is a triviality. For acquiring knowledge we have to start with something given, with sentiments and thoughts; as the starting point for knowledge acquisition, we liberally may call it knowledge of sorts. But the starting point of knowledge, of course, is not yet knowledge.

Chapter 5

Extraordinariness and the Two Stages of Rationality

THE CARTESIAN CONCEPTION PRESENTS THE SELF AS THE CAPACITY of an individual to freely choose the reasons for always fallible judgments that is necessarily embodied and identified by an organism but not identical with it. Descartes has been most important for the development of this conception, but is neither an infallible authority nor the only contributor. In this section I'll look at authors who prepared and confirmed the conception: Plato, Aristotle, Hegel, Freud, and Hannah Arendt. They will clarify what is not yet clear enough: By our selfs, we necessarily aim at extraordinariness.

Plato distinguishes three parts of the mind. To reason and desire, two parts long ago distinguished under various names, he adds *thumos*, which we may translate as "passion" or "spirit."[1] According to Plato, reason and desire propose to us actions that are often opposed to each other. Reason is a faculty enabling us to know nonempirical ideas that inspire action; desire is what pushes or pulls us to pleasure satisfaction. This distinction corresponds to my distinction of self and subject, because Plato's reason also is the power of judgment and his desire is something that happens to us. Plato regards desire's power to move us to action as stronger than that of reason. But reason in its fight with desire is helped by *thumos*. *Thumos* appears not only in adults but in children and dogs. They may passionately fight for a cause, also for reason, even though they are not themselves attacked.

Plato does not explain *why* reason gets support from passion. He seems to be more interested in the empirical fact, which is surprising indeed, that even children and dogs that lack reason may by their fury support reason. How are we to understand this? They certainly can become furious in favor of reason only when they have been conditioned to do so. But they can be trained only because

---

[1] "Passion" is the traditional translation; "spirit" has been chosen by G. M. A. Grube. Plato expounds his view of the tripartition of the soul in Republic IV, 435c–441c.

they have *thumos*. *Thumos* was known as the passion Homer ascribes to warriors when they become furious and overcome fear, weariness, and other hindrances to fighting. It is a passion that aims at defending one's value; an ambition of self-assertion. It helps reason by defending, not reason's standards, but the individual's self-respect. Plato presumes that reason and *thumos* share the aim of securing the individual's value. When a child gets furious, her *thumos* responds to what she feels is a violation of her self, which is still a proto-self, rather than a violation of reason. Her fury aims at restoring, not the standards of reason, but her own value. But how can she feel attacked in her proto-self when she sees a violation of what she has been trained to regard as standards of reason?

It is because Plato considers violations of reason the result of unchecked desire, and unchecked desire a danger to both the proto-self and self. Desire tends to dissolve the powers of both originating and deliberating action. So, because *thumos* is the passion for defending one's self and proto-self, it sides with reason against desire. Desire is their common enemy. But it is their enemy for a further reason. Both reason and *thumos* act against the ordinary. Following desire condemns people to stay on a level with animals, which to Plato and Aristotle is ordinary. In contrast, following reason or *thumos* makes a man extraordinary. This is obvious for *thumos* if we read about it in Homer. But it is obvious also for reason, as it proposes to us the extraordinary action-goals that we know by means of the transcendent ideas reason can present to us (because, as I remarked in the last chapter, we can decouple both us and our concepts from any predetermination).

Plato seems to have been the first to ally reason with the ambition of self-assertion. He does not argue, as I have done, that reason implies this ambition. He rather makes the ambition, in the form of *thumos,* an ally of reason. He is silent, though, on the danger that has become fairly obvious today: that the ambition of extraordinariness may as well lead to extraordinarily evil actions. He does not say anything either about a form of reason that might precede a mature form of reason.

Aristotle, however, distinguishes active and passive reason.[2] One reason for this distinction may have been to take account of the stage when the youth has to be trained by the advice of the adult.[3] In this stage, the youth's reason cannot yet be active. Only when he has acquired the habit necessary the intellectual virtues can he enact reason. If he has, he will actively use reason (and meet a condition for leading a life of *eudaimonia,* happiness), and will even do so in order to use his rational capacities *kat' areten,* "in excellence or extraordinarily."[4]

So we may speculate that Aristotle conceives of the full form of reason as a faculty necessarily preceded by a passive form that requires obedience to an

---

[2]   Aristotle, *De Anima,* 429b26–30a25.
[3]   Cp. Aristotle, *Politics* VII, 1334b19–29.
[4]   Aristotle, *Nicomachean Ethics* I, 1098a17.

authority. It is such a distinction that he may have found wanting in Plato. Plato's allying reason with *thumos* may have made problematic to Aristotle what Plato seems to have considered not a serious problem: that *thumos's* striving for extraordinariness can easily lead to vice rather than to virtue, and therefore, as it is allied with reason, makes it necessary to distinguish a passive authoritarian reason (by which people are trained to morality) from active reason (though this enables to reject even morality). So perhaps Plato triggered the two-phased concept of rationality that found its explication only in the twentieth century.

His recognition of *thumos* enables Plato to understand history and society not just as the struggle of reason and desire but as a more complex process in which *thumos*, or the ambition of self-assertion, plays its specific part. Similarly, Hegel rejects any explanation of history that does not take account of men's struggle for their individual recognition by other men, which again is a form of self-assertion. Such struggle does not aim at spreading reason and yet is the servant of reason, because it works for making reason the ruler of men. It starts from an individual's demanding of the other recognition of his superiority.[5] Plato's *thumos* puts individuals in opposition to each other as well, but it presupposes an offense for which they fight. The Hegelian individual demands from the other recognition of his superiority for no particular reason at all. He wants any other to recognize him to be superior, not just in fighting but in a quality specific to men. Such quality is that of overcoming the fear of his death that he risks in his struggle for recognition.

So while Plato's *thumos* is allied with reason, Hegel's struggle for recognition is allied with free will. The recognition the individual aims at implies the recognition that he is independent of any predetermination.[6] His perfect indifference to utilitarian considerations obviously risks general destruction. But Hegel wants to show that general destruction is prevented, not by abandoning self-assertion, but by finding a specific, universal form for it. It is just because the defeated do not abandon struggling for their recognition that the fight for recognition does not end in universal self-annihilation. If they gave up, only the victors would be left to give recognition; for recognition presupposes someone whose recognition has and can give value. In this case the victors would fight

---

5   The struggle is described in Hegel's *Phenomenology of Mind* IV, A (*Lordship and Bondage*). I partly follow Alexandre Kojève, *Introduction to the Reading of Hegel*, Cornell University Press, 1980, in my interpretation, but do not suppose that this interpretation exhausts Hegel's *Phenomenology* or his philosophy.

6   Does Hegel follow the Cartesian conception of free will? He starts his *Philosophy of Right* with a definition of will by three moments that organize both his philosophy of right and his entire system of philosophy. The first moment is "the element of *pure indeterminateness*, or of pure reflection, of the I in itself in which all restriction, all content given and specified by nature, need, desire, and drives are dissolved" (§5). This element is the aspect of indifference in the Cartesian conception. But there are also remarks in Hegel that do not fit well with the Cartesian conception.

with each other until no one would be left to get recognition from, and mankind would fall back on an animal state. Yet the vanquished find a new form of self-assertion in their serving the master. By making him dependent on their service, they become his equal and restart the struggle for recognition on a new level. Now extraordinariness is shown by indifference not to death but to the labor of serving a task that again does not follow utilitarian considerations.

It is in this way that the universalization of the struggle for recognition develops all constructive human faculties, producing discipline, creativity, and rationality. Max Weber was to develop this idea. Like Plato, Hegel finds support for the work of reason in self-assertion. But his self-assertion is not an independent ally of reason but its vehicle, an instrument of the cunning of reason.

In his presentation of the struggle for recognition, Hegel marks out an important character of the ambition of extraordinariness. People cannot aim at extraordinariness without presupposing a public, or at least one other person, who is to recognize their extraordinariness. Much as the individuals strive for extraordinariness just in order to leave behind the dependence on the judgment of the other, they can never free themselves from this dependence. Inescapably, they remain bound to the judgment of the world, but inescapably as well, they strive to overcome it.

Unlike Plato, Hegel developed a two-stage conception of the self and rationality, though a curious one. He presents historical agents as ruled by their desires and whims; they do not use reason but are its instruments. It is only the theorist who sees that men, just because of their follies, realize reason and freedom; that the heroes of history, Alexander, Caesar, and Napoleon, by their self-assertive, ruthless subjection of peoples, break the fetters of established societies and allow more and more people to find opportunities for enacting their capacities.[7] So we have two levels of rationality, that of historical practice and that of philosophical theory. In contradiction to Aristotle's distinction of active and passive reason, Hegel's superior philosophical reason is condemned to passivity. Philosophy puts knowledge on an Olympic height that people in the flats of history can never attain. It claims a wisdom that saves the wise from the pains of action.

Yet in a way of paradox that Hegel was fond of, this double-stage conception of rationality is the more condemned to collapse the more it seems convincing. For if we believe in it, we shall use our philosophical rationality for intervening in history and fight for a shortcut to the happy ending that avoids the repression and irrationality Hegel taught is unavoidable. This is what Marx and other Hegelians did. They switched back to Aristotle's model of rationality for which the higher stage is also the active stage.

---

7   Kant, in his *Idea for a Universal History*, transl. L. W. Beck, *Introduction* and *Eighth Thesis*, held a similar view, presenting mankind's future as following a "plan of nature" and even "Nature's secret plan." Cp. below, III 8.

The best confirmation of the Cartesian two-phased concept of rationality comes from Freud. The intention of psychoanalysis, Freud said, is "to support the ego, to make it more independent of the superego, to enlarge its scope of perception, and to extend its organization, so that it will be able to appropriate new parts of the id. Where there was id, there shall be ego."[8] Freud's ego includes self and proto-self. The process by which the ego extends its "organization" is the process by which a proto-self becomes a self. It is the passage from a first stage of rationality to the second stage, presupposed by both the Cartesian conception and by Freud. Freud has analyzed the process and its difficulties in a way that splendidly fits Cartesian expectations.

The passage from the first to the second stage would not so often need the help of an analyst if it were simple. Freud presumes it is difficult, not just in pathological but in normal development. We can locate the causes of the difficulty in the multifaceted role of what Freud called the superego. A first aspect of its role is that it is necessary for the proto-self to become a self. The child is a creature that has to learn to control its desires, because following them would often be fatal. Freud classifies desires as the id, unfortunately conceiving them as necessarily unconscious, though desires are of course not always unconscious. The child can learn to control the id only by following the judgments of individuals close to her. What she learns from them is the exercise of reason or judgment. Reason and control of desires are as inseparable for Freud as for Plato. The way parents control the child's actions and impulses becomes a model for the child of how to respond to her stimuli. It is the first model of rationality.

A second aspect is that this model is formed by the directions of the parents or other close persons who care for the child and attract her love. It presents to the child an interest in her own well-being that she identifies with and understands as the voice of her conscience. The model of rationality becomes a mental instance that pretends to be the child's self. Connected with this aspect is the third one – that the model cannot be founded on argument or insight but only on incontestable authority. But when the youth passes from imitating judgment to judging herself, what once was a necessary help for her development turns into a fetter. She has to grasp that rationality means following her own fallible judgment, but her first concept of rationality directs her to look for an authoritative form of rationality in another person. The opposition of new requirement and old habitude can produce the symptoms of inner conflicts that Freud so aptly described. Even if she learns to distinguish her own self from the pretended self of the superego, she will suffer from her rejection of it, for it threatens to punish her noncompliance with loss of self-respect. Such threat is

[8]　Sigmund Freud, *Vorlesungen zur Einführung in die Psychoanalyse*, 516 (31. Vorlesung: Die "Absicht" der Psychoanalyse "ist ja, das Ich zu stärken, es vom Über-Ich unabhängiger zu machen, sein Wahrnehmungsfeld zu erweitern und seine Organisation auszubauen, so daß es sich neue Stücke des Es aneignen kann. Wo Es war, soll Ich werden.")

possible because the superego has gained the role of a power to grant and refuse self-respect.

When Freud aims at dissolving the power of the superego, he does not imply that the power of granting and refusing self-respect should be dissolved. He rather aims at putting this power in the place where he thinks it belongs, namely, in the individual's own power of judgment. In the process of the individual's taming of her superego, we can recognize her emancipation from the ordinary world and its collectivism. It is an emancipation Heidegger described as the individual's turn from *das Man* to authenticity. It is perhaps Freud's greatest achievement for the basics of psychology that he pointed out in a particularly attractive way the (second) specific difference of man from animal (in addition to that of man's reason) that I am focusing on, the necessary break separating child and adult. Freud demonstrated not only that we need favorable conditions to replace the authoritarian model of rationality by the fallible way of the ego; he also demonstrated the power of the first model by convincing individual cases and intelligent reflection on them, not least by baptizing it superego. So we may well ask how its replacement with the ego is possible at all.

Here is Freud's answer. The ego has to mediate between "three severe masters": "driven by the id, hemmed in by the superego, repelled by reality, the ego wrestles for the accomplishing of its economic task of producing harmony among the powers and influences which act in and upon it."[9] The wrestling ego is the proto-self that starts discerning its own interests from those of the superego. How can it overcome its weakness? Though Freud does not give prominence to this point, the crucial step is that the ego learns that the power of id and superego depends on its consent to their demands. The more divergent these are, the better the ego (or the individual, by her capacity of judgment) can use its power of saying *no* or *yes* to them and strengthen itself against the threats of its masters. Saying *no* to a command of the superego threatens the ego with loss of self-respect. But against such a threat it can lean on the demands of the id or reality, whenever they diverge from the demands of the superego. The ego would be incapable of sticking to its rejection of the superego without the support it can take from one of the other original masters. Yet what constitutes the power source of the ego (and thus the self and no longer the proto-self) is its capacity of saying *no* and *yes* to the demands of its former masters.

So the Cartesian and Freudian agree that the development of the self is inseparable from the development of reason. They even agree that the mature form of rationality will be different in different individuals. They understand both rationality and the self not as capacities enacted in the same way in all individuals but as imbued with individuality and arbitrariness. The ego deliberates the

---

9　Ibid., 514f. ("drei gestrengen Herren": "vom Es getrieben, vom Über-Ich eingeengt, von der Realität zurückgestoßen, ringt das Ich um die Bewältigung seiner ökonomischen Aufgabe, die Harmonie unter den Kräften und Einflüssen herzustellen, die in ihm und auf es wirken.")

reasons its three severe masters can produce for following one of them, yet in
the end decides both rationally and arbitrarily for the special Cartesian reason
to demonstrate its capacity of liberating itself from any predetermining factor.
True, Freud (like Descartes) wants to secure the sphere of science from individual arbitrariness. Yet, also like Descartes, he can do so only conditionally.
Science presupposes egos that have emancipated themselves from the rule of
the superego, but an ego can become master of its former masters only if it also
is capable of opting for the Cartesian reason to demonstrate its liberty from all
predetermining reasons.[10]

Because we cannot have a capacity without enjoying its enacting, the individual will enjoy her power of liberating herself from all predetermining influences. So she will also enjoy acting against all expectations, for expectations
belong to the most powerful predetermining influences. Moreover, they represent to her the ordinary, because she is used to them. So she will enjoy doing
the extraordinary. Freud, it is true, probably would have claimed that psychoanalysis will free individuals from their craving for extraordinariness. But his
description of the way the ego "wrestles for the accomplishing of its economic
task" commits him to ascribing to the ego the ambition of extraordinariness.
The influences it has to wrestle down are all influences representing something
ordinary: reality in the first place, because reality represents the ordinary world;
and the id, because the desires and drives it represents are again what is ordinary. The superego, it is true, can represent the extraordinary expectations of
the parents. But what is extraordinary for the parents is ordinary for the individual, because she is used to them. For wrestling them down, she must oppose
to them what for her is extraordinary. So, if not Freud, then his psychology con-
verges with the Cartesian, the Platonic, and the Hegelian in assuming that man
has an ambition of extraordinariness that is indelibly allied with both his self
and reason.

There is an important property of the Cartesian conception of the self that
Freud's confirmation of it makes better if visible. It is that the conception is
applicable not only to individuals but also to groups. Just as individuals are capable of isolating their power of judgment from the rest of their mind and of pin-
ning self against subject, so are collectives. For doing so, there must be ways by
which actions of individuals come to constitute a collective and their individual
powers of judgment are transformed into a collective's self. Such ways can consist in a contract between individuals; they constitute rational collectives with
specified decision procedures that allow ascribing actions to the collective rather
than to an individual. But they can also constitute irrational collectives. They

---

[10]   Jean Piaget and Lawrence Kohlberg have introduced important stages in the transition from
       child to adult rationality and self. The crucial one is the passage from Kohlberg's conventional
       to postconventional stages.

are caused when individuals relapse into subjection to a superego that does not represent the will of their parents, but of a real or imagined person. Such relapses happen in publics under the spell of anxieties that make the individuals crave for an authority rather than rely on their own judgment, as in a panic and in situations that favor totalitarian movements.

In contrast, the Lockean conception of a self does not allow conceiving of a group self, because the self is defined by the consciousness of an individual and consciousness necessarily is the state of an individual. It implies that talk of group selfs is nonsense or metaphorical.

Hannah Arendt has pointed to another property of the Cartesian self worth noting. It necessarily aims at a particularly extraordinary goal modern philosophy avoids considering – namely, immortality. An individual who is capable of acting freely and rationally cannot accept any obstacle to her ambitions. Yet her self-assertion is inexorably stopped by death. Hence, she cannot accept death. Her knowledge of her self gives her an idea of what it means to be immortal. It means going on judging as the same judger on the never-ending, possible objects of judgments. Her self, rather than her extenuating and exhaustible desires, will press her to demand immortality.

True, most young people do not bother about mortality. The reason is not that they do not crave for immortality. Rather, they naïvely believe they are immortal. One day, they detect with horror that they are not. Once aware of this fact, they oppose to it their self-understanding as creatures that *ought* to be immortal. Immortality is *due* to a power that can grasp, expect, and enjoy immortality.

Therefore, the original goal of self-assertion, mastering the three severe masters of the ego, is complemented by the goal of immortality. The original goal has led to the utopian idea (liberalism's core idea) of a world everyone can act freely and rationally in; its complement demands the utopian idea of men's immortality. This aim has rarely been publicly declared. Philosophers often reject it because they think we should not aim at the impossible. But if we consider what is implied in poetry, religions, and technological fantasies, we cannot deny that immortality belongs to men's uppermost demands. And of course, the craving for immortality inherent in becoming aware of one's power of judgment is different from craving for a life after death. It craves for the immortality of a self incorporated in bones, blood, and brain and going on living in this world. Life after death is only the opiate ersatz for this original goal.

Hannah Arendt belongs to the few authors who have given due attention to the human craving for immortality. It may seem, though, that she ascribes to our time a loss of interest in it. Formerly, she says, men sought immortality, either in the world that would commemorate their feats, or in a supernatural afterlife; but after the separation of religion and politics in the seventeenth century, both options were rejected and "both life and world had become perishable, mortal, and futile. Today," she goes on, "we find it difficult to grasp this situation of absolute mortality could be unbearable." Yet, in fact, she assumes that today it is as unbearable as ever, even though few avow that it is. She attests to the modern world a "growing meaninglessness" that is exacerbated by the basic role of private property in modern society.[11] "Private interests which by their very nature are ... limited by man's natural span of life" can only "escape into the sphere of public affairs" by creating "a society very similar to that of the ants and bees," which loses all humanity, or by projecting "grandiose aims in politics, such as establishing a new society in which justice will be guaranteed forever, or fighting a war to end all wars or to make the whole world safe for democracy." She presupposes that such escapism "is incapable of guaranteeing men any kind of immortality."[12]

Arendt points to a requirement any attempt at understanding the self-understanding of the West (or any other tradition) should meet. It is to understand not only its avowed expectations but also its nonavowed ones. We can hope to do so if we understand human actions not only as the reactions to stimuli but also as the expressions of ambitions that are built into the constitution of our minds. Such an ambition is self-assertion and its ambition of extraordinariness, which includes the ambition of becoming immortal.[13]

Our ambition of extraordinariness is a necessary result of our capacity of judgment. It is a capacity that, from a means to serve the subject or the world, becomes an end in itself. So, using it for its own sake excludes its use for the subject or the world. As the subject and the world are the ordinary, its use for its own sake means its use for the extraordinary. The idea of the extraordinary results from our refusing any object of our will that makes the will its servant rather than its own cause. Such a refusal pits our self against the subject and the world.

But already our proto-self, the power of initiating (voluntary) actions, is thus pitted by the same refusal. The ambition of extraordinariness is connected already with the proto-self. In fact, Plato's *thumos* is this ambition of the proto-self. Therefore, as we shall see, the ambition of extraordinariness remains, even when individuals abandon their selves by abandoning their power of deliberate judgment.

The authors discussed in this section recognize a property of reason not duly taken account of in the prevalent philosophical psychology – namely, that it can be used for its own sake and necessarily inspires the ambition of extraordinariness. If we do not take account of it, we shall understand neither individuals nor

---

[11] Arendt, *Between Past and Future.* Cornell University Press, 1954, 73f and 78f.

[12] Arendt, *The Origins of Totalitarianism*, loc. cit. 145; and *Between Past and Future*, loc. cit. 78f.

[13] There is still another way Arendt confirms the Cartesian conception. I talk about it in Chapter 9.

societies, neither history nor the future. If we do not accommodate our institutions to it, still more disaster threatens than we had to experience.

Before considering how to accommodate institutions to the ambition, we have to perform another task. If, as I claim, the Cartesian conception is the best understanding of the self the West has produced, we should expect it to fit the facts. History should confirm that men act the way the Cartesian conception conceives of their actions. If we succeed in showing they do, we'll have both confirmed the Cartesian conception and advanced our understanding of history.

Part III

The Cartesian Self in History

Humanity does not strive for happiness; only the English do.
Nietzsche, Twilights of the Idols

I n this part, I look for traces of the Cartesian self in history. If individuals are Cartesian selves, they should have left their footprints. Notoriously, history bears many interpretations, so it would be pretentious to call such a search a test of the Cartesian conception by history. Yet if history becomes better understandable by looking at it with certain conceptual glasses, we may take such understanding for evidence that the conception is not falsified and the expected traces can be found. I dare say that the two-stage concept of the self and rationality makes history more understandable than one-stage conceptions.

By tracking the Cartesian self in history, it will also be possible to detail the two stages of rationality. As I aim at an assessment of the West and its potentialities today, and presume they are not independent of the self and the way it is grasped, it is necessary to understand the historical forms of rationality and the self. To understand them, Freud's and Heidegger's analyses have to be enriched by historical analysis. Yet a look at history needs to be guided by concepts. If I followed only the Cartesian conception of the self and rationality, I could not check it by history. I have tried avoiding prejudice by using both the Cartesian and the utilitarian conception in reading history.

As the most conspicuous characters of Cartesian selfs are their development from a childhood self and their ambition of extraordinariness, they should have left their marks in history. Because history is full of extraordinary feats, it is easy to find signs of this ambition. So we have to concentrate on a search for signs of the break between childhood and adult self and rationality. Freud and Heidegger described it as so difficult that it becomes improbable, but as it did happen, and the West is considered to be an incorporation of the adult self and rationality, our search should look for an explanation of how Western civilization could arise at all.

Chapter 6

The Cause and Content
of Modernity

ONE ROOT OF WESTERN CIVILIZATION IS THE CIVILIZATION OF THE Greeks of the fifth and fourth centuries BC. They started science, politics, and a form of rationality that have become models for the West. Nonetheless, ancient Greece is not the West. What distinguishes them is the idea that science, politics, and rationality are forms of activities that are open to and binding for everyone. For Plato and Aristotle, reason in its full active form was a capacity owned only by male Greeks; its lack in the barbarians entitled the Greeks to enslave them.[1] For them, mankind was divided in natural masters and natural slaves. What distinguishes the West or modernity (which I identify) from ancient Greece is its belief in the unity of mankind, the universality of reason, and the equal rights of everyone to decide on their life.

There is no sharp borderline between antiquity and modernity. We find the modern view already in Cicero and the Stoic philosophers he drew on, perhaps even earlier,[2] and the West is full of theorists and politicians who tacitly or openly reject the idea of universal reason. However, this idea prevails in and defines the West, just as the idea of a natural split of mankind into masters and slaves prevailed in and defined antiquity.

So when we search for an explanation for how modernity could arise at all, the first question is how the idea of universality of reason could arise. To be

---

[1]   Aristotle, *Politics* I, 1254b10–1255a2; Plato, *Republic* V, 469b-c, 471a. Plato rejects enslaving Greeks but seems to presuppose that enslaving barbarians is just. But Plato is certainly closer to a universalistic conception of reason than Aristotle. Hence, certainly against his intention, he undermined the closed society.

[2]   Cicero, *On Duties* III, 69, calls the law of nature, and by implication reason, "shared by all with all." His idea of shared reason even extends to that of shared natural resources: "everything produced on the earth is created for the use of mankind" (ibid., I, 22). The idea that active reason is given to everyone might have been held by sophists like the Athenian Antiphon, though it is difficult to decide. Cp. de Romilly, *The Great Sophists*, 182f and 122f.

sure, as we find the idea of active reason in ancient Greece and active reason represents the second stage of rationality, it is also worth asking how this idea could arise. But this question does not pose a serious problem once we grasp that an individual's reason necessarily first needs authoritarian training but then strives for independence, however hard the hindrances. We know that to reach it, conditions must be favorable, and we can understand that they were favorable in ancient Greece. What poses a problem is how the second stage of rationality could become an ideal to be attained by everyone. As long as the second stage is reached only by some happy individuals, it is the object of their pride and delight and a basis of their claims to rule the rest. But if it becomes a universal ideal, it turns into an obligation of everyone to respect everyone's deliberated views and a right of everyone to be respected, a right that bursts closed society. Historically we find this development in the shift from the often-praised Greek joy of life to the no-less-often-blamed Christian and Muslim gloom and gravity. How could a source of joy turn into a burden?

The solution perhaps most often proposed is that the delight in active reason first experienced by the happy few became attractive for the rest, as everyone tries maximizing their happiness, and enacting active reason is happiness. Yet this utilitarian approach has to take into account that enacting active reason means abandoning passive, authoritarian reason and is often enough burdensome. Karl Popper took it into account when he explained the attraction of totalitarianism as the attraction of closed societies (as he calls premodern societies). Closed societies are cozy, modern society is open, offering "anonymity and isolation, and consequently ... unhappiness." Nevertheless, "there is no return to a harmonious state of nature. If we turn back, then we must go the whole way – we must return to the beasts."[3]

Popper clearly recognized the attraction not only of closed societies but also of their authoritarian form of rationality and self, but trusted that people will see that the unhappiness of anonymity is outweighed by the happiness of the many activities and personal relations opened up by the open society. Ancient Greeks, Popper thought, for hard, egoistic reasons preferred the relative openness of Athens to the closeness of Sparta; so in the end contemporaries will prefer the open society as well.[4] This is a pious hope rather than an argument.

---

[3]   Popper, *The Open Society*, 174f and 200f. Popper 174f reads: "We could conceive of a society in which men practically never meet face to face – in which all business is conducted by individuals in isolation who communicate by typed letters or telegrams, and who go about in closed motor-cars. (Artificial insemination would allow even propagation without a personal element.) Such a fictitious society might be called a 'completely abstract or depersonalized society.' Now the interesting point is that our modern society resembles in many of its aspects such a completely abstract society ... There are many people living in a modern society who have no, or extremely few, intimate personal contacts, who live in anonymity and isolation, and consequently in unhappiness."

[4]   Ibid., 171–5. Cp. my "On Popper's Concept of an Open Society."

Moreover, it is an error to think that a return to a closed society is a return to the beasts. Closed societies can combine authoritarian rationality with high technology; they can conform to moral standards even better than the open society, if only they replace the ideal of universal liberty by religion; and they offer opportunities for extraordinariness for the proto-self.

Popper's explanation followed the similarly utilitarian explanation Marx had tried for explaining the disruption of what the Marxist tradition called the Asian mode of production. Its paradigms, ancient China and India, preserved its form of production (demanding subjection of the individual to the collective) until the beginning of the twentieth century and lost it only under the attack of modern capitalist society. But some societies that once had an Asian mode of production somehow managed by their own power to burst a form that in China and India had proved to be nearly unshakeable. How was this possible? Like Popper, Marx refers to individual self-interest. Yet unlike Popper, he thinks that normally, self-interest cannot break the communal bonds of closed societies. Only when it develops in trade between different societies can it become strong enough. In this case, it penetrates from intersocietal trade into societies and replaces communal bonds by market relations. This, Marx claims, happened in societies that burst the Asian mode of production.[5]

This explanation, more sophisticated than Popper's, can explain why Athens, strong in intersocietal trade, burst its traditional mode of production and developed nonauthoritarian forms of rationality in science, politics, historiography, medicine, mathematics, the arts, and other activities. But it cannot explain why the Phoenicians and Carthaginians, hardly less strong in intersocietal trade, did not develop along similar lines. Still less can it explain our crucial problem of how and why active reason could turn from an attraction for the happy few into an obligation for all; this started only when, in Cicero, the Roman republic ended.

Perhaps Marx was so much convinced that reason puts on us a universal obligation that he did not really see the problem. Today we can no longer overlook the attraction of closed societies. At his time, Marx rather saw the detestableness of closed societies. An open one, even though capitalist, is much better, as it rescues "the population from the idiocy of rural life" and other humiliations done to reason.[6]

---

5   Cp. Marx, "Forms Which Precede Capitalist Production" in his *Grundrisse*; cp. the following note.

6   Marx and Engels, *Manifesto of the Communist Party* (1848), ch. 1; cp. Marx, *The British Rule in India*, in Robert Tucker, ed., The Marx-Engels Reader, New York 1972, 577–82, justifying British rule in India where "man, the sovereign of nature, fell down on his knees in adoration of Hanuman, the monkey, and Sabbala, the cow" (582). Marx did not yet use the term *Asian mode of production* but described what was later so called. Cp. in particular his *Formen die der kapitalistischen Produktion vorhergehn,* in *Grundrisse der Kritik der politischen Ökonomie*

If we prefer the Cartesian approach to the utilitarian one, we should not be surprised that the utilitarian explanations fail. We should rather expect an explanation by individuals' self-assertion. But this line no less seems to be doomed. For we presuppose in it what is to be explained, namely, that individual self-assertion as a universal ideal has arisen. How could it arise in societies that leave as little room for individual self-assertion as the societies of the Asian mode of production? Still, following a philosophical trend of some decades ago we may try an explanation by recurring to the properties of propositional language.

Unlike the signal languages of animals, propositional languages distinguish descriptions and commands, and hence, what there is from what there ought to be. Signal languages operate by signals, that is, signs that indicate that a specific behavior is expected or appropriate. Propositional languages operate by propositions, that is, the expressions of a thought that represent a possible fact or a possible action. They demand of both the speaker and the addressee a decision – if the proposition is to be affirmed or rejected – that is, if the presented possible fact is true or false or the proposed action to be done or rejected. They structure the world in such a way that the basic operation in our coping with it is judging if a proposition is true or right.

This sows the germ of the authentic self. The basic operation of judging needs to start under authoritative guidance but tends to end with the knowledge that judgment requires independence and is never infallible. As propositional language opens up the ordinary world shared by all who understand it, the germ of individualism exists already in premodern societies.

This explains how individualism is possible. But it does not explain how it was universalized and reason turned into a burdensome obligation, nor how the attractions of closed societies could be overcome. The historical fact is that in all high civilizations the power of reason was detected but in most of them only by the happy few, who had no reason to universalize their detection. True, the use of propositional language gives birth to some ideas that are crucial for understanding reason: truth, moral rightness, necessity, and liberty. For, first, as long as we do not distinguish descriptions from commands, we cannot raise truth claims, as little as we can raise a truth claim for a command. Truth claims again give rise to the idea of falsity and pretension and to the ideal of truth and honesty. Animals can cheat, too. But lacking a propositional language, they cannot develop the idea and ideal of truth. Second, the distinction of description and command gives rise to the idea of moral rightness, as it makes possible validity claims on the rightness of actions and institutions. Such claims, like any validity claims, cannot be raised in a signal language, as it lacks the distinction between what there is and what there ought to be. Rightness claims give rise to moral criticism and justification and to the idea of a punishment that is different from revenge. Third, it gives rise to the ideas of necessity and freedom. Once we distinguish between what there is and what there ought to be, we can also distinguish between (1) what is, although it perhaps ought not to be the case, yet cannot be changed; that is, the necessary, (2) what is although it ought not to, yet can be changed; that is, the actual, and (3) what ought to be the case, although it is not, yet can be realized; that is, the possible. These distinctions give rise to the ideas of causal explanation, prediction, and rational projects.

Nevertheless, the ideas of truth, moral rightness, and freedom of necessity do not warrant the idea that everyone has an equal right to decide on their life. They are compatible with the ideas prevalent in closed societies and do not commit to the open one. Even if we take into account our "supernatural" capacity of conceiving truth and justice as independent of self-interest (that I talked about in Chapter 4), we do not arrive at a universal equal right to liberty.

Two more explanations of the birth of the core idea of modernity seem possible. One of them recurs to the Golden Rule, a principle of reciprocity that has been preached in nearly all high civilizations and therefore might be assumed to be built into our nature or language. It either positively demands we do to others as we expect them to do to us, or negatively forbids us to do to others what we do not want them to do to us. But traditionally, the Golden Rule has been understood, not as a principle of universal equality or equal liberty, but as one that demands us to respect status differences. It adapts to hierarchies and does not revolutionize them. Only once we accept universal liberty can we equate it with the modern law of nature, as did Hobbes.[7]

The other explanation recurs to religions that proclaim that God is father to all people and commands us to respect or love everyone. Though such religions have often respected status differences, sometimes they did not. So it is not just the belief in a divine father but another factor connected with religion that might explain the rise of modernity. Yet what is it?

One possible answer is that deep in our souls, if only we take the trouble of listening, we find a voice that we can ascribe to nature, reason, the conscience, God, or another authority that tells us to respect equally everyone's will, and that it is this voice that has been expressed by revolutionary religions. Such an answer raises more questions than it answers, but it has been given by Kant, when he despaired at finding an explanation for his categorical imperative of

---

[7] Hobbes, *Leviathan*, ch. 14; ed. Mcpherson 191; Swidler, "Towards a Universal Declaration," and Pralong, "Minima Moralia," 143, show that nearly all high religions agree in recognizing the Golden Rule as the essence of their message. They refer to formulations of it in Zoroastrianism (Gathas 43.1), Confucianism (Analects 12.2), in Mahavira (Sutraki-tanga 1.11.33), the *Mahabharata* (Anusana Parva 113.8), Hillel (Btalmud, Shabbath 31a); the New Testament (Matthew, 7, 12); it seems it is not quoted in the Koran but in Hadiths. The positive formulation of the Golden Rule is often taken as the basis for the universalization of love, its negative formulation, as that of justice.

universal respect and declared it a "fact of reason."[8] Heidegger, too, may seem to rely on it when he appeals to Being, as far as Being seems similar to a divine voice. This appeal is worth considering.

When Heidegger wrote his *Being and Time,* most Europeans believed in the superiority of their civilization though they were not free of doubts. They were feeling the superiority of their rationality as a burden rather than a privilege. Western states strove for colonizing what they considered the uncivilized, yet more and more Western individuals suffered from the costs they had to pay for their ambition. Utilitarian justifications for colonial ambitions were felt to be insufficient; rather, Richard Kipling struck the right note when, with both pathos and sarcasm, he called colonialism "the white man's burden." It is his burden "To wait in heavy harness, On fluttered folk and wild – Your new-caught, sullen peoples, Half-devil and half-child."[9]

What Kipling calls half-devil and half-child appears in Heidegger as the inauthentic self of *das Man*; what he calls the duty to take up the burden appears in Heidegger as the call of Being to answer what the historical situation requires. I do not claim that Heidegger knew of Kipling or thought of colonialism. What I claim is that his distinction of the inauthentic and authentic self fit the mood of the West, including Germany. The West regarded itself as more authentic, less illusionary, more in contact with Being (whatsoever was meant by that word) than the rest, but also in danger of losing contact with the ordinary reality that ordinary sullen people, half-devil and half-child, so cozily live in. Though a closed society built on illusions, it was a common world shared by all and producing happiness and security. Why then break it and take on individual responsibility? Well, listen to Being; it will tell you.

I do not think that this interpretation does justice to Heidegger, but it helps explain his success and illustrates the dangers in nonutilitarian explanations of universal rules. In his opposition of *das Man* and the authentic self, readers found mirrored the opposition of imagined non-Western naivete and Western burdensome civilization that it is a duty to be taken up by the now unhappy few. In his appeal to Being. they found a justification of an imagined duty.

However, there is more in Heidegger's appeal to Being than an appeal to some subjective voice, just as there is more in Kipling's appeal to take up a

---

8 Kant, *Kritik der praktischen Vernunft,* §7, Anmerkung, declares the "consciousness" of the categorical imperative is "fact of reason" one cannot deduce ("herausvernünfteln") from any data.

9 Rudyard Kipling, "The White Man's Burden." The first of seven stanzas, all beginning with the same first line, runs thus: "Take up the White Man's burden – Send forth the best ye breed – Go bind your sons to exile To serve your captives' need; To wait in heavy harness, On fluttered folk and wild – Your new-caught, sullen peoples, Half-devil and half-child." Some of them are still actual for development politics: "Take up the White Man's burden – ... To veil the threat of terror ... Fill full the mouth of Famine And bid the sickness cease; Take up the White Man's burden – And reap his old reward: The blame of those ye better, The hate of those ye guard ... Have done with childish days."

burden than sarcasm. If we understand Being as the reality that we can be more or less in contact with, it is no longer a mysterious voice, but a standard by which to measure forms of life. Though some theorists claim that any way of life is as illusionary and as close, to or far from, reality as any other, both Heidegger and the analytic philosophers who reject his philosophy as nonsense agree that some ways of life – that of science, for instance – are less illusionary and closer to reality than, say, a life of superstition. Similarly, Kipling thought the Western way of life closer to at least some aspect of reality than the Eastern is. In this interpretation we prefer the burdensome self, not because an authority commands it, but because we understand that it is the only way to escape a life that is further from reality than it might be.

Heidegger, it is true, explains neither how we find out that we are living less in illusion when living in authenticity nor why authenticity requires the concession of equal rights to everyone. The Cartesian, by contrast, can answer both questions by recurring to the requirements of judgment: Only by judging in perfect independence of the expectations of other people – and at the same time by conceding everyone the equal right to judge as independently as possible – can we hope to come closer to reality by detecting illusions and errors.[10] Despite these deficits, Heidegger's reference to Being can be understood as a step on the right way, while utilitarian, linguistic, reciprocity-oriented, and simple religious explanations for the universalism of rights fail. Moreover, by using the dark concept of Being, he reminds us that the judgments we need independence for can concern very different topics and that the illusions we hope to get rid of by everyone's independent judgments can be of very different kinds.

However, both Heidegger and the Cartesian again explain only the logic by which people in favorable conditions will recognize the obliging and burdensome consequences of the use of reason. They add to understanding this logic, but do not explain the historical conditions that broke the attractions of closed societies. Only if we find them can we both confirm the thesis that people have Cartesian rather than Lockean selfs and better understand the history and nature of the West. So, trusting we have understood the logic by which individuals detect reason, its joy and its obligations, let's go back to Marx who (as little as Popper) did not bother about a developmental logic of the use of reason. He found the cause of modern rationality in the self-interest favoring individualism that developed in intersocietal trade and then penetrated into the interior of societies. But he did not explain why self-interest penetrated only into the societies that were to become the West.

Now, Weber claimed to find the missing link in a new type of religion spreading in occidental societies that he called ascetic.[11] It is a religion that, first, denies

---

[10]   John Stuart Mill, *On Liberty*, ch. II, used the same argument for universal liberty.

[11]   Weber has scattered his most important remarks on salvation religion in his *Gesammelte Aufsätze zur Religionssoziologie*; particularly in his *Zwischenbetrachtung*. Also important are

this world lasting worth, ascribes such worth to a transcendent world open to virtuous people after death, and declares the ordinary world a lot we can be saved from. Second, it differs from other salvation religions by the idea that salvation is not attained by fleeing the world and retreating to realms of mystic meditation but in an ascesis that requires of the believer to stay in the world and subject it to the transcendent standards. Mystic salvation religion prevailed in the East; mundanely ascetic religion, tending to be monotheistic, in the West where market relations spread. Weber's thesis is that they spread because ascetic religion favored them. Subjecting the world to transcendent standards required the believer to control every step of her life so that in the end she would earn individual salvation. Ascetic religion broke the attraction of closed societies, not by opposing open society to the closed one, but by forcing individuals to live for their own individual salvation. Because salvation was paramount in their life and was individual, the collectivism of closed societies was broken. Utilitarian considerations that plead for retaining closed societies are invalidated because of the idea that the world and its happiness that alone count for the utilitarian are rejected as worthless, compared with the infinite value of salvation and the infinite bliss it gives. So far, I think, Weber's answer is brilliant.

But it also raises the question of why people could fall for the individual salvation idea. His answer seems to consist in a reference to the problem of theodicy, of how to understand the evils of the world. He holds there can be several rational answers to this problem: Zoroastrian dualism of the eternally fighting powers of good and evil, monotheism combined with predestination that ascribes to God responsibility of the evil, and the Hindu idea of mystic self-salvation.[12] The salvation idea the involuntary initiators of modernity fell for is a consequence of the monotheistic solution; the one almighty God commands every individual to act for the subjection of the world to his will and promises them the reward of immortal bliss.

This explanation provokes, again, questions; first, why people preferred the monotheistic solution of theodicy; second, why theodicy was so important for them at all. Moreover, any solution to the theodicy problem is compatible with the closed society. Even the divine command to subject the world to divine standards does not imply that individuals have to look for their individual salvation. Perhaps Weber thought that scientists have not to answer the question of why the adherents of individual salvation religion fell for its distinctive idea; they have just to state what happened. However, for understanding history and the present the question is important. Our ancestors may have fallen for this idea for

his *Religionssoziologie* in his *Wirtschaft und Gesellschaft* and other essays, in particular his *Wissenschaft als Beruf*. – Weber's historical analyses are no longer in high esteem; for a forceful defense see David Landes, *The Wealth and Poverty of Nations*, and his contribution to Harrison and Huntington.

12   Max Weber, *Zwischenbetrachtung*, 571f; also in Weber, *Soziologie*, 481ff.

some irreducibly religious reason; in this case, modernity is inspired by a genuinely religious idea. Or they may have fallen for it for a not specifically religious reason; in this case modernity is inspired by an idea that had a religious wrapping only. We may also put our question this way: Did the revolutionary ascetic salvation religion respond to a need that we can understand without recurring to religious ideas, or do we need to recur to specifically and irreducibly religious ideas? I think we do not, for this reason.

What I have called the developmental logic of judgment can be given a more sociological form by the following scheme for the development of societies. People in successful societies, in societies that solve the problems they are expected to solve, get weary of the ways by which the problems are solved. They get sick of them because they crave for the enactment of capabilities that they become aware of in the successful society but cannot enact, because the society has not been built for the enactment of these new capabilities. We can consider this a universal tendency of human nature. Once the most urgent of our problems are solved, new demands arise because our capabilities are inexhaustible – but they are not met by the established social form. Marx called such capabilities forces of production, but understood them in a predominantly economic sense.[13] We have to understand them in a broad sense that includes any capability by which we change the world and ourselves, also the capability to change ideas about man and the world; therefore I call this developmental scheme Marxian rather than Marxist. Tribal societies solve their problems by enmeshing individuals in a close web of blood relations that subordinates them to the tribe and suppresses individual aims. This organization form proved particularly successful in Mesopotamia and the Mediterranean civilizations and led the most powerful among their members to raise claims for their individuality. This is what most conspicuously happened in ancient Athens.

For an individualistic and still universalistic religion to arise, people were required who were as sick of tribalism as the Athenians but, unlike them, incapable of abandoning the religious form of understanding the world. We may say that it required people less enlightened but as sensitive to the insufficiencies of closed societies as the Athenians. Such people existed. One of them was Ecclesiastes of the Old Testament. This is what he said:

> Vanity of vanities, saith the Preacher, vanity of vanities; all is vanity. What profit hath a man of all his labour which he taketh under the sun? One generation passeth away, and another generation cometh: but the earth abideth for ever. The sun also ariseth, and the sun goeth down, and hasteth to his place where he arose.[14]

---

[13] Marx assumed that societies consist of forms of production that organize human productive forces but will be burst by new forces just because the forms of production have been successful in organizing the old ones.

[14] Eccl. 1, 2–5. According to the prevailing opinion of critical scholars the *Ecclesiastes* was written around 250 BC.

Here speaks someone who is sick of the tribal order that subordinates the individual to the tribe. The daily reappearing sun is the image of the ever-passing and reappearing generations; it is an image that reminds us of the absurd activity of the boulder-rolling Sisyphus.[15] The eternally abiding earth stands for the tribe in whose chain of generations the individual seems vain. The words express the despair at the lack of meaning the individual finds in the closed society, at his submergence in the chain of generations. Salvation religion answered to this despair by the evangel that the individual is immortal, hence, has the very quality of immortality for which the tribe was the hub of the world. It required of everyone to look for a life that would be judged in the end of their days as their individual product.

Therefore, the cause and content, the origin and aim of modernity, was the idea that the life not only of the happy few but of everyone consists in living not for the well-being of one's tribe but for their own sake. This was the universalistic individualism Athens lacked. Athenian individualism could destroy the closed society but not replace it by a sustainable form. The sustainable form that arose under the guidance of a universal individualistic salvation religion was not an open society but incorporated the principle that everyone has to live for their own individual salvation. This principle is not based on religious presuppositions but on the disgust of the individual at being submerged in the chain of generations in closed societies. This origin of salvation religion made it possible for societies guided by salvation religion to give birth to an open society, though only after a long time.

If it is true that people become sick of their life just because their society has been successful in organizing their productive powers and raised the new capability of living without the idea of belonging to an immortal chain of generations, then we can expect modern society to run into trouble once it has been successful in satisfying their demand for recognizing their infinite individual value. This expectation, unfortunately, will not be disappointed.

[15] The nineteenth-century Sanskrit scholar Max Müller interpreted the myth of Sisyphus, like many other myths, as a solar myth. This interpretation, much ridiculed in twentieth century, finds support in this passage, though for reasons that are quite different from those Müller adduced. For Müller's solar interpretation, cp. Dorson, 1955, 393–416.

Chapter 7

The Second-Stage Rationality in History

A S THE CAUSE OF MODERNITY, WE HAVE FOUND A HISTORICAL EVENT that presupposes the Cartesian conception of two stages of the self and rationality but separates antiquity and modernity, not just by these two stages, but by the universalization of the second stage. So we can regard Western civilization as an effect of an ascetic salvation religion that made the second stage of rationality a universal obligation. But does history confirm that the second stage of rationality implies the ambition of extraordinariness? Weber found evidence for an excellence, unequalled in any other civilization, in the development of science, art, the state, and *"capitalism,* that most fateful power of our modern life" in the West.[1] I think there are no good reasons to deny that the West was extraordinary.[2] But the question is: Was it due to the cause Weber assumes, the burst of the closed society by ascetic religion? Whether we date the beginning of the heyday of Western civilization in the seventeenth century or some centuries earlier, there is always a distance of more than a millennium from the birth of ascetic salvation religion. Still worse, how can we understand excellence in the nonreligious spheres of science, the arts, politics, and the economy as due to a religion that started with the intention of subjecting all spheres of life to its religious ideas?

Curiously, Weber did not explicitly discuss these obvious problems to his thesis. But we can reconstruct an answer from the tendency of his ideas. The two problems help to solve one another, and the solution confirms that the core idea of modernity is not essentially religious but had a religious wrapping necessary

---

[1] Weber, Vorbemerkung zu *Gesammelte Aufsätze zur Religionssoziologie*, vol. 1, 1–4.

[2] Weber used the term of *Außeralltäglichkeit*, extraordinariness, in his sociology of religion to mark out the striving for extraordinariness as a character of religious activity. But he did not use it in describing Western civilization.

for its being accepted, yet becoming a burden once it had broken closed societies. The long time from the birth of ascetic religion to the heyday of Western civilization was necessary for individuals to become aware that their struggle for salvation could be realized only by their struggle for perfection of their capabilities – most of which are not religious.

The solution to the two problems is this. The believer in ascetic salvation religion, having gazed at the true value of a transcendent world, like the Platonic philosopher who had seen the light of the sun, turns back to this world and tries forming it after her religious ideals. But only at the price of ending all human life can she neglect to care for the next generations. However, if she accepts the duties of caring for the future, there is no reason not also to recognize duties of judges, politicians, traders, soldiers, and of all the other life orders. Ascetic religion, though, will conceive of them as special forms of religious duties. It will confer on them religious value and teach that, what formerly was done for the tribe's sake, is now done for the sake or greater glory of God. This is what Johann Sebastian Bach and the Jesuits did – Bach when he signed his compositions, the Jesuits when they chose the motto for their order, "ad maiorem Dei gloriam." Now, God's glory can become greater only by perfecting the activity we use for magnifying his glory, but when is an activity perfect? Obviously, not when it becomes more useful for people; hence, utilitarian standards fail. Rather, the perfection must be measured by the activity-immanent standards of music, economy, politics, or another kind of activity. So, after a long time necessary for understanding what it means to serve God, ascetic religion gave rise to the idea of activity-immanent perfection standards and their emancipation from, and autonomy against, all conditions that do not conform to these standards.[3]

What exactly such standards are could be detected only when individuals started acting not for the preservation of the community but for the glory of God. It belongs to the emancipation of individuals from authorities to detect perfection standards and specific values of activities. Their uncertainty about the standards did not prevent them from following the idea that what they did, they did for the glory of God or the perfection of the activity they performed, be it music or diamond trade. A first step in the detection of activity-immanent standards was the differentiation of possible activities into value spheres, realms whose values proved irreducible to each other. We follow this distinction when we distinguish science and economy, politics and art, religion and the family. Each of them seems to have its own function, value, and perfection standard, even if it is not clear what exactly they are. In fact, the answers to this question have changed till today.

---

[3]   Olivier Roy, *Globalized Islam*, 40f, describes this process as "secularization through religion" in his description of contemporary Islam: "When everything has to be Islamic, nothing is," but the spheres of society are intensified, differentiated, and promoted.

Weber, perhaps, thought that the idea of activity-immanent perfection standards could only arise under the influence of an ascetic religion. Yet if, for whatever reasons, people have the opportunity to use their capabilities without being regulated by utilitarian or other ideas external to an activity, they will detect its immanent perfection standards, as, for instance, happened in ancient Greece in activities like mathematics, rhetoric, and philosophy. New in the West was the idea that everyone's life can and ought to follow perfection standards. This was a consequence of the idea of individual salvation, but it was not necessarily a religious idea that made the innovation possible.

So far we have confirmed that the West developed under the influence of ascetic salvation religion, incorporates the second stage of rationality in a universalized form, and is bound to the ambition of extraordinariness. But history can teach us more, something that shows the destructive side of the second-stage rationality. When we now start considering it, I'll not restrict my interest to historical and conceptual analysis. Rather, I'll look for ways to reduce the destructiveness of rationality.

The curious effect of ascetic religion to give birth to the idea, and in the end the practice of emancipated value spheres, had a disastrous effect. The autonomy of the value spheres established a set of sphere-immanent rationalities, but left society without a generally recognized universal rationality, stopping the glorious development of the West and today threatening its survival. In premodern societies, all life orders served the collective, or what its rulers declared to be the common good. The same is true of all societies we may call postmodern, that is, societies that have abandoned the ideal of equal liberty. In modern society, activities follow their own standards. All standards to judge conflicts by are standards of a specific value sphere. If there are sphere-independent standards, they do not fit sphere rationalities, hence, do not fit modernity either. But we need a universal sphere-independent standard. This seems to be a fundamental contradiction of modernity.

As long as modern society was busy detecting and developing its sphere-immanent perfection standards, traditional standards sufficed to solve conflicts between the sphere standards. Once economy and the state, the most powerful spheres, had established their standards and eliminated the traditional ones, they became imperialistic and attempted to impose their rationality on the rest of society. Economy has been most successful in this effort, both in practice and theory. I'll consider its success in theory in the next chapter. Today, though, it has lost credibility because it produces unemployment that wastes productive powers and contradicts the claim of modernity to allow everyone equally to use their capabilities. The state, no less, has lost credibility because it did not prevent two horrible World Wars and proves incapable of imposing rules on economy that would stop the waste of productive powers. Small wonder, then, that religion has restarted to claim priority, though the history of religion should have made it clear that if it imposes the will of God on society rather than the whims of its leaders, the effect

is the emancipation of value spheres and the reintroduction of the very problem
that it is thought to solve.

Yet we find two more attempts at establishing a universal standard for
modernity that are worth considering. One of them resumes and systematizes
the standard of the closed societies, the well-being of the collective. This is the
utilitarian approach. It was favored by economic rationality, because economy
pursues an aim of maximizing a value, though not happiness but production;
but this difference was dissolved when economic theorists argued for the social
utility of their principles (cp. Chapter 12).[4] Yet utilitarianism is incompatible
with the autonomy of value spheres. It subjects them to the standard of utility that can never get rid of its origin in closed society. Yet science, art, politics, sport, sexuality, religion – and most things we do – do not aim at utility or
happiness, however happiness may be understood. Strict utilitarianism poisons
modernity. Most times, though, it is used and understood in a watered-down
form that defines the fulfillment of an individual's interest, however unhappy
she may become, as happiness. In this case, solution of sphere conflicts by a utilitarian standard is either purely arbitrary or a decision by the vote of the majority. In the latter case, it may produce a good solution but also violate minority
rights.

The second attempt consists in instituting the sphere of justice. You may
wonder why I call it an attempt; isn't there a well-established sphere of justice
in any modern society? There is not. Both Weber and Hegel, who preceded
Weber in considering value spheres, do not list justice as a value sphere. They
rather ascribe the task of enforcing justice to the state that they identify with the
sphere of justice. This fits the historical facts; justice enforcement is a task the
states have annexed. But the state, though political philosophy justified its existence by teaching that it does the necessary job of justice enforcement, pursues a
lot of other tasks. Its original task is the administration of all affairs that require
a person or institution that can manage them better than those immediately
concerned, such as river regulation for agriculture, military defense, expansion
of a territory, and conflict arbitration. Yet, though justice enforcement can be
reckoned among the state tasks, sphere autonomy that characterizes modernity
demands the pursuit of different tasks in different spheres, according to their
different perfection standards. Because justice enforcement follows standards
other than services for the infrastructure or military goals, modern society
requires of justice enforcement organization in one sphere and infrastructure
services in others.[5]

If justice enforcement was organized in its own sphere, there would be no
major problems with sphere autonomy. It would be the very task of the justice sphere to prevent a sphere from imposing its standards on other spheres, to

---

4   Cp. Chapter 12, in particular n. 1.
5   I'll be more explicit on these points, and those mentioned in the next paragraph, in Chapter 11.

adjudicate conflicts between different spheres, and to intervene in a sphere when it violates the rights of equal access to it and its services. Judges are expected to be independent of the rest of the state apparatus, and for this reason are entitled to certain privileges. So, to some extent, justice enforcement has gotten a kind of sphere autonomy. Yet the extent is far from sufficient. What is necessary is the separation of the task of justice enforcement from that of administrating a territory. Today, justice enforcement is obviously severely hampered by the borders that define state territories, not to mention the wars and other crimes that only states make possible. But we can also observe today that law, in particular private law, becomes more independent of states and states lose more and more of their arrogated powers.

So there is a solution to what seemed to be a fundamental contradiction of modernity. Modernity does not suffer from lack of a sphere-transcendent universal rationality standard; rather, it possesses a sphere-immanent justice standard by which to solve any conflict between and within the spheres. Before looking at the details of this solution, let us have a look at the attractions of a society that would be guided by the sphere of economy. These attractions have certainly hindered the institution of an autonomous sphere of justice enforcement.

Chapter 8

Economic Rationality

THE EARLY POLITICAL ECONOMISTS BERNARD MANDEVILLE AND Adam Smith proclaimed the rationality of the market to be the universal form of rationality and justice that society should follow in all its spheres. It was not the only attempt at raising a sphere-immanent value to a universal one. Similar attempts were made by adherents of the rationality of bureaucratic administration and of that of science. But they were less explicit, less interesting, and less momentous.

Can't we exclude the possibility of universal rationality from the beginning? This is what Weber seems to imply when he distinguishes "rationality of means" (*Zweckrationalität*, instrumental rationality) from "rationality of value" (*Wertrationalität*, practical rationality). He assumed that only the former can claim universal obligation but cannot raise justice claims, while the second can raise justice claims but cannot claim universal obligation.[1] There is an obvious objective standard for deciding whether it is right to choose a means for a given end, but there seems to be no such standard for deciding if it is right to choose an end. Nevertheless, political economists argued that economic standards are such standards.

When in 1714 Mandeville republished his *Fable of the Bees* under the subtitle *Private Vices, Publick Benefits*,[2] he marked out the fable's claim to reform our moral ideas: What traditionally have been considered vices – egoism, lavishness, exploitation, pride, and aggressiveness – are vices only in private. In public, that is, when we have to attend to justice, they are benefits, for they promote

---

[1] E.g., Michael Schaefer, Die "Rationalitaet" des Nationalsozialismus, Weinheim (Beltz) 1994, 112f.

[2] Mandeville published his rhymed fable first in 1705 under the title *The Grumbling Hive: or, Knaves Turn'd Honest*; there have been later editions between 1724 and 1732, each of them again expanded. For a critical edition, see *The Fable of the Bees*, Oxford, 1924, 1957.

the wealth of a nation more than the contrasting virtues of altruism and modesty.[3] Similarly Smith, though he tried to distance himself from the reviled Mandeville, taught that the wealth of nations is promoted by a morality not of "benevolence," but of "self-love." As he said in this famous statement:

> It is not from the benevolence of the butcher, the brewer, or the baker that we expect our dinner, but from their regard to their own interest. We address ourselves, not to their humanity but to their self-love, and never talk to them of our own necessities but of their advantages.[4]

The idea, well known today, is that egoism and only egoism drives people to be productive and inventive, and that everyone's unhampered business leads to competition that transforms the egoism of the individuals into wealth for all. Today most people consider Mandeville and Smith's thesis a typically economic view that distinguishes attitudes of economic man from noneconomic or normal man. But in the eighteenth century, it became an evangel of universal rationality for reasons probably not foreseen by its first prophets. It declared action motivated by egoism, hence evil, to be productive of universal welfare, hence good. Salvation was attained not by virtue but by the vice of universal egoism.[5]

The greatest attraction of the new evangel was that it offered a justification for both man-made and naturally given evil. It achieved what so many theologians and philosophers had aspired to in vain: a justification of God, a theodicy. How could he, who is infinitely powerful and good, admit evil to his creation? Well, looking closer, the evil proves good. The economists' ideas are taken up by Alexander Pope in 1733 when he writes:

> All Nature is but Art unknown to thee;
> All chance direction, which thou canst not see;
> All discord, harmony not understood;
> All partial evil, universal good:
> And spite of Pride, in erring Reason's spite,
> One truth is clear, *Whatever is, is right*.[6]

---

3 Cp. first edition of Mandeville, 1705, line 409–416; partly corrected by the 1714 edition text: "Then leave Complaints: Fools only strive /To make a Great an honest Hive. / T'enjoy the World's Conveniencies, / Be famed in War, yet live in Ease / Without great Vices, is a vain / Eutopia seated in the Brain. / Fraud, Luxury, and Pride must live; / Whilst we the Benefits receive." In Mandeville we still find the pride of and delight at the extraordinary that Smith denies.

4 Adam Smith, *The Wealth of Nations* (1776) bk 1, ch 2, ed. A. Skinner, Penguin 1986, 119.

5 According to Gynnar Myrdal, *The Political Element in the Development of Economic Theory*, 1955, 194f, behind the "harmony of interests" in liberal economics stands always the "communist fiction" of one interest. This is a misunderstanding that Arendt, in *The Human Condition*, 43ff, unfortunately followed. The early economists presumed rather a conflict of interests that only competition transforms to a harmony.

6 Alexander Pope, *Essay on Man*, End of First Epistle.

Pope added, no less in Mandeville's spirit:

> Two principles in Human Nature reign,
> Self-love to urge and Reason to restrain;
> Nor this a good, nor that a bad we call;
> Each works its end, to move or govern all:
> And to their proper operation still
> Ascribe all good, to their improper, ill. ...
> Self-love and Reason to one end aspire,
> Pain their aversion, Pleasure their desire ...[7]
> Thus God and Nature link'd the gen'ral frame,
> And bade Self-love and Social be the same.[8]

The echo of the economists' message resounds no less impressively from Germany. Goethe, in his *Faust,* lets the devil Mephisto introduce himself by the description that he is "part of the power that always strives for evil and ever creates the good."[9] That he creates the good is of course against his intention, but he cannot help doing so, thanks to a social mechanism that transforms bad intentions into good results, a mechanism disclosed by Mandeville and Smith.

Philosophers respond no less attentively. Already in 1739, Hume remarks that the virtue of sociability was motivated by the "passion of self-interest" and adds that whether it "be esteemed vicious or virtuous, 'tis all a case; since itself restrains it: So that if it be virtuous, men become social by their virtue; if vicious, their vice has the same effect."[10] Kant follows in 1784 by praising men's "unsocial sociability" and thanking nature for planting in men "the insatiable desire to possess and rule," because only by this vice are men spurred "to the manifold development of their capacities," "thereby perhaps showing the ordering of a wise Creator and not the hand of an evil spirit."[11] Hegel concentrates on the economic aspect that vice produces, or even proves to be, virtue. "Political economy," he teaches, "is a science that honors thinking, since it finds laws to a mass of accidents. It is an interesting spectacle to see the feedback between all connections."[12] Modern economy seems to be

---

[7] Ibid., part 2 of Second Epistle.

[8] Ibid, end of Third Epistle. Giacomo Casanova, *History of My Life*, vol. 1, 26, probably also was influenced by Pope or Mandeville when he wrote in 1797 "that both in this physical world and in the moral world good comes from evil as evil comes from good."

[9] "Ein Teil von jener Kraft Die stets das Böse will und stets das Gute schafft," Goethe, Faust, Studierzimmer, line 1335+.

[10] Hume, *A Treatise of Human Nature*, bk. 3, pt. 2, sec. 2, 492.

[11] Kant, *Idea for a Universal History from a Cosmopolitan Point of View*, Fourth Thesis. The translation follows L. W. Beck.

[12] G. W. F. Hegel, Grundlinien der Philosophie des Rechts §189 Zusatz. He adds: "At first one does not believe in this reciprocal transformation since everything seems dependent upon the individual's arbitrary decision. But that is what is most remarkable. It is similar to the planetary system which also shows only irregular movements to our senses but follows nevertheless laws

chaotic, because it depends on decisions of selfish individuals, yet is proved to be virtue by the economist, just as the astronomer proves what seems to be chaotic to sense-impression to be admirable order.[13]

There is another revolutionary aspect of the argument that vice turns into virtue if everyone is vicious for which we do not find documents as impressive as those of Pope and Goethe. If egoism, practiced by everyone, proves a benefit for society, then a society needs neither masters nor morality in the sense of rules that prescribe how to attain a good life. Then people can secure to themselves more liberty, equality, democracy, autonomy, and hence justice in the sense of equal consideration than ever before. Only markets allow for true democracies. States will be superfluous.

In the traditional view, still accepted by modern political philosophy from Hobbes to Kant, society is an association of individuals that need masters and morals to flourish. The masters are often split into warriors and priests, so that the traditional model of society is composed of the three estates of producers, warriors, and priests or philosophers that we know from philosophical theories since Plato and from practice in many societies. It is attractive for thugs and theorists alike who both find a comfortable niche in which to live on the producers. But the insight into the vice-becoming-virtue mechanism gives insight into what is really necessary for society and allows us to see that theorists and thugs or priests and princes are not.

What is necessary is that society solves a problem that I'll call that of tuning of interests. Any society has to tune the potentially divergent interests and inclinations of its members. What is not necessary is that the problem is solved in the traditional way. Political economists presumed, quite convincingly, that there are two (and only two) principal solutions to the problem of tuning and a bunch of mixes or compromises of the two principal solutions. They associated traditional societies with the one and a market society with the other principal solution.

---

knowledgeable to our thinking." ("... Staatsökonomie, einer Wissenschaft, die dem Gedanken Ehre macht, weil sie zu einer Masse von Zufälligkeiten die Gesetze findet. Es ist ein interessantes Schauspiel, wie alle Zusammenhänge hier rückwirkend sind ... Dies Ineinandergehen, an das man zunächst nicht glaubt, weil alles der Willkür des Einzelnen anheimgestellt scheint, ist vor allem bemerkenswert und hat eine Ähnlichkeit mit dem Planetensystem, das immer dem Auge nur unregelmäßige Bewegungen zeigt, aber dessen Gesetze doch erkannt werden können.") My translation.

[13] Hegel's admiration for modern political economy did not hinder him from finding an indelible flaw in it. Unlike the liberal economists, he did not believe that the market system works without state intervention. He was one of the first to understand its virtue, that it stimulates production, again as a vice, namely, as a surplus production that cannot be consumed by the population, makes a "great mass" (§ 244) of it superfluous in production and leads to their pauperization and exclusion. Such necessary effect of the market can only be countered, says Hegel, by the state and new forms of virtue (ibid., §§ 243–5, 254–6).

The solution of traditional societies presupposes rulers. We can distinguish within the problem of tuning the problem of how to allocate the resources available to society and the problem of how to reward individuals for their contributions to what is produced in a system of a more or less differentiated division of labor. In traditional societies, whether they are authoritarian or democratic, the rulers impose on the producers the ways of how resources are allocated and work is evaluated. Even if the rulers are democratically elected, the producers remain objects of administration. Let us therefore call this first principal solution the administrative way. Only if this solution is the only one possible can states justify their existence.

The market society leaves the decisions on resource allocation and work rewards to the producers. What at first sight seems to result in chaos soon proves harmonious. Egoistic buyers will control egoistic producers so that their demands are completely satisfied. Tuning by administration is replaced with tuning by the market, for the vice-becoming-virtue mechanism is the unhindered market. I'll call this the market solution.

The market is an institution that is well known from earliest times. But formerly it was *embedded* in political, religious, or other institutions. By contrast, a society that needs neither prince nor priest needs an unembedded market.[14] The market allows producers to offer products at prices they are free to demand and consumers are free to reject. What is produced in which quality and at what price it is offered, is decided in dependence on the relation of supply and demand. As long as markets were subjected to regulation, neither what was produced nor at what price it was sold depended only on market decisions. Once we grasp that regulations hinder the hidden harmony of a system of self-interest, we must abolish them.

No other activity is needed in such a society than economic activity. Some administration and education will be necessary, but they have to be conceived as preparations for, hence, as parts of production. The society knows no class distinctions, because there is only the one class of producers. Nor does it recognize value spheres aiming at specific and irreducible aims. Moreover, because everyone contributes more or less to the social product, there is a simple principle of *distributive justice*: Everyone gets as much out of the social product as she contributes to it. She gets back the amount and quality of labor she has put into the social product in the form of the amount of money that represents the amount and quality of her labor.

By contrast, societies that follow the administrative way are split into the classes of administrators and producers. Even if the producers elect the administrators, the difference of their functions is a source of class division. Amazingly for modern ideas of equality, few philosophers before Adam Smith took offense

---

[14] Karl Polanyi, *The Great Transformation*, called deregulated markets *disembedded* to mark out that they had been embedded in noneconomic institutions.

at the privileges of the ruling classes. Locke, by making labor the condition for appropriating natural resources, belongs to the few who express concern, but by including commanding into labor blunts his point.[15] Smith takes offense at what the rulers rob from the producers and extensively describes the economic consequences of their injustice.[16] His market society leaves no place for rulers and priests and other parasites on the producers. It cares for itself because everyone pursues her own interest and thereby both flourish and makes everyone else flourish. This idea of an autonomous and classless society was defended later by political liberals and socialists alike.

In Mandeville and Smith, economic theory becomes both a new salvation religion and a utopia of a classless society. Universal egoism supersedes both morality and the classes that are necessary in the administrative solution. Marx radicalized the new utopia by his thesis that even the social mechanism of the market would become superfluous by the time it would have stimulated productivity to a degree that riches would be abundant and neither administrative nor market justice would be any longer necessary for solving tuning problems.

Even without Marx's thesis, the market solution to the tuning problem is captivating. It seems more elegant, more efficient by avoiding cumbersome bureaucracy, and more just, as it allows people their own decisions on how to allocate resources and evaluate work. Yet in the model of Mandeville and Smith, the market does not do without justice. It strictly distinguishes between justice and morality. Justice is the sum of enforceable rules that secure everyone equal liberty in production and distribution; morality is the sum of rules for leading a good life. Such rules are a private affair without effect on the functioning of society.

Historically, there may be many compromises between the market and the administrative solution. But if we are to decide on the principles of society, it seems we should aim at the market solution, as it is supported by reasons of beauty, utility, and justice. It is even compatible with Cartesian rationality, as it does not exclude that individuals aim at extraordinariness in their activities. Though Adam Smith presents market activities as aiming at happiness, Mandeville delights in the greatness of vice and the varieties of goals.[17] But can their market model keep its promises?

---

[15] Locke, *Second Treatise of Government*, §§27f. He includes commanding into labor when he says: "Thus the Grass my Horse has bit; the Turfs my Servant has cut ... become my *Property* ..."

[16] Smith, *The Wealth of Nations*, loc. cit., among many other passages. Cp. 152f and 484–9.

[17] Cp. note 3. Later economists, however, presented economic activities as aiming at happiness and found in this aim a model for all rational activities. Marx and Engels similarly liked to present economic activities as an ordinary striving for profit maximization. But in their Manifesto of the Communist Party, Part 1, in Marx and Engels, *Selected Works*, Volume One, Progress Publishers, Moscow, USSR, 1969, pp. 98–137, they praise the extraordinary feats of the bourgeoisie as in a litany: "The bourgeoisie, historically, has played a most revolutionary part. The bourgeoisie ... has put an end to all feudal, patriarchal, idyllic relations ... It has accomplished

Perhaps the argument most successful in turning the mind of the public favorably to the market model is the appeal to the baker, brewer, and butcher who will supply us with the best bread, beer, and beef if they follow self-regard. It's a captivating image. Yet as soon as we replace bakers, brewers, and butchers by doctors, lawyers, and teachers, plausibility dwindles. Can there be good doctors, lawyers, and teachers who are led in their professions by egoism?

Smith and Mandeville presupposed that all professions can control each other by competition in the same way as they thought bakers, brewers, and butchers can. Yet this is an error. The position of patients, clients, and customers is necessarily weaker than that of experts. They would not ask the professionals if they knew as much of medicine, law, and education as them. There is no place for competition between experts and their dependents, as there may once have been between producers and consumers. So there is no mechanism to transform egoism into a virtue. Once we recognize that we will not be well served if experts are egoists, we can no longer believe that the problem of work evaluation will be best solved by the unregulated market. How can it secure to the good lawyer or judge the salary that corresponds to the quality of her council? At least in addition to market criteria we need perfection standards.

As to the problem of resource allocation, the market can seem the best solution, because it rewards the most effective use of resources and spurs inventions that exploit latent capacities in natural resources. But even here the market cannot be the only factor to decide on resource allocation. There are two related obstacles. First, natural resources are considered by most theorists the common property of mankind that may be privately appropriated only if they are used in the interest of the whole society and future generations. Their reason is that, because they have not been produced by anyone, no one can claim a right to their exclusive use. Second, allocation of resources affects the health of the environment, which according to most theorists is a public good not to be left for its protection to market principles.

Whereas the second obstacle is generally recognized and has led economists to propose economic means that compel producers to take account of the damage they cause, the first one has received little attention. Yet it is no less important. Civil society can only care for itself if any of its resources can be assigned to a proprietor who is entitled to decide how to use it. If there are goods that must

wonders far surpassing Egyptian pyramids, Roman aqueducts, and Gothic cathedrals; it has conducted expeditions that put in the shade all former Exoduses of nations and crusades ... The bourgeoisie has through its exploitation of the world market given a cosmopolitan character to production and consumption in every country ... The cheap prices of commodities are the heavy artillery with which it batters down all Chinese walls, with which it forces the barbarians' intensely obstinate hatred of foreigners to capitulate. ... The bourgeoisie has ... rescued a considerable part of the population from the idiocy of rural life ... The bourgeoisie ... has created more massive and more colossal productive forces than have all preceding generations together."

be used in the interest of mankind, society is in need of nonmarket institutions that decide what the collective interest of society and future generations is.

Nor can we stick to the idea that everyone in a deregulated market system gets out of the social product exactly the amount in the form of money that she has put into it in the form of labor. For the input is not only labor, but also natural resources that she consumes in her labor, and these resources have not been her private property. Moreover, her input depends to a high degree not on her but on the social milieu that formed her; on the education her parents and institutions provided her with, and more generally on the quality of the cultural resources of mankind that she happens to have access to. The individualistic idea of distributive justice cannot take account of the collective factors in the individual's input in the social product.

The economists did not deny that natural resources are common property. They followed Locke and assumed like him that the value of natural resources is so small that we can forget it.[18] They considered labor the only relevant factor of production.[19] Today, when states fight wars for oil and may soon fight wars for fresh water, this view has proved erroneous. It has become clear again that mankind as a whole is dependent on the resources we find in nature. Therefore, the idea that distributive justice can be realized by giving to everyone exactly what she has produced is an illusion. There are things to distribute that no one has produced.

The market model does not only fail in theory. In historical reality, its political champions tried to realize it by stripping the historical markets from the "embedment" that was to prevent its destructive potential. Yet whenever they brought a society close to the ideal, as Karl Polanyi has shown,[20] they brought it close to its collapse. Moreover, up to now most often the strongest Western societies, rather than believing in the universal idea they purported to believe in, have used the idea of the free market as a means to open the markets of the countries they exported their cheaper products to, while they protected their own markets from world market competition.[21]

---

[18] Locke, *Two Treatises of Government* II, §§ 37, 40, and 43, estimates the portion of the value of the natural resources in the total value of a product compared to that of labor one tenth, one hundredth and finally less than one thousandth.

[19] This idea was criticized by Marx in his *Critique of the Gotha Program of 1875, Selected Works*, vol. 3, Moscow, 1970: "Labor is *not the source* of all wealth. *Nature* is just as much the source of use values ... as labor, which itself is only the manifestation of a force of nature ... The bourgeois have very good grounds for falsely ascribing *supernatural creative power* to labor; since precisely from the fact that labor depends on nature it follows that the man who possesses no other property than his labor power must, in all conditions of society and culture, be the slave of other men who have made themselves the owners of the material conditions of labor. He can only work with their permission, hence live only with their permission." (Part I, first point)

[20] Polanyi, *The Great Transformation*. Polanyi introduced the concept of market embedment.

[21] Cf. the work of Immanuel Wallerstein and Noam Chomsky, e.g., Wallerstein, *World Systems Analysis*.

In short, economic rationality is an amazing blunder. Far from meeting the conditions of a universal rationality standard it does not even meet the conditions of rationality in economy. Why did so many intelligent people nevertheless fall victim to it? Because, first, the economists' theory is a wonderful theoretical construction that fascinates intelligent people susceptible to theoretical construction. Second, it fascinated because of its more literary and utopian aspects that promised a solution to the problem of theodicy and projected an autonomous society. Third, modern society needs sphere-transcendent universal rationality so badly that they could easily fall for the economists' claims. But this was possible only because no alternative was seen; in particular, the alternative of a state-independent sphere of justice enforcement has not been recognized.

According to the Austrian-American management theorist Peter Drucker, economic rationality lost its status as universal justice and rationality at the turn of the nineteenth to twentieth centuries, when Marxism lost its attraction. Because Marxism represented for the masses and the intellectuals Economic Man, "the collapse of the society of Economic Man was inevitable as soon as Marxism had proved itself unable to realize the free and equal society."[22] Drucker describes the ideological and psychological consequences thus:

> Through the collapse of Economic Man the individual is deprived of his social order, and his world of its rational existence. He can no longer explain or understand his existence as rationally correlated and co-ordinated to the world in which he lives ... The function of the individual in society has become entirely irrational and senseless. ... Europe – and Europe alone – has successfully attempted the rationalization of the whole cosmos ... (I)n the order of Economic Man the rationalization of the world is driven to a point where everything becomes not only understandable as part of a rational entity but calculable as part of a mechanical sequence ... In the same way in which the physicists cannot find a new rational substitute for their mechanically conceived law of causation, society has not found a new rational basis to replace the mechanical rationalization of the world.[23]

Drucker was right in asserting the lack of orientation and the feeling of the meaninglessness of life that befell many Europeans after the collapse of Economic Man, though this feeling was in fact due rather to their uprootedness and economic superfluity, as described by Arendt, Riesman and other authors.[24] But he was not right in his presumption that Europe had "success-

---

[22] Peter F. Drucker, *The End of Economic Man. The Origins of Totalitarianism*, 50. Drucker became interested in management "because I saw in the big business enterprise the new integrating social agency," all other candidates for integrating society having failed, a view he later abandoned. See Drucker, *Isao Nakauchi, Drucker on Asia*, 149.

[23] Drucker, *End of Economic Man*, loc. cit. 55–8.

[24] Drucker, ibid., 59ff also refers to the experiences of World War I, uprootedness and unemployment, as contributing to the feeling of meaningless but also asserts: "They are exclusively

fully attempted the rationalization of the whole cosmos"; the rationalization of society by the economists was no success. Nor was he completely right in claiming the model of Economic Man had collapsed; it is still believed in by today's neoliberals and in some respects even by anyone who defends modernity or the open society, as Drucker himself did. For the model of economic rationality shows traits dear not only to the neoliberal.

The core ideas of modernity are closely connected with the market model of society. The modern idea of liberty is more than the idea that people should not be tyrannized. It is the idea that individuals can and should be free in the choice of their life and the pursuit of their ideas of a good life; that they can and should choose their profession and way of life without regard to the expectations of the others. Such liberty is dubious in any society that follows the administrative solution to the tuning problem, as it endangers the power of administrators. But it seems to be possible in societies that follow the market solution, as the market needs no administrators to prevent actions unwanted by society.

Similarly, the liberal idea of *equality* is more than the idea that all men are children of God, more than the idea that without regard to rank, color, and sex they have an equal claim to decent treatment and to participate in public affairs. It is the idea that differences even in morality, as distinguished from justice, do not count, and that everyone has a right to pursue their ideas of a good life. Equality, it seems, can become real only in a market society, for such a society needs not morality, but only justice. Only the strict distinction between justice as the sum of enforceable rules that secure liberty to everyone and morality as the sum of ideas of a good life that belong to the private realm made the

due to the disintegration of the belief in the foundations of our society... As far as modern war is concerned, it will, of course, always be regarded as a terrible evil. But that it appears irrational and senseless is not a necessary consequence... The World War came to appear senseless and chaotic only because it revealed the main foundation of the social order as illusory. Otherwise the war would have made sense as part of this rational order ... in the same spirit in which they were regarded by the soldiers of the French Revolution or by the Prussian and Austrian volunteers who rose against Napoleon in 1813." Drucker neglects the relation felt by those who experienced the World War and unemployment between the evils suffered and the reasons given for why they had to be suffered. It was felt to be incongruous or disproportionate in the World War but less so in 1813, and hence corroded the "belief in the foundations of our society." Though Drucker here explains "the origins of totalitarianism" – the subtitle of his book later also chosen by Arendt for her book – by ideological or philosophical changes preceding historical experiences, he reproaches Arendt for "blaming Hitler and Nazism on the systematic German philosophers of early nineteenth century: Fichte, Schelling, or Hegel" (xi). Nothing could be more amiss; I wonder if he had read Arendt's book. (In his second book, Drucker even claims that "There is a straight line from Rousseau to Hitler," and says "Fundamentally, rationalist Liberalism is totalitarianism"; *The Future of Industrial Man*, 1942, London 1995, 137.) In some important points his explanation of totalitarianism is close to Arendt's: in his insistence that "the masses" prefer "security" to freedom and equality (78); and that "Nazism is the real totalitarian revolution whereas Italian fascism is just an imitation" (127). Moreover, he is as much a critic of bureaucracy as Arendt.

radical modern ideas of liberty and equality possible, and this distinction is an offspring of market society.

Belief in the radical ideas implied an ideological revolution that made explicit ideas already implied in the rejection of the closed society. Morality is no longer accepted as a rule imposed by an outward power on the individual, whether mundane or divine, because this contradicts the ideas of liberty and equality. It is instead considered the choice of the individual herself: it is to be autonomous. Nor is society accepted as an order upheld by rulers, no matter how just they may be. Rather, it is considered an order arising from the free choices of equals: an autonomous civil society. As these views make explicit what the rejection of the closed society implied, they are the core ideas of modernity, shared by liberals and socialists.

But how can we keep them, if belief in the market society is wrong? Though this belief is untenable indeed, we cannot conclude that all ideas inspired by the idea of economic rationality are untenable as well. What we cannot abandon without abandoning the core idea of modernity is the idea that everyone has an equal right to decide on their life. This idea implies the ideas of autonomy as presented in the market model, of an autonomy of morality and society that is not in need of priests and princes, administrators and bureaucrats. If such autonomy cannot be realized by the market model, we have to look for other models to realize it. The model I propose is that of autonomous spheres. As the market model radicalized the social reality of embedded markets, the model of autonomous spheres radicalizes the social reality of the more or less autonomous spheres of economy and politics; not in order to strengthen them, but on the contrary, to restrict them in favor of the spheres that today are shrunk by the powerful ones.[25]

Yet before turning to the sphere model, we have to finish our task of looking for traces of the Cartesian self in history. For when we look at the twentieth and the twenty-first centuries, we may well think that there is no chance for modernity to survive at all, and conclude that to consider any model of modernity is love's labor's lost.

[25]   Cp. Chapters 11, 12, and 21.

Chapter 9

The Cartesian Self in the
Twentieth Century

I F WE LOOK FOR TRACES OF THE CARTESIAN SELF IN HISTORY, THE twentieth century is its best and saddest confirmation. It may seem that the most horrible crimes in human history that characterize it had to be committed for theorists to be forced into a clearer articulation of the Cartesian conception. Never before have there been such favorable technological and social conditions for enhancing happiness, and never before has evil of this degree been perpetrated. This at least is what many contemporaries think; rightly, to my judgment. The Cartesian conception provides us with a general explanation for the crimes and for why the chance of happiness has not been used, as it presumes that happiness is not the first aim in humans but the morally ambivalent ambition of extraordinariness. Such explanation of course is too abstract to be a historical explanation. Though we can always find a reason to prefer the bad in the intention of proving our freedom even of morality, and there will be always some individuals who choose this reason, this cannot explain the specific moral disasters of the twentieth century. Societies differ in moral abjection because they differ in the conditions that favor crimes.

The Cartesian conception can help identify such conditions. It assumes as a basic fact that we will always strive for extraordinariness. If we do not find ways for being extraordinarily good, we will prefer being extraordinarily evil to renouncing our ambition of extraordinariness. In the course of the nineteenth century, fewer and fewer people found a way to be extraordinarily good. Weber described this lack of action possibilities as the house of bondage.[1] Peter Drucker described it as a spiritual emptiness after the collapse of Economic Man. Most

---

[1]   Weber, *Parlament und Regierung im neugeordneten Deutschland*, 319f, calls contemporary society the "steel-house of modern professional work," "the housing of that future bondage … to which perhaps men will be forced to bow impotently, like the fellahin to the state of ancient Egypt."

differentiated is the description given by Hannah Arendt in her book on the *Origins of Totalitarianism*. In spite of their deeper differences, the earliest theorists on the origins of totalitarianism, Drucker and Arendt, agree that "not in spite of its being contrary to reason and in spite of its rejecting everything of the past without exception, but because of it ... the masses flocked to fascism and Nazism."[2] They agree that the acceptance of the Nazi revolution by the masses was a "revolt ... against 'realism,' common sense, and all 'the plausibilities of the world' (Burke)."[3] It was a revolt against utilitarian standards. But no less was it a revolt against all sphere-immanent value standards.

Not only the Nazi revolution was a revolt against utilitarian standards; World War I already was. With an enthusiasm shocking today, individuals all over Europe accepted the decision of a minority to start a war. They literally died for sacrificing their lives for their countries, even though enthusiasm cooled when the first battles slaughtered masses of soldiers. The Cartesian explanation that people were eager to leave the ordinary world of peace and prove their extraordinariness at least has a point.

Utilitarians are again in trouble when they have to explain why so many Germans and Austrians accepted the Nazi revolution. They might argue thus: Standards of living had risen in most parts of Europe since the nineteenth century, but the feeling of security had shrunk, since more and more people no longer lived by their work on fields they and their children could be sure to cultivate in future, but by work in factories and offices, where they could be fired at any time and often enough were. They felt, and indeed were, uprooted and economically superfluous, and the more they felt so, the more they were inclined to accept ideologies like communism or Nazism that promised radical change. Because of their defeat in war, "uprootedness" was particularly strong in Germany and Austria. Communism was particularly unacceptable for them because it was the ideology of an enemy country; hence, they opted for Nazism. This explanation leaves out the fact that the program and actions of the Nazis before 1933 allowed no doubt that they were dangerously anti-Semitic, fanatical about ideas of an Aryan race most Germans did not take seriously at all, and contemptuous of elementary moral rules most Germans held inviolable. There could be no doubt that people so fanatical and so ready to commit and admit crimes[4] (to the eyes of those born later so strongly resembling gangsters), would do anything but maximize happiness.

---

[2] Drucker, *The End of Economic Man*, loc. cit. 84.

[3] Arendt, *Origins of Totalitarianism*, loc. cit. 352. It is curious that Arendt does not mention Drucker, though he had used the title Arendt chose for her book nearly a decade earlier as the subtitle of his book.

[4] Cp. Arendt, *Origins of Totalitarianism*, loc. cit. 344ff, on the open way the Nazis acknowledged the crimes committed by their adherents before they took over the government.

The problem for utilitarians is: How could people accept a revolution that so clearly was against their interests? If we follow Arendt we find an explanation that confirms the Cartesian conception of the self and rationality. Her explanation is that their "uprootedness" and economic superfluity made people unwilling of having selves. Not finding a use for their selfs in conditions where there was in fact no use for them, it was not necessary but understandable (and in this sense rational) for them not only to renounce their selfs that might burden them with responsibility, but also their self-interest. But renouncing self-interest does not imply abandoning the ambition of extraordinariness. This ambition survives the death of the self, because it is already a property of the proto-self.

"The fanaticism of members of totalitarian movements," Arendt stated, "so clearly different in quality from the greatest loyalty of members of ordinary parties, is produced by the lack of self-interest of masses who are quite prepared to sacrifice themselves."[5] This phenomenon was not a postwar product. Arendt observes the "peculiar selflessness of the mass man" before the war, but also in individuals who, like Lawrence of Arabia, yearned for "losing their selves"; or who like Bakunin confessed, "I do not want to be *I*, I want to be *We*."[6] Talking of the "masses," she explains it as "the result of their atomization, of their loss of social status along with which they lost the whole sector of communal relationships in whose framework common sense makes sense."[7] Such loss or uprootedness, as she calls it, was suffered not only by the masses but also by individuals of upper classes. Nor is it a temporary phenomenon characteristic only of the first decades of the twentieth century; rather, it has increased till now in proportion to the threat of unemployment.

If Arendt is right, the Nazis' open contempt for morality and rationality has been attractive because it presents a form of life that, alongside morality and rationality, despises the very conditions of self-responsibility, self-respect, and having a self. But the Nazis did not only offer the dissolution of the self; at the same time they promised something Arendt does not give due regard to, though without it a totalitarian movement cannot even start. They promised extraordinary actions the world would never stop talking of: the conquest of the world; the killing of the Jews; the transubstantiation of the average ugly, flabby, dull German into a vigorous, brilliant, blond beast.

The absolute necessity for totalitarian movements to promise extraordinariness may seem paradoxical, for if we dissolve the self, how can we hope for glory? But if our self ends, our ambition of extraordinariness need not end as well. The self is the result of a difficult passage from the childhood stage of rationality. Its dissolution is easy, for we may fall back on the proto-self and

---

5   Ibid., 348.
6   Ibid., 327–30.
7   Ibid., 352.

rely on a superego or another absolute authority, as we necessarily did as children. The relapse does not extinguish our ambition of extraordinariness. As I explained, already the proto-self is pitted against the subject, is ambitious of extraordinariness and eager to prove its superiority. The more self-assertion is denied us, the more we will incline toward using our freedom of the will for the final decision to stop judging and surrender to the self-less extraordinariness of a mass movement.

This explanation is no exculpation. The decision to abandon one's self, though favored by the lack of opportunity for self-assertion, is a freely willed option. Arendt's conception of the will is perfectly Cartesian: "We are *free* to change the world and to start something new in it. Without the mental freedom to deny or affirm existence, to say 'yes' or 'no' – not just to statements or propositions in order to express agreement or disagreement, but to things as they are given, beyond agreement or disagreement, to our organs of perception and cognition – no action would be possible."[8] By stressing that the freedom to say both *yes* and *no* not only to propositions but also "to things as they are given," Arendt wants to point out that this power enables us to say *no* to the entire world (or to deliberate the "possibility of the impossibility" of anything at all, as one might say with Heidegger) and to change it (though actually both are implied by reference to propositions).[9] She gives back to the power of free will the capacity of deliberately changing the world most of her contemporaries denied. She even marks out the aspect in the arbitrariness of free will that complements its dangerousness: that it starts something new in the world. This may be an evil; hopefully it is a good.

Is there a chance at all for modernity or the West to survive? Like Max Weber and so many other observers of the twentieth century, Arendt sticks to modernity's core idea of equal liberty but thinks that if we have a chance at all for saving equal liberty it is only if we see as clearly as possible the immense dangers immanent in the given social conditions. Though she reckons unemployment and other economic failures among the most obvious causes for the dangers, she does not think that regulation or even abolishment of markets would suffice to cure society. She diagnoses the causes as failures of an understanding of the

---

[8] Arendt, *Lying in Politics*, in *Crises of the Republic*, 5f.

[9] Calling the decision to say *yes* or *no* to a proposition *thinking*, Arendt, *Origins of Totalitarianism* 473f, like Descartes, considers it "the freest and purest of all human activities," and opposes it to "the self-coercive force of logicality" that she sees fully developed in totalitarianism. She is close to Descartes's view on judgment and to Heidegger's and Wittgenstein's view that the world is accessible only in interaction when she claims that repression of this free activity by insisting on "cogent deduction" disables men to distinguish fact and fiction. For logical "consistency … exists nowhere in reality" (ibid., 471) and is excluded when we are "in contact with other men," upon which "even the experience of the materially and sensually given world depends" and "without which each of us would be enclosed in his own particularity of sense data which in themselves are unreliable and treacherous" (ibid., 475f).

world and the self that the economic and political disasters are symptoms of. To cure such failures, a revolution in the way to grasp oneself and the world is necessary.

Let us look at some of her remarks to understand better what such a revolution would consist of. Because the conditions of uprootedness have not changed until now, but unemployment has even grown, "What we are confronted with is the prospect of a society of laborers without labor, that is, without the only activity left to them. Surely, nothing could be worse."[10] Nothing could be *better* under conditions we might call normal than that people become superfluous in economy and labor becomes scarce; labor is painful or boring. When not threatened by unemployment, people hate and avoid it as much as possible. What should be delightful is a cause for despair today. Today, for everyone without patrimony, unemployment is loss of income, of esteem (including self-esteem), often of meaning in life. Labor has become the only activity left to most people that can give them meaning, although it is an activity that "normally" functions only as a necessary means for activities that have a meaning. So the problem of unemployment cannot be solved by job-creation programs or higher unemployment benefit. Nor can it be solved by a purely mental change, say by becoming negligent to unemployment and content with an unemployment compensation. This would not stop labor from being the only activity to give meaning to most people's lives. It can be solved only if there are other activities that can give meaning to people. Whether there are, does not depend on an individual's will but on social conditions that form and are formed by individuals.

Such dependence of the not-just-economical but more general mental calamity of individuals on social conditions is similar to the dependence on social conditions two millennia ago, when individuals despaired at the absurdity of a life that dissolves in generating generations for generating generations. Their despair could be overcome only by a social form that offered them the chance of living for causes other than for generating generations. Such a social form alone, without the individuals' ambition of living for more than just generating generations, would not change anything. But there was such ambition; so the new social form that arose after the collapse of the closed society in ancient Greece and republican Rome was capable of satisfying the needs the closed society was not.

The need the open society had satisfied was itself a productive force in the wide Marxian sense described previously.[11] Once this force found the social conditions it needed, it pushed modernity to its feats in science, politics, and other spheres. Similarly, the calamity of finding no meaning in a world whose labor runs short cannot be overcome just by changing social conditions. It can be overcome only if the change finds a social form in which all or nearly

---

[10] Arendt, *The Human Condition*, 5.
[11] Cp. Chapter 6.

all individuals find sufficient opportunity to enact their specific ambitions of extraordinariness. Today, for most people there is only the opportunity to enact this ambition by labor. As labor runs short, the social form of organizing our productive forces, first of all our ambition for extraordinariness, must be organized in a way that opens up far more opportunity. If this succeeds, a similar push might bring modernity to new feats, though the time necessary for such a success might be similarly long as in the past.

Arendt did not use the Marxian terms I have used for describing the calamity she finds in contemporary modern societies, but her ideas are similar. To point out the specific dependence of the present calamity on both social and mental conditions, she refers to ancient Athens, which offered its citizens action opportunities that are not only closed but have lost their meaning to modern individuals. Athenians knew more meaningful activities than labor. They knew that the most perfect, most meaningful form of activity is action, an activity that is shared by a community and is extraordinary enough to be remembered by the following generations. It alone can give "human affairs a permanence they otherwise do not have"; they can "immortalize" people.[12] Arendt's idea is that meaning, whether of words or in life, always arises from actions; they are the original source of any significance.[13] Yet they are most significant (or significance-producing) when they are performed in common by the community for which they have meaning; such are political actions like the foundation of a city or a war, but also celebrations of games like those in Olympia. The knowledge of the importance of this form of activity was broken by the Christian turn to a transcendent world that denied this world meaning; it was lost when the polis dissolved in the empires of Alexander and Rome. But there was still left another kind of activity more meaningful than labor, namely, work, the production of things that can last as long as the memory of great actions and is as meaningful as its products can be.[14] Even this activity has lost its significance today, because work has been dissolved in labor, which does not produce lasting things but serves the ever-regenerating needs and desires of our lives. Labor is just the activity that offers least opportunity for extraordinariness.

Arendt's judgment is that contemporary modernity fails in allowing people to enact and even detect their capability of finding meaning in activities. She reproaches it with stifling a capacity that is the most valuable and human one. Such a capacity is the most important productive force, in the wide Marxian sense. It presupposes the ambition of extraordinariness, as both action and work aim at immortal fame. Only labor does not, but this is just the reason why it cannot satisfy people and leads them to seek extraordinariness in destruction.

---

[12] Arendt, *The Promise of Politics*, 97.

[13] This view has also been held by Wittgenstein; see my *Wittgenstein über den Willen*.

[14] Arendt, *The Human Condition*, loc. cit. 301.

So, unemployment will not stop being a danger as long as people do not redetect the meaning of action and work. Lacking these conditions, this is what we have to reckon with:

> The frightening coincidence of the modern population explosion with the discovery of technical devices that, through automation, will make large sections of the population "superfluous," even in terms of labor, and that, through nuclear energy, make it possible to deal with this twofold threat by the use of instruments beside which Hitler's gassing installations look like an evil child's fumbling toys, should be enough to make us tremble.[15]

What we have to fear most, she says, is not just the extinction of mankind:

> "For we know today that killing is far from the worst that man can inflict on man, and that death is by no means what man most fears."[16] As she had explained earlier, "in their effort to probe that everything is possible, totalitarian regimes have discovered without knowing it that there are crimes which men can neither punish nor forgive. When the impossible was made possible it became the unpunishable, unforgivable absolute evil."[17]

Yet here we may doubt if she is right. Isn't death "what man most fears"? Is there absolute evil?[18]

Arendt seems wrong even when she meant to say that death is not what man *ought* to fear most. For, aren't the crimes of the totalitarian regimes absolute evil because they killed so many innocent? One may perhaps not even be a utilitarian to think so. She rejects this idea, as well as doubts in absolute evil. The "absolute evil" is what totalitarianism "aims at." What it aims at is "the transformation of human nature itself. The concentration camps are the laboratories where changes in human nature are tested, and their shamelessness therefore ... is the concern of all men. Suffering, of which there has been always too much on earth, is not the issue, nor is the number of victims. Human nature as such is at stake."[19] Totalitarianism aims at man's transformation into "a specimen of the animal-species man," a being with the properties of men but without their power of judgment, condemned to live "in a world of conditioned reflexes, of marionettes without the slightest trace of spontaneity."[20]

---

[15] Arendt, *Eichmann in Jerusalem. A Report on the Banality of Evil.*
[16] Arendt, *Men in Dark Times*, 126f.
[17] Arendt, *Origins of Totalitarianism*, loc. cit. 459.
[18] Arendt's talk of absolute evil has become fashionable. Take this example of a comment on George W. Bush's talk of "the axis of evil": "there is, in fact, ... an absolute 'evil' whose threat, whose shadow, is spreading. Absolute evil, absolute threat, because what is at stake is nothing less than ... life on earth and elsewhere, without remainder." (Jacques Derrida in G. Borradori loc. cit. (fn. 6), 99).
[19] Arendt, *Origins,* loc. cit. 458f.
[20] Ibid., 457.

So what totalitarianism aims at is the abolition of human nature. We can abolish it by destroying mankind, but this is not what Arendt fears most. The danger she wants to point to is that human nature is abolished by reducing man to an obedient animal without judgment. It is what we ought to fear most because it is aimed at not only by totalitarian regimes. It may even be the unintended result of actions that aim at profit, entertainment, or medication.[21] We have to fear it most because the danger springs not from extraordinary monsters like Hitler but from societies that do not know what meaningful activities are. Lacking this knowledge, they do not feel the value of human nature and are ready to abolish it.

The danger Arendt describes should be feared most indeed, because it is rarely seen. It is just the danger we have to expect when we recognize the importance of the ambition of extraordinariness. Finding no other meaningful activities but those of labor by which life is maintained for life's sake, our ambition of extraordinariness will look for extraordinariness in changing human life. But changes will be the more extraordinary the more radically life is transformed into something it has not been. Hence, because political interest in taming people will always be strong, we have to expect that ambitions will concentrate on transforming humans into kind and happy animals.

So chances for the survival of modernity are somber. But this is certainly not sufficient not to think about ways to escape from what seems bad fate.

---

[21] Cp. Martin Rees, *Our Final Hour*, 2–13: "By mid-century … [people may] have different attitudes from those of the present (maybe modified by medication, chip implants, and so forth). …Nongenetic changes could be even more sudden, transforming humanity's mental character in less than a generation, as quickly as new drugs can be developed and marketed. The fundamentals of humanity, essentially unaltered throughout recorded history, could start to be transformed within this century."

Part IV

Value Spheres

Man can relish nothing but what is eminent.
Hobbes, Leviathan

Chapter 10

A First Diagnosis and Therapy for Modernity

L ET US LOOK BACK AT WHAT WE HAVE DISCOVERED ABOUT THE Cartesian self in history. The break between the childhood and the adult self finds a historical correspondence in the break between closed and open societies. Quite a few individuals develop an authentic self whether they live in a closed or open society (Greek philosophers and sophists are a splendid example). But it is only in an open society that the authentic self is recognized in institutionalized equal rights to decide on one's life. The break to modernity was motivated not by a desire to enhance happiness but by the desire of the individual to find a non-Sisyphean meaning of life. It took a religious form that imposed on everyone the duty to use their own judgment in their struggle for salvation and to respect everyone's judgment, transforming the ancient Greeks' pride in reason into a burdensome duty.

The new non-Sisyphean meaning was found in perfecting activities and brought forth the idea of sphere autonomy, yet this idea was only partially realized. Modernity suffers from lack not of a sphere-transcendent rationality but of a sphere of justice strong enough to adjudicate sphere conflicts and watch over equal liberty within the spheres. The disasters of the twentieth century demonstrate that today we do not only suffer from too weak a justice sphere but also from loss of understanding what the activities are that can give meaning to life. This loss has social causes and cannot be overcome without regaining social conditions in which the meaning of action and work and its distinction from labor can be understood. Otherwise we have to expect a transformation of human into animal nature, if not the extinction of mankind.

Up to the nineteenth century, modernity excelled in science and technology, economy and state power. Its core idea of equal liberty has found general recognition in most other civilizations that detected the propagation and suppression of similar ideas in their own past. And yet it took a disastrous turn in the twentieth century, contradicting its core idea. Does this mean that modernity has collapsed; that we should abandon it and try a new civilization? What has gone wrong?

As long as we do not see an idea that might replace that of equal liberty, how could we abandon modernity? Equal liberty, to be sure, is not an exact idea; allowing everyone an equal right to decide on his or her own life can be understood in a couple of ways that political theorists quarrel about.[1] Yet ideas that guide a civilization cannot be exact; they need to allow various interpretations. With all its broadness, it is sharp enough to mark out that most past societies did not conform to it and that most contemporary Western societies do not either. Does this show that it is not the guiding idea of the West? Or that it is an illusion? This is not plausible. Once the idea that everyone has a right to be equally respected in their will has won the consent of the masses, as it has, only minorities will be capable of believing that they are entitled to a right they can deny the rest. The idea of equal liberty will remain a guiding idea.

If we stick to this idea, we cannot abandon modernity. Rather, we have to find out what has gone wrong with modernity and how it can be saved. There are a lot of explanations, conservative and Marxist, some claiming that modernity failed because it has undermined religion, others, because it did so too little; some that capitalism is the culprit, others that it is the state that interfered too much with economy. I'll look for the cause in the imbalance of the values spheres, in the domination of the most powerful of them, economy and the state, over the other spheres. It led society into colonialism, imperialism, exploitation, and uprootedness of the masses that brought forth wars and totalitarian regimes. Like Arendt, I'll also take account of the meaning that activities have for people. I presume it is a historical fact that Western individuals lost an understanding of those activities that give meaning to life, action, and work and now crave for extraordinariness in narrow categories that breed still more horrible disasters.

But does looking at the meaning activities have for people really give us a better understanding? It will not allow falsifiable predictions, as we ascribe to people free will that renders their actions unpredictable anyway. But it allows us to understand how people felt and judged the economic and political conditions that more traditional explanations point to for explaining history. Even if we do not assume, as Arendt did, that feelings and judgments can cause historical change, we would still understand more of history. Anyway, reference to the meaning of activities has another recommendation.

I have found the most convincing solution to the problem of how modernity could arise at all in the answer that it was born out of individuals' disgust at their dissolution in the chain of generations. I presupposed that feelings relating to the meaning of activities can explain history. If this is too speculative for passing as sound historiography, Arendt's theses on the effects of lack of meaning

---

[1]   I'll present a more detailed understanding in Chapter 20. Cp. also my own *Gleiche Freiheit*.

in modernity is certainly not. Her theses imply that modernity was not able to keep its promise of giving meaning to life. As she claims that the ancient Greek poleis still understood what is meaningful in activities and that Christianity (and Platonism) contributed to the loss, she implies that it was modernity, its individualism and obsession with saving the individual's soul, that reduced people to the narrow-mindedness of finding meaning only in the poorest activity of labor. In fact, her provocative thesis that today "suffering, of which there has been always too much on earth, is not the issue, nor is the number of victims,"[2] is based on her view that saving mere life is the present orientation that robs life of meaning.[3] Her explanation of the disasters of the twentieth century is an uncompromising rejection of the claim of modernity to give meaning to life, though no less uncompromisingly she defends equal liberty, the core idea of modernity.[4] So, reference to the meanings of activities is necessary: first, for understanding a civilization and how it attracts its members and, second, for deciding if it can redeem its promises.

For this reason it is not any kind of meaning of an activity that is of interest to the historian and the analyst of modern society. It is only a meaning that indicates success or failure of the social form of organizing productive forces in the wide Marxian sense. The despair at the Sisyphean absurdity of generating generations for its own sake is an example of a meaning, that of absurdity, that indicates a failure. The specific meaning labor has today is another example. It expresses both an interest to cling to some meaning when any meaning is threatened and a disgust at the nullity of labor and thus indicates again a fundamental incapacity of the present form of organizing our productive powers. Like the despair millennia ago at the nullity of generating generations, disgust at labor indicates that the form of organizing productive forces fails to include forces that would bring about a new flourishing if only they could find opportunity for nondestructive enactment.

If this is a correct diagnosis of the misery of modernity, the therapy is not too difficult to find. It consists in promoting institutions in which people can experience the meaning of activities that are meaningful not because, like labor, they help saving life for survival's sake, but because they are themselves meaningful. Yet activities that are meaningful in themselves have an activity-immanent perfection and can be performed extraordinarily. If we could promote institutions

---

[2]   Arendt, *Origins*, 458f.

[3]   She opposes the concept of world to that of life to mark out that, when people lost an understanding of action and labor, they lost an understanding of the world and considered everything, in particular society, part of the "life process." While formerly only the family had served life, now everything belongs to it (*Human Condition*, 256).

[4]   This becomes clear in her discussions of contemporary politics, e.g., her comments on the Pentagon Papers in *Lying in Politics* (in *Crises of the Republic*, 1972), but also in her attitude to the conflict between Israelis and Palestinians, for which she, being a Jew, was attacked as a traitor of Judaism.

that favor such activities, we would succeed in squaring the circle. We would organize productive forces in a form that would escape the unavoidable: That organization forms, just because of their success, breed productive forces that rebel and play havoc with the form that bred them. We would escape it because the form would challenge any kind of constructive ambition of extraordinariness and use it for strengthening society. The resulting society would stick to the core idea of modernity, equal liberty, and save modernity. But it would organize productive forces in a form very different from the present one. It would be a very different society.

What could be the institutions that enable people to experience the meaning of action and work, challenge their ambition and still strengthen society? Such institutions have been conceived in the values spheres of which Weber showed that they have been emancipated from their service to the closed society and developed to autonomy rather than being subjected to a religious system. Value spheres can follow their specific perfection standards only because they are experienced by their agents as having an inherent meaning that enables them to find their specific perfection standards. The broad variety of nonabsurd meanings of activities is experienced in the broad variety of value spheres. Every one of their specific values is experienced as a specific meaning of the activity. Only if we experience such meaning can we learn the specific perfection standard of a sphere. Such a standard challenges the ambition of extraordinariness of all and only individuals who have a talent for the specific sphere. If the spectrum of value spheres is broad enough, we can hope that everyone will find at least one sphere they have a talent for. So for developing our idea of a modern society that uses the inexhaustible, potentially destructive source of productive forces (which is what the ambition of extraordinariness is) for strengthening modern society, we have to consider value spheres more closely and check whether they can really be used the way I propose.

Chapter 11

Value Spheres Defined
and the State

L ET US START WITH ASKING WHICH KIND OF ACTIVITIES CAN BE recognized as value spheres at all, what is implied by their recognition, and by which criteria we can distinguish them.

In answering this question, we can refer to Weber. He understood that the past glory of the West was based on value spheres that attracted individuals and challenged their ambition of extraordinariness by their specific meanings. He was not the first to understand this. Hegel had already distinguished spheres in his system of modern civilization by both the functions they have for society and the meanings they have for the individual. He distinguished what he called the *objective* and the *absolute* spirit and differentiated the first into family, civil society (which is economy), and the state, and the second into religion, art, and science. His distinction of objective and absolute spirit points to an important difference among value spheres not mentioned by Weber. All sphere activities require judgment, so they are "spirit." But those of the first class (of the family, economy, and politics) objectively serve the survival of a society, however much they are subjectively felt to be done for other reasons. Those of the second class are activities that find their meaning in themselves and are served by the activities of the first class. This is why Hegel calls their spirit absolute. I'll follow Hegel's distinction, though not his terminology, and call the spheres of the first class serving, and those of the second class nonserving, spheres.

The distinction does not exclude the activities of the first class from being performed for their own sake. But economy, families, and even justice would be without a point if there were no activities for which they secure the conditions. Such nonserving activities need not be the sublime activities of religion, art, and science that Hegel lists; we may as well think of more vulgar activities like playing tennis just for fun. Only the second class gives a society meaning. Its activities are the hinge life turns around if it is not to become Sisyphean. Both kinds require the judgment of the self, but the second gives more consideration to the subject. Its activities pursue interests that presuppose passions and sentiments of the agent. They are the place to reconcile the subject to the self and realize individual autonomy; for autonomy requires a harmony of self and subject and social conditions that allow the enactment of the individual's talents, which belong to the subject. Subjectivity is important also for the activities of the first kind – economy, politics, and technology exploit and adapt to it, families live on it, justice takes account of it, the media get into it. But here it is important as a means to the aims of the serving spheres rather than as an end. In the nonserving spheres, it becomes the object of investigation, as in science, and of presentation, imagination, exploration, experimentation, stimulation, as in art, religion, sport, and love.

Weber added to Hegel's six spheres sexuality, which he also calls eroticism.[1] In fact, erotic activities are no less nonserving activities than those of art and religion; but should we not add more? For instance, is not twirling one's thumb or enjoying the smell of one's sweat a nonserving activity as well? Yet Weber conceived value spheres as *life orders*, that is, activities of the professions of a society. The activities of sexuality are those of the profession of prostitution; a "life order" hardly less old than the profession of priest, soldier, or merchant. But prostitution is a serving activity; only if sexuality is performed not for money but love, can it be classified as nonserving; maybe this was a reason why Weber did not distinguish serving and nonserving value spheres. Anyway, twirling one's thumb and enjoying one's sweat obviously are not life orders, so fail as value spheres in Weber's conception. Yet should we accept Weber's condition?

Weber was interested in history; in history the differentiation of values originally corresponds to a differentiation in professions. Because my interest is in history as well, I'll follow Weber, yet because my interest also is in possible historical developments, I'll bind value spheres to possible professions and presume that an activity is a possible profession if it (1) aims at a value that is not reducible to the value of another sphere and (2) can be perfected. This implies that the activities of a value sphere follow a specific perfection standard. It is not necessary, and rarely the case, that the agents of a sphere can explain what its standard is, as little as they need to formulate the aim of their sphere. Nor is it necessary that they agree what the standard is. In historical fact, the standards of many spheres are controversial up till today. What is necessary, however, is their agreement that their spheres have a specific, irreducible aim and perfection standard.

The agents of a value sphere learn its perfection standards by practice. This requires of value spheres that they introduce their agents in a way that enables them to learn what is essential in the activity and what is not, that they discipline the beginners so that they can get aware of what counts and where the specific

[1]   In an insertion after his study of Confucianism, the so-called *Zwischenbetrachtung* (cp. note 11 in Chapter 6).

meaning of the activity comes from. An example for such necessary disciplining in a value sphere is teaching a child to play the violin. It is a hard process and can fail when talent is too small or discipline too rough. Yet often enough it succeeds and makes playing the violin an activity the player knows how to evaluate. In this case, the child has understood the meaning of playing the violin, learned the perfection standards and knows what extraordinariness in her field is. She has acquired a virtue in the sense in which Aristotle describes virtue: a disposition to choose and do the right actions with excellence and joy.[2] A similar discipline and favorable circumstances are necessary in all other value spheres, as will become clear later on. This means that value spheres need a degree of institutionalization that allows schooling.

So let us define a value sphere as a kind of activity that requires judgment, can be the activity of a profession, allows schooling, and pursues a value irreducible to the value aimed at in any other kind of activity. This is a definition that needs examples. We may doubt if a musician and a novelist aim at the same value, though I'll understand it to be the same value of art. Similarly, I'll understand the values aimed at by a physicist and a historian as the same value of science. I'll try showing what the values of art and science are, but I start from the view that there are specific values of art and science. I think the differences between the values of music and novels and those between physics and historiography can be understood as resulting from the differences of the matter used for showing what the artist tries showing and of the objects investigated by the scientist.

Using this definition, which activities make up value spheres? Can we accept Hegel's list, added to by Weber's sphere of sexuality? This list is too short, for technology and sport are activities for possible professions and aim at values irreducible to any other sphere. You may argue that science and technology aim at the same value, but I'll try showing that this is an error. Entertainment might be regarded as another value sphere, but the values it aims at are reducible to the values of economy, sport, and sexuality. Morality and military affairs might also be proposed as value spheres. But military activities can serve very different aims and pursue different values. If we do not think there is a specific value of military courage or honor or another quality that we do not find aimed at in any other nonmilitary activity, and I think we cannot, then we cannot recognize military activities as a value sphere of their own.

As to morality, though some philosophers think that by acting morally we aim at a specific value, this is a mistake, probably due to the confounding of morality and justice. Justice can be aimed at for the sake of justice indeed; that is what judges ought to do. But when, say, we help a friend, we act morally, yet do not aim at the specific value of morality (or the idea of goodness). Rather, we aim at the well-being of the friend; any other aim would stop the help from being a moral act. For this reason, there is no value sphere of morality. It is true,

---

2   Aristotle, *Nicomachean Ethics* I, 1098a7–18; II, 1106b4ff; 1107a1ff; X, 1177a11ff.

though, that actions can be done for the sake not of morality but of love; a love that aims at the well-being of the loved one and not at the morality of the lover. Such activities belong to the value sphere of love.

Do at least the value spheres proposed by Hegel and Weber conform to our definition of a value sphere? There can be little doubt as to the spheres of the family, economy, religion, art, and science. But as I have already argued (in Chapter 7), the state is a sphere of activities pursuing very different values. There is the value of justice, no doubt irreducible to any other value and pursued by judges and other individuals in the profession of justice enforcement. And there are the aims of administration, of managing the many ordinary and extraordinary affairs that can be better managed, or are only claimed to be better manageable, by mediators than by the people directly concerned. Administrative activities, like military ones, pursue a lot of different aims with different values, hence constitute no value sphere.

One reason that is adduced for considering the state a value sphere is that its irreducible and specific value is power. It needs power for performing both its administrative and judicative tasks; hence, securing and maximizing power becomes its defining value. Though power is also pursued in other spheres, such as economy and religion, the power pursued in the state might be considered a specific one, as it serves administration and justice. This view is often ascribed to Weber. Yet Weber was aware of the ambiguity of the state's aim, for he struggles with answers. He says indeed: "the whole process of interior affairs of the state machine ... is inescapably regulated ... by the objective pragmatics of Reason of State: by the absolute ... intrinsic end of the preservation (or transformation) of the inner and outer distribution of power."[3] He is talking here only of the interior affairs, but has been understood as identifying the state's specific aim with power. Yet he continues his sentence thus: "The state opposes to the principle of the Sermon on the Mount 'Don't withstand the evil by the use of force' the principle 'You shall help that Right will win even by using force – bearing yourself responsibility for doing wrong.' Where this would be absent, the state would be absent: pacifist anarchism would have been born."[4]

Here he ascribes to the state the ultimate aim of justice enforcement. He leaves no doubt that states would be illegitimate, even "absent," if they did not pursue this aim. The power that is used in its pursuit is indeed defined by the aim of justice, while the power that is pursued in "the objective pragmatics of

---

[3] Weber, *Zwischenbetrachtung*, 547, ed. Kröner, 453f: "... der gesamte Gang der innerpolitischen Funktionen des Staatsapparates ... reguliert sich ... unvermeidlich stets wieder an der sachlichen Pragmatik der Staatsräson: an dem absoluten ... Selbstzweck der Erhaltung (oder Umgestaltung) der inneren und äußeren Gewaltverteilung)."

[4] Ibid,: "Dem Widerstehet nicht dem Übel mit Gewalt' der Bergpredigt setzt er das. Du sollst dem *Recht* auch mit *Gewalt* zum Siege verhelfen – bei eigener Verantwortung für das Unrecht' entgegen. Wo das fehlte, da fehlte der 'Staat': der pazifistische Anarchismus wäre ins Leben getreten."

Reason of State" is not. So Weber and the reference to power is of little help in arguing for recognizing the state as a value sphere.

Another reason for such a recognition is that the state is the sphere of the political, understood as public affairs or the public; affairs that concern everyone. Though such affairs pursue a lot of different aims with different values, we may ascribe to dealing with them the pursuit of an irreducible aim, that of serving the common or public interest. Such an aim, we may go on arguing, is particularly important if we want to develop the autonomy of value spheres. Without a public sphere, they would fall apart into isolated value spheres, and such isolation would stunt the development of capabilities. Though the value sphere of justice forms a bridge between all spheres, by looking after justice in and between them, this would not suffice for counteracting their islolation. We need a specific sphere for identifying, discussing, and managing public affairs. This is what the state aims at.

My reply to this defense of the state is this. If it defends an ideal the state should conform to, we should ask if other spheres or institutions are not better capable of looking after public affairs than the state. If it implies that the modern state of history is or can become the sphere of public affairs, historical facts do not confirm this expectation. Until the nineteenth century, the modern state was successful because it excluded important parts of the public affairs from its sphere. Political philosophers succeeded in presenting the state as the protector of both justice and public affairs and at the same time argued for the exclusion of parts of the public affairs from the state sphere. They could convince themselves and the public because they believed in the state as an irreducible value. Let's look at their arguments.

The belief in the state is based on the major premise that we need justice enforcement and the minor that only the state can deliver justice enforcement. The major is true; we can never abandon the task of justice enforcement and will always need means of coercion, because there will never be a time, as Fichte and Marx believed, when people will no longer commit crimes;[5] doing evil is too much of a challenge for an authentic self. The minor is false, as justice need not be enforced by one central institution that has the monopoly of force. Hobbes argued for the minor, because he had specific historical reasons for preferring to the diffusion of power its concentration in an institution that by definition is the modern state.[6] In medieval times, economic and religious institutions

---

5 Johann Gottlob Fichte, *Die Staatslehre*, 599: The state that he calls a "government of coercion" (Zwangsregierung) will "little by little fall asleep because it will not find anything to do at all (allmählig einschlafen, weil sie durchaus nichts mehr zu tun findet)." For Marx's and Engels's views on the death of the state and their efforts at delimiting their position from anarchism, see Hal Draper, *The Death of the State in Marx and Engels*, 281–307.

6 Hobbes, *Leviathan*, ch. 13 and 17, ed. Macpherson loc. cit. 185 and 227: Without one "common Power to keep them all in awe" and "terror thereof," men will sink into "such a warre, as is of every man, against every man."

and different political institutions like towns and princes had their own means of coercion to enforce justice on lawbreakers.[7] This pluralistic form of justice enforcement may not have fitted the needs of later times, but the monistic form has proved disastrous in the twentieth century when crimes formerly unthinkable have been committed by the horrible means of coercion concentrated in the states.[8] True, the Hobbesian argument is getting fresh nourishment today by the threat of terrorism.[9] But though force is necessary to defend justice, state power is not. It may be the only force available today to protect justice, yet it is more likely to provoke new terrorism than stop it.

In fact, Hobbesian monistic justice enforcement served the emancipation of the sphere of economy. The modern state owed its rise to a division of labor with economy that caused its later fall. Ironically, this division of labor was recommended by the very philosopher who became famous for his radical defense of an absolute state. Hobbes gleefully shocked his contemporaries when he called the state, for the powers he granted it, by the name of the biblical monster Leviathan. But his boosting of state power contrasts with his restriction of it in economy. Talking of a citizen's "controversie with his Soveraigne, of Debt, or of right of possession of lands or goods," he is as much a defender of citizens' rights as Locke and later liberals. The citizen, he says, "hath the same Liberty to sue

---

7   Cp. Jessica Tuchman Mathews, "Power Shift": "In the Middle Ages, emperors, kings, dukes, knights, popes, archbishops, guilds, and cities exercised overlapping secular power over the same territory in a system that looks much more like a modern, three-dimensional network than the clean-lined, hierarchical state order that replaced it." (61) "NGOs ... are better than governments at dealing with problems that grow slowly and affect society through their cumulative effect on individuals – the "soft" threats of environmental degradation, denial of human rights, population growth, poverty, and lack of development that may already be causing more deaths in conflict than are traditional acts of aggression." (63) Stating that "States are the only nonvoluntary political unit, the one that can impose order and is invested with the power to tax," she implies that their legitimacy may be rejected just for this reason. No doubt she is right to predict: "The shift from national to some other political allegiance, if it comes, will be an emotional, cultural, and political earthquake." (65) M. Hardt, A. Neri, *Empire*, xii f, find in the "declining sovereignty of nation-states ... one of the primary symptoms of the coming of Empire" and understand empire as "the realization of the world market." This is an important warning from equating the end of nation-states with the end of political sovereignty.

8   Francis Fukuyama, *After the Neocons*, 10, argues: "The state ... remains the only source of power that can enforce a rule of law. But for that power to be effective, it must be seen as legitimate; and durable legitimacy requires a much higher degree of institutionalization *across* nations than exists currently"; cp. 215, n. 2. He also states that there are already "jurisdictions" needed in a "multi-institutional world" (180), like the International Organization for Standards (ISO) that function without a "mechanism of enforcement," though they pay for their efficiency by lack of legitimacy (162–5).

9   V. P. Naipaul, *India*, 484f, presents the view of a Sikh terrorist who declares that "we want to apply that system [of religion] to the whole of the world," arguing: "Animals have got their leaders ... Similarly, Khalsa (the Sikh brotherhood, as established by Guru Gobind Singh in 1699) wants to be the leader of the world, as it has got the inseparable elements of that leadership in its character." The last bracket is Naipaul's.

for his right" against the sovereign "as if it were against a Subject,"[10] In economy, the state stops being a Leviathan. The Leviathan's power must not be used for the state's but for economy's sake.

Locke follows the same idea. He shrinks the state but does not weaken its power of protecting merchants and producers from any intervention, political ones included. He is explicit that government's *"absolute* Power, where it is necessary, is *not Arbitrary* by being absolute." An officer can "command a Souldier to march up to the mouth of a Cannon ... where he is almost sure to perish," but not "command that Soldier to give him one penny of his Money."[11] Mandeville and Adam Smith reduced the state further to a night watchman. Amazingly, at the very time when Europe's economy made everyone dependent on everyone and hence became the most public affair, Hobbes, Locke, and the economists succeeded in presenting it as a private sphere that the state, far from understanding it as its own sphere, has to protect from political intervention. This was possible for two reasons.

First, when Hobbes and Locke started the separation, religion also began to be considered a private affair. Objectively, religion belongs to the public affairs no less than economy does, for the way divine powers are revered and appealed to concerns everyone; this shows even today in ceremonies when state authorities commemorate a public event (most often the death of soldiers) and appeal to whatever divinity seems appealable. Though sovereign and his subjects were expected to confess the same religion, the public confession was distinguished from faith. Faith was excluded from the state sphere, not because people believed that in fact it was not a public affair, but to stop the bloody religious wars. The exclusion of economy from the state followed this example: Treat economy as a nonstate affair, not because it is private but because private individuals are better in producing wealth than the state is. The consequence was that nonstate institutions, the market and the churches, took over central public tasks. Objectively, the public sphere was no longer the state sphere but the state plus economy and religion. Nevertheless, the state remained the only sphere recognized as public.

Second, economy was regarded as a sphere of private property rather than of wealth. As Arendt said, "prior to the modern age ... all civilizations have rested upon the sacredness of private property." So if in economy such private property was used, it would be a sphere not to be interfered with by the state. But what in fact is used is wealth, and as Arendt also remarked, "wealth ... whether privately owned or publicly distributed, had never been sacred."[12] Property that was considered sacred was the hearth, house, and field an individual needed for being recognized as a member of society. It was private for the political reason

---

[10] Hobbes, *Leviathan*, ch. 21, ed. Macpherson, 271.

[11] Locke, *Two Treatises of Government* §139; loc. cit., 362.

[12] Arendt, *The Human Condition*, 61; cp. ibid., 253.

that it secured an individual membership in society. By contrast, wealth is the sum of the resources that exist independently of the conditions of recognized social membership. It is these resources that economy attempts to increase. The way individuals use wealth is a public affair to be discussed as a political problem; as Aristotle did in his *Politics* when he criticized the use of money for increasing money.[13]

What in addition helped turn the notions of public and private upside down was the fascination of the market ideal expounded by Mandeville and Smith. It fascinated by its promise to remove masters and morality. The ideal market society was the first utopia of an association of autonomous individuals who, by doing what they like, produce wealth. The unregulated market captivated the open or secret admiration of theorists who did not suffer from its reality. They believed it might become the core of a better society, despite the disasters it produced of which they only heard. Similarly, theorists in the twentieth century who did not suffer from the reality of the socialist countries believed they would become the core of a better society in spite of the disasters they produced.

The powerful states never followed the rules liberal theorists produced to justify the states' existence and activities; rather, they went on arrogating as many tasks as they could get hold of. But the liberal theories expressed the historical fact that the modern state had ceded to a specific class the right to organize economic activities, a right no institution that claims to promote the interests of the public can ever justly surrender. Politicians tried to take influence on economy but never succeeded in regaining their old right. In the end, the separation of state and economy ceded politics to economy. Since the crucial public affair of how the actions and interests of men are tuned is decided by markets, economy has become the most important political sphere.

The state did not lose its right to organize economy to the bourgeoisie by treachery or conspiracy. Rather, the bourgeoisie proved superior to the state in organizing productive forces. This historical fact shows that public affairs are best organized, not by bureaucrats or administrators, but by those who perform the activities that administrators claim to be competent for. The early bourgeoisie organized trade and the input of labor better than state administrators because they have been merchants and entrepreneurs. Today they have been replaced by bankers and finance experts, who no less are administrators than former state bureaucrats. Public affairs are again not decided by those concerned but by administrators. This is one cause of contemporary miseries.

The history of the modern state is puzzling because it shows both the success of the value sphere of economy in managing the public affair of economy and the dangers of the arrogation of a public affair by value spheres that do not pursue their aims as a public affair. Yet despite this puzzle, it seems clear enough

[13] Aristotle, *Politics* I, 1257b-58b.

that the modern state follows neither a perfection standard of its own nor the aims of public affairs.

Today, we lack clarity if either the economy or the public needs the state monopoly of power for justice enforcement any longer. What they need is, first, an autonomous sphere of justice. To avoid the temptation that necessarily accompanies the power monopoly, its justice enforcement is better entrusted to institutions of legislation, judicature, and execution that are independent of each other even though they belong to the same value sphere. Second, they need a sphere in which to identify, discuss, and manage public affairs. Perhaps this task can be performed by the value sphere of the media, but this sphere may well be insufficient for accomplishing this task. Moreover, for a very long time, state institutions might prove irreplaceable for protecting modernity. I am painfully aware of the insufficiency of these comments.

You may raise another objection to my discussion. I am investigating value spheres because they might be the institutions for activities by which individuals can attain extraordinariness. Why is it important that such activities pursue an irreducible value? Why can't it be a mishmash of values? The reason is that activities aiming at a mishmash of values lack unambiguous perfection standards; different values require different standards; so the individuals cannot know how to attain extraordinariness in an activity that is split by two or more aims. Actually, this is a reason why it is difficult for politicians to attain extraordinariness and for a public to judge on their extraordinariness; they may be extraordinary in several respects, none of which seems specifically political. It is also a reason why, in the process of globalization that increases differentiation of social functions, state institutions are "disaggregated" into task-oriented and often international institutions – a process that decreases national sovereignty.[14]

Moreover, activities are to give meaning to the agents; they are to show them what has been lost in modern societies that know only the value of labor and rightly do not find much meaning in it. Only if individuals are attracted to

---

[14] Anne-Marie Slaughter, *A New World Order*, describes an aggregation of global institutions along economic, legal, legislative, and information "issues" that "makes a global system of checks and balances possible" (254), as well as a "subsidiarity" that she calls "the European Union's version of Madisonian checks and balances" (255f); both subsidiarity and checks and balances conform to an organization that is oriented to value spheres. On the retreat of the states from their former role in legislation and law enforcement, cp. Susan Strange, *The Retreat of the State*, Cambridge University Press 1996; Saskia Sassen, *Losing Control?* New York 1996; Wolfgang Reinhard, *Geschichte der Staatsgewalt*, Munich 1999; Bertrand Badie, *Un monde sans souveraineté*, Paris 1999; Virginia Haufler, *Private Sector International Regimes*, in Richard A. Higgott et al., eds, *Non-State Actors and Authority in the Global System*, London (Routledge) 2000, 121–137. Philosophically important is Allen Buchanan, *Justice, Legitimacy, and Self-Determination*, Oxford University Press 2004, rightly describing itself as "a serious erosion of sovereignty – a diminution of the powers traditionally accorded to states under international law" (6).

activities whose meaning is so obvious that it obtrudes itself on them when they are trained to it (as on children who learn to play the violin) will their ambition be constructive and further the society rather than bursting its organization form. Such obviousness is absent in activities with mixed aims and values.

In the following sections I'll look at some of the value spheres. I want to show that they can function as institutions that make obvious the meaning of their activities and allow individuals to enact their ambition of extraordinariness.

Chapter 12

The Serving Spheres

THE SERVING SPHERES AIM AT QUALITIES THAT ARE OBVIOUSLY USEFUL and wanted: wealth, health, security, justice, education, information. No one doubts of their worth, no one wants to miss them. What is less obvious is that they would be useless and threatened by Sisyphean absurdity if there were no nonserving spheres or activities that are done for their own sake and not for their utility. Economists agree that economic activities pursue, as Adam Smith expressed in the title of his economic work, the wealth of nations, which means, as a nineteenth-century economist said, they serve to "maximize the utility of the produce,"[1] and utility presupposes something it is useful for.

This does not exclude that the activities of the serving spheres are done for their own sake. On the contrary, values, whether serving or nonserving, would

---

[1] W. S. Jevons, *The Theory of Political Economy*, Penguin 1970, 254. Yet economists lack agreement on what their own job is. Cp. R. H. Coase, "Economics and Contiguous Disciplines," *Journal of Legal Studies* 7, 1978, 202–11, 210; cit by O. E. Williamson, "Introduction to O. E. Williamson," S. G. Winter, eds., *The Nature of the Firm*, Oxford University Press 1993, 3: Economics is "simply a way of looking at the world." Lionel Robbins, *An Essay on the Nature and Significance of Economic Science*, London (Macmillan) 1932, 116: "Economics is the science which studies human behaviour as a relationship between ends and scarce means which have alternative uses." Alfred Marshall, *Principles of Economics*, London (Macmillan) 1986 (1920), 1: "Political Economy or Economics is a study of mankind in the ordinary business of life; it examines that part of individual and social action which is most closely connected with the attainment and with the use of the material requisites of well being. Thus it is on the one side a study of wealth; and on the other, and more important side, a part of the study of man." Richard A. Posner, *Economic Analysis of Laws*, Boston (Little Brown) 1977, 3: "Economics, the science of human choice in a world in which resources are limited in relation to human wants, explores and tests the implications of assuming that man is a rational maximizer of his ends in life, his satisfactions – what we call his 'self-interest.'" Daniel M. Hausman, *The Inexact and Separate Science of Economics*, Cambridge University Press 1992, 95: "Economic phenomena are the consequences of rational choices that are governed predominantly by some variant consumerism and profit maximization. In other words, *economics studies the consequences of rational greed*."

not be values if they could not be pursued for their own sake. Nonetheless, without the existence of nonserving values, even the pursuit of justice would be futile. The fact that people pursue justice for its own sake does not free justice enforcement from its dependence on actions outside the sphere of justice enforcement that can be performed justly or unjustly. True, justice is something sacrosanct, as it must not be violated. But it is false to conclude that it does not serve other activities, in particular such as become possible only because justice is enforced. Similarly, merchants and managers often enough aim at increasing wealth for its own sake. Yet this does not stop the value they strive after from being a utility value that would lose its value if there were no activities it is useful for. All serving spheres show the same dependence that still does not prevent pursuing their values for their own sake.

This may seem paradoxical but can be easily explained. Any activity that challenges capabilities is delightful if we possess the capabilities challenged, and is delightful to the degree the capabilities allow to perform extraordinary actions. Such delightful activities are normally done for their own sake. Moreover, to be challenged by an activity it is necessary that it has its specific meaning and perfection standards – and this is the case with sphere activities, as by definition, they pursue their specific values with their specific standards. Modern societies even are built on this kind of attraction, as is most obvious in the economic sphere. While in traditional societies economic activities are often burdened with noneconomic tasks, such as that of helping relatives or strengthening military power, in modern societies nearly full sphere autonomy has been realized in the economic sphere. If this is disgusting from a moral point of view, it is attractive for the ambition of extraordinariness.

Administration lacks this attraction because there is no one value it aims at. As the word says, it has to administer to or serve people, and what it has to administer depends on the needs of a territory and the wants of its population; so it is no one value sphere. But as a historical fact it has been made an institution, the state, that is similar to and often arrogates the tasks of the value spheres of economy, justice enforcement, and religion. It challenged and profited from the ambition of extraordinariness, in particular of those enjoying power.

Its explicit valuing of power, however, puts the state in a necessary opposition to all value spheres, as by its striving for power it has to subject the activities of all other spheres and hence cannot but violate their values. This distinguishes the state from the sphere of economy. Though as a historical fact the agents of economy have often subjected other spheres, not least the state, to their value, this is not necessary, because wealth maximization can be coordinated with the pursuit of the other value spheres. Yet sphere autonomy is incompatible with the existence of the state. If sphere autonomy is necessary for saving modernity, as I presume it is, states have to be abolished and the tasks they have arrogated have to return to the spheres they belong to.

The activities of a family can again be regarded as having a meaning that is independent of any other activity. In fact, caring for one's children can be so satisfying that it seems absurd to think its meaning is dependent on activities that they serve. But if we think of Ecclesiastes, it may become clear that there is a dependency. If the life of the children we care for had no meaning at all or only the meaning that they are again to care for their children, the care would look pretty Sisyphean. What is remarkable in the activities of the family is that their standards of perfection are so little known. Yet education and child care can be better or worse, though the criteria for such qualifications are difficult to define and certainly not uncontroversial.

One reason for the undeveloped state of clarification of the perfection standards of the family is the ambiguity of its meaning and value. Its social function is generally considered to be the rearing of the new generation, but as a historical fact the family, in this respect similar to the state, has more functions than this one. In most classes it also serves emotional needs of the parents, in particular their sexual interests. Weber has here been more consistent than in his treatment of the state by assigning the value of sexuality to a sphere of its own. Thus, he restricts the value of the family to child care and implicitly proposes a social organization in which parents are not bound to look for their sexual satisfaction in the family. Though a revolution in theory, in practice it is rather an adaptation to social facts. There are a lot of complaints about the separation of the functions of child rearing and sexual satisfaction. Yet rather than destroying the family, the separation will strengthen it in its most important role of child rearing. Ambiguities of meaning will always reduce the attraction of an activity; so the less ambiguous its meaning the more the family will flourish.[2]

Are we to classify the sphere of sexuality as a serving or a nonserving sphere? This sphere offers the interesting case that a value aimed at in a value sphere with a long historical past can shift its meaning. In premodern societies, sexuality was a serving value; it served either child rearing or an emotional pacification that enabled men (women had been rarely considered) to follow the tasks that counted. Yet today, sexuality is often regarded and experienced as a nonserving value, having a meaning that saves life from Sisyphean absurdity; for some it is even the only meaning possible. So we should be open to recognize a value sphere that oscillates between a serving and a nonserving sphere and have a closer look at this phenomenon.

Is also technology such an oscillating sphere? Considering the fascination of technology, we may believe so. As technology is so important for modernity, let's start our review of some value spheres with a discussion of it.

[2] Cp. Chapter 23.

Chapter 13

Technology

TECHNOLOGY HAS ALWAYS BEEN IMPORTANT FOR THE SURVIVAL OF mankind; so, it is a serving sphere. Yet for modernity it seems to have a meaning that goes beyond its serving function. It is generally recognized that modern society is necessarily dynamic in the sense in which Marx said of the bourgeoisie that it "cannot exist without constantly revolutionizing the instruments of production, and ... with them the whole relations of society."[1] It is not just technology that is necessary for securing modern society; rather, it is a technology that needs unremitting growth and promotion. Because much energy and attention has to go into technology, for many people it has turned from a means to an end. Moreover, social theorists of the twentieth century as different as Karl Polanyi and Peter Drucker agree that the disasters of their century were conditioned by the misfit of the rise of modern industry, which is a form of technology, and the prevailing social and mental conditions. Polanyi aimed at the *Great Transformation* from the preindustrial to a functioning industrial society, and Drucker at the *Future of Industrial Man* after the *End of Economic Man*.[2] Both of them expected technology to dictate the character and meaning of future society.

[1]   Marx and Engels, *Manifesto of the Communist Party* loc. cit. ch. 1, transl. Sam. Moore.
[2]   The first term in italics is the title of Polanyi's most famous book, the last two the titles of Drucker's two earliest books. Drucker proclaimed the end of economic man and the future of industrial man, understanding by economic man, the man of the economic theory of Mandeville and Smith, and by industrial man, the man who works in the modern plants, though today he may be threatened by "technological" or "industrial unemployment" (*The Future*, loc. cit. 81). The "economic as the socially constitutive sphere" has been replaced by the "techno-economic engine" (ibid., 78 and 196) "the industrial plant has become the basic social unit" that, though "not yet a social institution," "must be made into a functioning, self-governing social community. It must be made capable of serving industrial society, just as formerly the village served the rural society and the market the mercantile society" (ibid., 207). Drucker hoped for a transformation of industrial society into a society that "gives the individual member social status and

Before them, Marx claimed that "modern industry ... imposes the necessity of recognizing, as a fundamental law of production, variation of work, consequently ... the greatest possible development of his [the worker's] varied aptitudes." It is not the people who subject technology to their will; rather, "it becomes a question of life and death for society to adapt the mode of production to the normal functioning of this law."[3] Happily, the dictate of technology, "the greatest possible development of (man's) varied aptitudes," coincides with the interest of the people, but this is just good luck. What is clear to Marx, Polanyi, Drucker, and a lot of other theorists, is that modern society has to adapt to technology. Hence, technology is no longer a means for modern society; it belongs to its ends; it gives modern society content and meaning. Actually, this is how technology is regarded by many people. If they are not ready to say they live for the development of technology, they are ready to say having the newest car or laptop gives meaning to their life like good sex or their favorite sport.

The development of modern technology has been influenced by Descartes's proposal of a "practical" philosophy that replaces the "scholastic philosophy by one that teaches us the power and effects of fire, water, air, the stars, the sky, and of all other bodies around us as exactly as we know the various activities of our artisans so that we can use them in the same way for all the aims they are fit for and thus make ourselves quasi masters and possessors of nature."[4] He goes on to express the expectation that we thus can postpone ageing and death. His proposal, confirmed by similar ideas of his contemporaries, put its stamp on seventeenth-century thought, on the Enlightenment, on natural science, the state, and the economy, all favored by and, again, favoring the idea that control of nature is the common aim of mankind and a criterion of progress. In this idea, technology remains a means. However, there is widespread fear that, by subjecting nature, man will be subjected himself to his drives, or at least the majority will be subjected to the arbitrary will of a minority.

The reason theorists adduce for this fear is that, when a person is used to controlling nature, she will also develop mechanisms to control her own mind and become herself a slave. She starts with controlling some inclination and ends up

---

function" and integrates her in "the purpose and meaning of society" whose "decisive social power is legitimate power" (ibid., 28). Few twentieth-century theorists recognized as sharply as he that contemporary social power lacks legitimacy and that, because of this lack, the Nazis were successful and further disasters threaten. Yet he was mistaken in expecting that substituting one "constitutive sphere" by another could provide social power with legitimacy. The problem of unemployment cannot be solved as long as a sphere of labor, whether "mercantile" or "industrial," is "socially constitutive." This is only possible if, rather than only one sphere, a system of value spheres is socially constitutive. Technology, no less than economy or politics, will be destructive if it is the prevailing sphere.

3 Marx, *Capital*, vol.1, transl. Moore and Aveling; chap. 15, sec. 9 ("The Factory Acts"). In the German Marx und Engels Werke edition, vol. 23 (MEW 23), Berlin (Dietz), 1971, this is not chap. 15 but chap. 13, sec. 9, pp. 511f. Cp. Chapter 23.

4 Descartes, "Discours de la méthode," sixième partie.

in being controlled by her own control mechanisms. Horkheimer and Adorno, the most prominent mouthpieces to this fear, describe the process thus:

> Man's domination over himself, which grounds his selfhood, is almost always the destruction of the subject in whose service it is undertaken; for the substance which is dominated, suppressed, and dissolved by virtue of self-preservation is none other than that very life as a function of which the achievements of self-preservation find their sole definition and determination: it is, in fact, what is to be preserved.[5]

It is true that man's domination over himself grounds his self-hood. But Horkheimer and Adorno do not distinguish the dominating part as the self from the dominated part as the subject. They follow the Lockean conception that cannot distinguish the parts, defining the self as consciousness. So they call the subject that, in fact, is dominated the "substance." Yet the substance is the self. Also, it is the self and not the subject "in whose service" domination "is undertaken." The self is not dominated at all when it dominates the subject. If the self had to be conceived in the Lockean way, the analysis would be correct. But this conception is mistaken, and so is the analysis. If we distinguish self and subject, we must not assume that by becoming masters over nature we *therefore* become slaves. We certainly can become slaves when we become masters, but if so, then not *because* we have become masters but because we have not learned how to control ourselves.

In fact, the important and true reason for fearing technology is not the argument adduced by Horkheimer and Adorno; it is much too abstract to be effective. Until today, technology has been ruled by elites of science and economy. Its development did not follow democratic principles or the interests of the masses at all. This is the perfectly justified reason for the fears of technology. People have learned that the introduction of technology in production has made them a negligible quantity in economy. In the nineteenth century, they had to fear becoming an appendage of machinery. Today they have to fear extinction. Therefore, technology can be justified only if it is ruled by democratic principles that allow everyone an equal voice in its development and application. Rather than lamenting the dangers of technology, and conjuring up nightmares of Frankenstein monsters, we should look for means to control technologies that indeed might bring societies still closer to a Brave New World. What we have to presuppose is that technology is only a serving sphere.

How can technology be subjected to democratic principles? Would it mean that the world population votes on the admission of any technological innovation? If so, technological innovation would become difficult. But stopping technological innovation would today condemn a great part of mankind to starvation. Yet there are other ways than voting to adapt technology to the

---

5   Max Horkheimer and Theodor W. Adorno. *Dialectic of Enlightenment.*, 54f.

interest of mankind. The rules by which patent offices admit innovation can be subjected to public discussion and, in the end, decided by the populations. It is improbable that they would vote for rules that allow innovations to make them jobless. They would rather attach to any innovation the string that, if it robs anyone of their work (other innovations, whether social or technological), give them opportunity for decent work.[6] Such a restriction would not reduce technological innovation but channel it in a direction compatible with the interests of most people. Another control of innovation, already practiced in many areas of technology, are ethics committees staffed by both experts and laypersons. They can be easily extended to watch over any kind of technology.

Granting to the people so much influence on the development of technology will still seem to many a freakish idea. But it is a requirement that springs not only from ideas of democracy but also from the idea of technology itself. Its idea is the subjection of nature to man's self, and the self has here to be understood as the self of mankind. If elites claim to represent the self of mankind, they need reasons for justifying their claim. If they introduce technology in a way that threatens the survival of the majority of mankind, as it does today, any reason they might put forward is unacceptable from the beginning. There is no other way to consistently pursue technology than that of subjecting it to admission conditions of the "freakish" kind described.

So let it be settled that technology is a serving sphere, the sphere that serves the self to control nature, including the subject, and that despite its dangers we cannot reject it from the spectrum of possible activities that offer opportunities for the ambition of extraordinariness. Obviously it has an enormous attraction for individuals who are talented in invention and technology and eager to excel; so it is unacceptable for a society defending the idea of equal liberty and integrating the ambition of extraordinariness to forbid extraordinariness in technology, not to mention the argument that mankind would have to shrink considerably in numbers if technology were not promoted. The question is still how far technology should be allowed to change the world and mankind. This is a question that particularly concerns biotechnology and the medical sciences. They seem to possess the skill and knowledge to produce completely new forms of life and to change humans into creatures that are very different from what we are today. Is the only condition to be imposed on technology that it is democratically controlled; that the self that technology is to serve as the master of nature has to be the self of everyone and not of a minority?

---

[6] This condition is not fantastic. Peter Drucker demanded "that the employer takes responsibility for replacing redundant employees in new jobs"; in *Drucker on Asia*, 37, following his dictum from 1942: "It is absolutely certain that we shall have to prevent a recurrence of large-scale chronic unemployment after this war. Otherwise, we shall surely disintegrate into chaos or tyranny" (*The Future of Industrial Man*, 83).

This is certainly not sufficient. There is another and even more important condition: that the changes effected by technology never change the capability of judgment. This capability is the self; its change would be the end of the self and hence of what technology is to serve. Yet we'll find some more conditions that technology must meet. Let us consider what they are and concentrate on biotechnology. Unfortunately, we have to go into some detail.

There are pragmatic and principled objections. Pragmatic objections reject or restrict technology for reasons of risk or other contingent circumstances that suggest abstaining from a technology, but only as long as the circumstances are given. Principled objections reject it under any possible circumstances, for reasons that concern technology itself and not its circumstances.

The most important *pragmatic objection* to biotechnology is that it can easily lead to the destruction of all life on earth. In fact, all kinds of modern technology, weapons of mass destruction no less than genetic engineering, will produce damage beyond imagination if they are misused, or not used cautiously, or even, as in the case of weapons of mass destruction, used for the aim they have been produced for. Therefore, all modern technology is the object of this objection. Most often it is not formulated in a way that quantifies the risk. Nevertheless there is a forceful logic in it. It is the same logic we follow when we forbid children from playing with fire. We cannot reduce the risk of their fire misuse to zero. Yet the damage done by fire is too great to allow them to play with fire. If it is insane to allow children to play with fire, it is insane to allow adults to use technology, because its risk can never be reduced to zero either. Although it is pragmatic, in effect, this objection prohibits modern technology in any circumstances.[7]

Obviously, without a good reason we should not use high-risk technology. But if rejecting high-risk technology does not reduce the risks of life we are incurring anyway, or even raises such risks, then it would be irresponsible not to accept and even promote technology. We would irresponsibly shrink back from our duty to protect the following generations from the risks they are incurring. Yet there are such risks, whether we admit technology or don't. There are diseases that we risk suffering and which genetic engineering attempts to rid us of. There is overpopulation and malnutrition whose risks we can reduce by invading the genome of plants and animals to open up new resources. There is the rural exodus that feeds misery in many megacities and might be stopped by biotech.[8] Life on Earth has always been risky and always will be. If we try reducing the risks, this is not reckless but wise. And the best means for doing so is modern technology.

The critic might correctly reply that even though life is always risky, technology often makes it still riskier. Yet if technology can reduce risks that we

---

7   Thus argues Hans Jonas, *Technik, Medizin und Ethik.*

8   Cp. Freeman Dyson, *The Sun, the Genome, and the Internet,* Oxford University Press 1999, and Freeman Dyson, "Our Biotech Future," *New York Review of Books,* July 19, 2007.

have incurred up to now, the rational answer to this objection is not to forbid all technology but to introduce or strengthen ethics committees and similar institutions that watch over it and admit only applications that are likely to reduce the risks that we incur also without them.

There is another pragmatic objection to biotech that is similar to the one just discussed, as it is directed against modern technology in general and the risks connected to it. But it concentrates on a specific risk, that of entailing involuntary unemployment and capital concentration leading to mono- and oligopolies that make people dependent on them.[9] I have already argued that such risks make it necessary for reasons of both consistency and justice to impose strict conditions on the admission of technology.

So from the pragmatic objections considered we can draw two legitimacy conditions: Biotechnology can only be justified if it can reduce the average life risks of people and does not worsen their dependence on the powerful that is caused by involuntary unemployment and mono- and oligopolies. These conditions, in particular the second one, are not met today. Hence, for pragmatic reasons, technology lacks legitimacy.

Most of the *principled objections* to biotech appeal, in different guises, to the idea that we play God or commit blasphemy when we use genetics. However, we have to take account of the different guises, and there is an objection that points to aspects that are not concentrated upon in the admonition not to play God. This objection is that technology in general, and biotechnology in particular, alienates us from nature, and that we ought not to be alienated from nature. The idea is that technology inserts between men and nature a wall that prevents us from experiencing nature in its immediacy, yet that experience is necessary or useful for human life. Without it, the roots of our existence will be cut off.[10]

It is true that technology raises a protective wall between man and nature. But it is an illusion to believe that we can experience nature in its immediacy. We experience nature always through the filter of our interests and expectations. Before men developed their protective wall of technology against nature, they did not love nature. They venerated it in the form of piety and obedience to their gods, but their veneration was fear rather than love; for they suffered from the arbitrariness and incalculability of nature, cruel properties that reappear in the character traits of the former polytheistic and monotheistic gods. Love of nature started only when the protective wall of technology had become reliable

---

9 Cp. Freeman Dyson. "Our Biotech Future," *New York Review of Books*, July 19, 2007: "The public distrusts Monsanto because Monsanto likes to put genes for poisonous pesticides into food crops … It is likely that genetic engineering will remain unpopular and controversial so long as it remains a centralized activity in the hands of large corporations. I see a bright future for the biotechnology industry when it follows the path of the computer industry … becoming small and domesticated rather than big and centralized."

10 This is an objection I met in courses on technology and applied ethics.

and allowed changing the character of the monotheistic god from an irascible master to a benign father. Only then could one believe that the protective wall hinders us from experiencing true nature. Pulling down the wall would be like leaving a ship in space without a spacesuit. Therefore, we shall love nature, if and only if we can present it in a form that suits our senses and instincts: as lovely gardens; as a sublime wilderness that we can flee from into our gardens; as pets on our couch and tigers behind bars.

Yet the objection is right if it insists on the falsity of the idea that technology can make us completely independent of nature. Some champions of technology adhere to this fantasy. Actually, the more important technology becomes in our life, the clearer it becomes that, far from making us completely independent of nature, we are in some respects totally dependent on it. We can become nature's masters but must respect its conditions. We shall always need matter or energy for our metabolism; we shall always need a place to stand or lie on and even time to endure. None of these elementary existence conditions can ever be changed by us. They are both a gift and a dictate of nature whose products we remain, however much we can intervene in it. The sharper our eye becomes for how to solve problems by technology, the more evident become its limits. If the objection reminds us of these facts, it does a good job. But then it is no argument against biotechnology.

There are two senses of the objection to biotechnology that one should not play God. The first is that it is as risky as when children play with fire, and that if adults nevertheless promote it, they pretend to achieve what only God can do, namely, reduce its risk to zero. In this sense, the objection is directed to all forms of modern technology and can also be formulated without reference to the idea of playing God, as I did when I was discussing it. In its second sense, the objection is directed against gene technology only. It rejects it not for its risks but for its intervention in life processes that the critics maintain are to be decided on and fixed only by nature or God or chance, but not by men and their choice.

Now, to be worth discussing, the blank assertion that the way gene technology intervenes in life processes is an arrogation of a privilege of God or chance is insufficient. It needs an argument. Three kinds of arguments are presented. The first claims that God has forbidden men to intervene in life processes by biotechnological means. The second argues that it is better to leave the combination of genes to chance rather than to choice. The third argues that there is a violation of human rights or of human dignity when men are the objects of genetic engineering.

The first kind of argument, appeal to an interdiction by God, has little chance of being taken seriously. The reason is not that belief in God should not be taken seriously. The reason is that belief in a god who forbade biotech implies that the god has given men their capacity for biotech in vain, or as a seduction they should not yield to. This implies belief in quite a malicious god. If we believe in a creator divinity, it should have given us our capacity for biotech for a better reason than for not using it. So, if we take belief in God seriously, the consequence is not to abstain from biotechnology, but rather to use it as perfectly as possible.

Arguments of the second kind, those for chance rather than choice, are strong indeed. The way genomes are composed by natural evolution is an object that merits admiration, because it is the incredible result of the combination of elementary forces that produce creatures like us who get insight into their natural origins. Scientists would not be scientists if they did not consider nature and men the result of chance processes governed by laws that happen to be what they are. But this (as we'll see) methodological condition of doing science does not prevent them from finding deep sense in natural evolution, because it has produced us – beings who start understanding natural evolution. For this reason we would be fools to disregard nature and its chance processes.

However, the way genomes are composed and the world was built by natural evolution, admirable though it is, allows for accidents that we suffer from or are threatening us: diseases like cancer; scarcity of resources like fresh water; and climate catastrophes that can turn a flourishing planet like Earth into a desert planet like Mars. Nature has given us a sense for admiring its beauty and sophistication. But this very sense demands us to intervene in processes that we know are disastrous and degrade nature's beauty. Moreover, it even requires us to do science and develop technologies, so that we are better capable of preventing natural disasters. The very reason we admire nature and its chance processes is a reason for intervening in natural processes and even developing our capacity of doing so.

So, the first two arguments for why we should not play God turn into a justification for biotech if we consider them more carefully. The justification is that because we are capable of understanding, and to some extent controlling, the processes of nature, we would not live up to our capabilities if we abstained from technology. Actually, principled criticism of biotech has concentrated on arguments of the third kind, which appeal to human rights or human dignity. These arguments apply only to biotechnology for humans, not for animals and plants, so they can only result in prohibitions of biotech applied to human beings.

Now there is consensus among friends and foes of biotech that it would violate human rights if it produced men with properties that restrict them in their capabilities or life options, that is, if it handicapped them. As far as ethics committees have the competency to veto biotech projects, they would strictly forbid any project that would produce or risk producing men with restricted capabilities. Formulated in this general way, there is agreement on the limits of gene technology. But as soon as we get more specific, dissent starts.

A first difficulty occurs when we try to define the concept of restricted or reduced capabilities or life options. Cases are clear if people lack an arm or are blind, but is it a loss of capability if someone has twelve fingers and a talent for the piano? Yet we can solve this problem by taking recourse to the capability approach developed in political philosophy by Martha Nussbaum and Amartya Sen.[11] Its idea is that the life people have a right to must enable them to use a healthy body and mind, communicate with whom they like, detect and deliberate alternatives to actions, choose among them for reasons, stick to their choices, and yet be able to revise them. We may leave the list vague; it is sufficient to know that for deciding on the legitimacy of genetic engineering we have to look at not how many fingers people have but whether they are capable of doing what well-developed people do.

The capability criterion seems reasonably reliable. But its application leads to results that do not find favor with many critics. One example is human cloning, a technology that does not even require intervening in the genome. Many people are horrified at the thought that men are procreated from a single parent and thus share his or her genes. But the mere fact that persons have the same genes does not damage them or condemn the later one to leading the same life as the earlier one, as so many monozygotic twins prove. If we follow the capability criterion, and if cloning humans is not risky (which actually it is and probably will remain so for some time), then the cloning of humans cannot be condemned.

We might, though, argue that receiving the genome of only one parent makes a clone worse off than a naturally born child, because she has a less broad spectrum of talents. If this is true, cloning would violate a human right. Yet many authors argue that even if clones are not thus disadvantaged, they suffer a specific right violation, that of the right to ignorance of one's genetic endowment. They argue that individuals who know the life of the person they are cloned from will be restricted in their life options, because they will be obsessed with the life of that person and be incapable of leading their own life. As they presuppose that it is immoral to keep the fact they have been cloned secret, they conclude that producing human clones violates the right to ignorance.[12]

This is a poor argument. The clone obsessed with the life of the person she is cloned from can be cured by informing her about the restricted influence of genes on choosing one's life. Monozygotic twins have more genetic matter in common than clone and clonee. Of course cloning is immoral if it is used for dominating the clone. But in that case there is damage done to her, and it is the damage that makes it illegitimate. If there is no such damage, there is no reason not to follow our capability criterion and declare the cloning legitimate. In this case we should judge the horror at cloning an emotional reaction similar to the horror people once felt when courageous anatomists started dissecting corpses.

---

[11]   Nussbaum, 2000; Sen, *Development as Freedom*; Sen, *Commodities and Capabilities*, Equality of What? http://www.tannerlectures.utah.edu/lectures/sen80.pdf.

[12]   Cp. Jonas, *Technik*, 194; Jürgen Habermas, *Die postnationale Konstellation*, 253f; and for criticism my papers "Zur Legitimität des Klonens" and "Kritik der Kritik des Klonens."

Accepting the capability criterion has another practical consequence that diverges from popular opinion. Many commentators think that genetic engineering might be legitimate if it serves the curing of disease but not if it serves the enhancement of human capabilities. It is not only for reasons of risk that they think so, but also because they consider enhancement of capabilities an aim that intervenes too far in life processes or is too godlike. Yet if biotech raises resistance to disease and fatigue or the capacity of concentrating attention, it would neither cure a disease nor do damage to anyone, but rather would enhance capabilities. Hence, by the capability criterion, it would be legitimate. However, enhancing capabilities must be prohibited as long as access to it depends on wealth or status, as it actually does today, because this exacerbates existing inequalities. Only if access to it were equally open to everyone would capability enhancement be legitimate.[13]

Now, the distinction of what violates a human right and what does not is only the first difficulty in setting limits to gene technology. The second one is to distinguish what is a human and what isn't. The best-known example of this difficulty is the case of early embryos. If they are human individuals, it will be difficult to justify experiments using early embryos made by gene technology to cultivate embryonic stem cells. Many authors claim that the human individual starts with the zygote. But until an embryo reaches the stage of its gastrulation and axis formation around its fourteenth day, it is a *dividual,* not an individual. Its cells can be separated and put together without harming it; it may also fuse with another embryo into a single one and split into independent embryos, as do those that become monozygotic twins and other multiples.[14] Therefore, the human individual cannot begin its life before the fourteenth day of the embryo. Indeed this is the date recommended for stopping experiments with embryos by the British Committee of Inquiry into Human Fertilisation and Embryology.[15]

Establishing a date for the beginning of a human individual is only part of establishing who is a human individual and what isn't. Another part is establishing the end of a human being; yet this problem is of little interest to biotechnology. But there is also a problem of distinguishing human beings from animals. Let's consider some puzzling examples.

Some people dream of interstellar journeys by humans who by genetic engineering are reduced to the functions needed for navigating a spaceship and informing earthlings of their adventures. Even if humans were made happy by drugs or genetic engineering but were unable to walk, their capabilities would be severely reduced and their right to unrestricted capabilities crassly violated. So far, no serious differences in the moral assessment of the example arise. Now

[13] Cp. Chapter 20.
[14] Cp. Norman Ford, *When Did I Begin?*; Ulrich Steinvorth, "Über den Anfang des menschlichen Individuums."
[15] Set up in 1982, chaired by Baroness Warnock and reported in 1984.

imagine a second case. Our jolly navigators are so far reduced in their capabilities that they are incapable of deliberating and judging alternatives. They
look like humans, are clever as foxes in responding to unexpected accidents,
and operate the instruments by which to navigate and send data to earthlings
without ever making a mistake. Yet, they lack the power of reason to decide if
an action is right or an idea is true. They understand signal languages, as dogs
and chimps do, but no propositional language, as men do, because using such
language, as I have argued previously,[16] implies and is implied by the capability
of judgment.

In this case we cannot classify them as humans; they are animals. If people are incapable of distinguishing true and false and right and wrong, we do
not grant them the active rights of contracting and voting, and commit them
to a guardian. Yet we grant them the passive rights of being treated like men
because they belong to our species. The jolly navigators of our second example,
by contrast, are a new species that lack reason as dogs do and have no claim to
treatment different from that of dogs. So the consequence is that, in the first
example, we have a less radical intervention in the human genome but a human
rights violation, and, in the second example, a more radical intervention but no
rights violation.

This looks like a paradox. To avoid it, we might classify the second intervention as even more illegitimate than the first one. But how can we do so if there is
no human being whose rights might be violated? A possible answer is that the
rights violation is done not to the navigators but to the humans whose genome
has been used to produce them. Yet this is implausible, because the navigators
could be produced from stem cells that the donor has given voluntarily to the
genetic engineers or from cells that have been cultivated in a lab and can no
longer be traced back to a human donor. So what is wrong with producing nonhuman navigators that look like humans but are not humans? Or is there nothing wrong with it?

Let's take a third case and imagine that genetic engineers produce fox-clever,
ever-cheerful, nonhuman navigators, not only for specific astronautical aims,
but for the purpose of replacing mankind by this new species. They agree with
the rest of mankind that living as a member of this new species is better than
living as a human, or that at least all but the genetic engineers should live so.
There would be as little violation of human rights in this as in the second case,
because the victims of the engineering would again not be humans, and no
human would have been forced to abstain from having human children. But
unlike the second case, this case seems condemnable. Transforming all or most
humans into a subhuman species looks as horrible as bewitching a man into an
animal. But is the horror we feel at this possibility not as irrational as the horror

---

[16] In Chapter 6.

people feel at cloning? Would it be legitimate to bewitch a man into an animal if he agrees to his bewitchment?

In fact, the transformation described cannot be a human rights violation for want of a violated human. Yet human rights violations are not necessarily the only atrocious crimes. Rather, abolishing the self (or power of judgment), even if the victim consents, is most atrocious (the absolute evil, according to Arendt). Moreover, if we accept the capability criterion by which we forbid genetic engineering that reduces human capabilities, we cannot accept the extinction or diminution of humanity, even if everyone consents, according to the principle of criminal law that consent is no defense.[17] For extinguishing or diminishing the human species implies extinguishing or diminishing human capabilities.

Once we understand why the third case is a crime, we can understand why the second example is difficult to judge. It is ambivalent, as it leaves it open whether the jolly navigators are a species that is the model for what all humans will become or only a new kind of cattle that is to serve the use and development of our human capabilities. In the first case, procreating them would be a crime; in the second case it would not. The example demonstrates also the ambivalence of gene technology, for which it is justly feared. Its products can serve the use and development of our specific capabilities, yet some of them may turn into models of our future existence. Though this risk is no reason for a principled objection to gene technology, it is a reason for distrusting any application of genetic engineering to man, particularly under the given conditions of inequality and the economic superfluity of more and more people.

We can deduce from the preceding discussion a provisional rule for deciding when genetic engineering and cloning criticized as "playing God" is illegitimate in principle. It is illegitimate if it either offends someone's right or diminishes human capabilities. If it diminishes human capabilities, it need not offend a right, because the diminishing may occur with the consent of the victims. Still it is a crime; it may even be absolute evil. We may subsume crimes that do not violate a right under the concept of violation of human dignity and thus give this concept a clear, definable meaning.

We find violations of human dignity also outside genetic engineering. Two obvious examples are cannibalism and slavery that the victim has consented to. They are rightly proscribed because they prevent the victims from either acting autonomously or acting at all, hence, reduce and degrade men's specific qualities.[18]

Yet such cases are not typical of the appeal to human dignity. The typical case is rather a form of gene technology that offends feelings of piety or decency but

---

[17] Hillel Steiner used to point to this principle in seminars at the University of Manchester.

[18] In 2001, in Rotenburg, Germany, a man who had been asked by another one to kill and eat him did so. Cp. *Frankfurter Allgemeine*, Jan. 30, 2004. He was sentenced for manslaughter to eight and a half years in prison.

neither human rights nor human dignity. Most prominent among such cases is the cloning of men that neither violates one of the recognized human rights nor reduces human capabilities. Other typical cases are those of fusing human and animal cells to produce animal-human hybrids or chimeras. There are reports of "pigs with human blood flowing through their bodies" and of "mice with human brains."[19] In these cases, the product is not a human being but an animal with some human cells or genes. No human right can be violated by producing them, nor are human capabilities reduced. Nevertheless, as they seem illegitimate to many observers and somehow to contradict what is due to man, they are said to offend human dignity.

However, there are also reports on breeding monkeys with a substantially human brain.[20] The result might be a species capable of reason and judgment. In that case, we would have to treat them like humans and give them the protection of law including human rights. Moreover, it would be as unconditionally forbidden to reduce their capabilities as it is forbidden to reduce the capabilities of humans. But it is improbable that this condition can be met if they are produced for a purpose of genetic engineers. In such a case, therefore, their production is illegitimate, yet not because it offends human dignity but because it violates human rights.

To draw a conclusion from our lengthy discussion, let us state the conditions under which technology is illegitimate. It is, first, if it abolishes our power of judgment; second, if it reduces other capabilities than our judgment. Normally, such reduction is a human rights violation and must be prohibited as such a violation. But, third, even if a person consents to a reduction of her capabilities, the reduction can be a crime (the only case the term *violation of human dignity* should be applied to) and must be prohibited. Fourth, technology is illegitimate if it raises the risks under which we are living. Fifth, it is illegitimate if it is not subjected to democratic control. So preservation of the self and human capabilities, respect of human rights, risk-minimization, and democratic control are the five conditions that technology must meet.

But we cannot stop discussing technology yet. There are two more points to discuss that relate to the question of how far technology should be allowed to change the world and us. They even challenge the Cartesian approach this book is defending.

---

[19] Maryann Mott in *National Geographic News*, January 25, 2005.
[20] Cp. http://www.news.com.au/story/0,10117,15891104-13762,00.html.

Chapter 14

Utilitarian or Cartesian Approach

T HE FIRST POINT IS A FUNDAMENTAL OBJECTION TO THE PRECEDING discussion. I appeal to the self and capabilities, as a criterion for distinguishing legitimate from illegitimate genetic engineering and as a gift we are entitled to use and improve. But isn't it obvious that *utility* is a superior criterion and grounds for the value of gene technology? Isn't utilitarianism a more adequate foundation for biotechnology? Isn't it more convincing because it is less metaphysical? When we talk of our capabilities as a gift we are to live up to and therefore entitled to use, perhaps even obliged to perfect, we imply metaphysical ideas. By contrast, the utility criterion legitimates all and only biotech that maximizes happiness. If this implies metaphysics as well, at least it seems to be a generally accepted one.

We are here again confronted with the competition of the utilitarian and the Cartesian approaches. But now it seems clear that we do and ought to use technology for making our life as comfortable as possible. Isn't this the best proof we may imagine for showing that we use our capabilities in order to be happy rather than for the sake of perfecting them and our activities? So here the utilitarian approach proves its soberness and its unpretentious metaphysics, if we have to call its belief in the finality of happiness metaphysics at all. The Cartesian approach, by contrast, seems caught in the implausibility of its presuppositions and consequences. But if we cannot accept it here, we should completely reject it.

The utility criterion does not exclude what the capability criterion unconditionally forbids, namely, the use of technology for removing the faculty of judgment or other capabilities from humans if they prevent or reduce happiness. In fact, the probability that judgment reduces happiness is pretty high. Our judgment is often enough a source of trouble rather than happiness. Kant argued that Nature would not have given us reason if she had intended our happiness.[1] But it is not only a source of unhappiness but of crime. Without a power of judgment, we would be incapable of knowing good and evil and could not be seduced to do evil. It is only because we can judge that we can commit crimes. So, replacing mankind by a species like the peaceful and cheerful space navigators that lack judgment would cleanse the world from human crimes. True, we abhor the idea of being reduced to puppets programmed by some mastermind. Black utopias like Huxley's *Brave New World* and Orwell's *1984* have expressed and confirmed this horror. This horror is used as an argument against the utility criterion. But we can turn the tables. There is a widespread conviction that if there is a god who is both morally good and has the power to prevent Auschwitz he *must* have prevented Auschwitz. So if we have the power to prevent another Auschwitz by genetic engineering, how can we dare say that we should not use it? The logic that requires an almighty god to prevent Auschwitz requires us to transform humans into happy animals incapable of judgment.

What this argument certainly shows is that the crucial question is whether we live for using our capacities in order to maximize happiness, or for perfecting them and the activities they enable us to pursue. Howsoever we decide, we commit ourselves to teleology and metaphysics. And whatever we opt for, the decision seems based on insufficient reasons. The Cartesian may argue that it is incoherent to delete the very capacity of moral distinctions that convinces the utilitarian of the rightness of its deletion. The utilitarian will reply that there is as little incoherence in such an act as in a suicide by which the agent, by his power of action, prevents himself from acting in the future. To this, the Cartesian will answer that suicide is incoherent indeed unless it stops a life that does no longer offer opportunities for action. The utilitarian may argue that the Cartesian is immoral in protecting a power that he admits is likely to produce Auschwitz-like crimes again. The Cartesian will reply, as Descartes did in commenting on Medea, that the capability of doing evil is a sign of the greatness of the agent, because action by free will is greater than action without free will, and a universe with organisms capable of free will is preferable to one without.

Obviously both approaches are embedded in incompatible world views. The Cartesian admires a universe for its quality that a product and part of it is capable of knowing what the universe is that its part is capable of intervening in it by actions based on this knowledge, and that the actions are decided by a faculty of acting independently of any predetermining factor. She feels that for its specific complexity, such a universe is more admirable than a less complex one. The capacity of knowledge adds to it another level, a mirror to make its own greatness known to itself. The capacity of free will adds even a further level by which the universe takes an unpredictable course and delivers itself to the agents. That

[1]   Kant, *Grundlegung zur Metaphysik der Sitten*, 1. Abschnitt, ed. Vorländer a.a.O., 12.

such capacity makes crime possible does not reduce but enhance the grandeur of the universe.

The utilitarian admires a universe to the degree it enhances happiness. She cannot see greatness in a constitution that allows for unhappiness, at least if the unhappiness is as deep as that created by Auschwitzes. If by its constitution unhappiness is produced, she will look for ways to remove the source, even if she has to delete the power of judgment. If the Cartesian reproaches her that her world view is too shallow, she will reply that the Cartesian admiration of complexity is cruel and insincere, because also the Cartesian cannot tolerate an Auschwitz. So it seems rationally undecidable which world view to prefer.

It is important to know the incompatible world views of the two approaches, but we can thus easily overlook a rational solution to the problem of whether to judge technology by the standard of happiness or that of capabilities. Despite her diverging world view, the utilitarian will agree that a universe with free will would be better than one without, if happiness were enhanced by free will. So if there is a probability that free will contributes to enhancing happiness, she will agree that in proportion to the probability degree we should refrain from abolishing free will. But it is improbable that free will never will enhance happiness. We cannot exclude the possibility that people learn from their crimes and prevent the repetition of Auschwitz. Even if there is only a minimal degree of probability that free will enhances happiness, its deletion would definitely stop a possible way to enhance happiness. Yet its deletion would definitely stop a way to delete those sources of unhappiness that it needs reason and free will to detect and remove. Hence, a utilitarian calculus of happiness would favor the decision to keep human nature as it is.

This argument does not prove the superiority of the Cartesian world view. It shows that in practice the utilitarian will agree with the Cartesian if she takes into account the chances that using our power of judgment can raise happiness. Yet this pragmatic point proves a pragmatic superiority of the Cartesian approach. Whatever our capabilities are, they are a source of happiness as well as of unhappiness. Whether they produce more happiness than unhappiness depends on social and psychological conditions that we can, and according to the utilitarian even must, act on once we know them. Again, that we ought to attempt to learn them and change them in a way that we can enjoy the use of our capabilities are two principles the utilitarian and the Cartesian agree in. They agree, although for different reasons: the Cartesian because she presumes that the enactment of capabilities is the ultimate aim, the utilitarian because she presumes that maximization of happiness is the ultimate aim, but also that, if capabilities are constructively enacted, they will produce happiness.

Hence, even by utilitarian standards, it is better to follow the criterion of capabilities that looks at whether capabilities can be enacted and enhanced for as many people as possible and absolutely forbids endangering the capability of judgment. Even the utilitarian has a pragmatic reason to recognize the practical superiority of the Cartesian approach to the utilitarian one.

The second point left for consideration is whether we are to use technology for the goal of immortality. Our five legitimacy conditions of technology – preservation of the self and human capabilities, respect of human rights, risk minimization, and democratic control – do not necessarily forbid such use. But *is* the goal of immortality acceptable? Isn't this too much of playing God? Moreover, by this question we can check if it is true that in practice, even utilitarian standards demand of us to follow the capability criterion.

According to both the utilitarian and the Cartesian standard, there is no principled objection to pursuing immortality, because it may well enhance both capabilities and happiness. But the utilitarian is exposed to the objection that life becomes intolerably boring after a more or less long time and hence will dry up as a source of happiness and even turn into a source of pain.[2] She can counter this objection by arguing that life becomes boring only if we lose the curiosity of the young and that we'll not lose it if biotech succeeds in engineering our nature so as never to lose curiosity. Yet then she has to accept that capabilities may lead to doing evil; curiosity makes curious of experiencing the evil no less than the good. Hence, it seems the Cartesian who takes such danger for a reason of admiration can defend the pursuit of immortality more consistently. For the critic of the pursuit of immortality, this of course is a point that counts against the Cartesian approach.

There are more reasons for the utilitarian to distrust the aim of immortality. Judging our actions by the happiness criterion implies the distinction between actions that follow an illusion of happiness and those that do not. Activities that aim at immortality seem to follow a natural illusion. The illusion is produced by the experience of pleasure that is accompanied by the desire that it should stay; no feeling is pleasurable if we do not want to keep it. We may even measure the degree of pleasure by the intensity of our wish that it stay. To quote an authority, "But joys want all eternity, Want deep, profound eternity."[3] Yet, we know it is not possible incessantly to experience ecstatic joy. Or if it is, it will be the bliss of drugs or pleasure machines that many utilitarians today regard as a goal unworthy of pursuit.[4] So, if life is the pursuit of happiness, the pursuit of immortality is an illusion, as immortal happiness is unattainable.

Moreover, for the utilitarian, death cannot be something intrinsically bad. Death is the end of happiness, but also of unhappiness. The death of an individual is balanced by the birth of another one; the chances for maximizing happiness are not really changed. As we are born *mortal* organisms, we should even welcome death when it comes after a fulfilled life. We may fear the pains that may accompany dying, but as Epicurus argued, death does not "concern either

---

2   B. Williams, *The Macropoulos Case.*
3   Nietzsche, *Thus Spake Zarathustra*, transl. Thomas Common (1891), pt. 4, sec. 79, § 12. The German text reads: "Doch alle Lust will Ewigkeit, will tiefe, tiefe Ewigkeit."
4   Jonathan Glover, *What Sort of People Should There Be?* Cp. Chapter 22.

the living or the dead, since for the former it is not, and the latter are no more."[5] Yet Epicurus could never convince the majority, who are not indifferent to death but prefer to go on living. It seems that both Epicurus's and the utilitarians' understanding of death misses something important. Unlike animals, we know that death is the end of all our possibilities. This is what we hate, not the end of happiness. The Cartesian can easily explain this hate; the utilitarian cannot.

To be without possibilities is abhorrent to us. Death is the end of challenges to our capabilities. Creatures with a self cannot but feel mortality to be a deep failure in the construction of nature. The faculty of judging by which we respond to challenges does not look like being made for ceasing; immortality is our due. For the Cartesian our craving for immortality is far from being condemnable; it is a consequence of our constitution. Only immortality warrants that we will never be without possibilities. To understand our craving for immortality, we have to take on the Cartesian viewpoint. This viewpoint favors technology. For the Cartesian, the attraction of immortality is the attraction of having possibilities. This is the very attraction technology has. Technology promises to give us new possibilities again and again. Just as we are craving acting and judging possibilities, we are craving possibilities that are opened up by technology.

In practice, the utilitarian will not exclude immortality from the goals of technology either. She will think of the possibility that by an immortal life the chance will rise that people learn from their mistakes and crimes; hence, that the chance of increasing happiness will arise as well. So again, in her practice she will follow the Cartesian consideration of possibilities and capabilities, though her theory pulls her rather in another direction.

Immortality is not one aim among others of technology; rather it is its aim *par excellence*. Hence, condemning the pursuit of immortality would be a grave restriction of technology. First, all technology aims at freeing us from the fetters of nature, and mortality is the strongest fetter by which nature binds us. Freeing us from it would be the most conspicuous act by which we cut the fetters of nature. Second, all technology aims at enhancing human powers; aiming at immortality aims at a power to give us infinitely more time to enhance any other power. Third, all technology aims at enhancing our powers regardless of what we will use them for. Such disregard finds its paradigm in the striving for immortality regardless of what we will use our immortal life for. The mere prospect of immortality makes many of us happy, even though we cannot exclude that, in the end, eternal hell awaits us.

Of course, that immortality is a paradigmatic aim of technology is not sufficient to recognize it as an aim. But as we are interested in instituting a broad spectrum of value spheres that attracts as many people as possible and reduces the destructiveness of the ambition of extraordinariness, we need strong reasons for excluding this aim. So let's look at the arguments for its exclusion.

5   Cyril B. Bailey, *Epicurus. The Extant Remains*, Oxford (Clarendon) 1926, 124f.

A simple objection is that immortality would lead to the overpopulation of the earth, if people did not stop having children; if they did, this would be a reduction of both capabilities and happiness. But if technology were capable of bringing humans closer to immortality, it would also be capable of offering the means to colonize the universe and thus fulfill another dream of mankind.

A more sophisticated argument is what we may deduce from Heidegger. As Heidegger seems to have assumed, as immortals we would not be able to grasp our lives as tasks that we have to accomplish, as little as the Olympian gods were. If our life does not end, we cannot organize our life by a goal. We would have not too little but too much time to do something valuable with our life. Perhaps we would even lack selves that give us individual identity over time.[6] In any case, immortality would reduce our capabilities; hence, we must not aim at it.

This argument rightly points out that, first, if we are freed from the burden of considering what we should use our life for, we would be reduced in our capabilities, and, second, our mortality favors such a consideration. But the argument overrates technology. The immortality technology can offer will always remain endangered. Unlike the Olympians, we will never be exempt from the danger of death. Even if we could stay eternally young, a meteorite could crush us any time. In a somewhat humiliating way, we would only attain the immortality of bacteria or cancer cells that can for ever go on living (and fissioning) though this does not secure them Olympian immortality. Moreover, we would have no more chance than bacteria of escaping the death of the universe that science says is inevitable. Even if we can delay it, as some scientists dare to think,[7] we will still have to reckon with the possibility of a definite end, with Heidegger's "possibility of the impossibility of any existence at all." Therefore, even if technology gives us eternal youth, we are still under the pressure mortals are under, namely, to consider what we should use our life for. Hence, the immortality that technology might open up to us will not dissolve our self nor reduce our capabilities.

What the Heideggerian argument does show is that immortality, if we could ever attain it in the non-Olympian form that alone is possible for us, would be but a blank we must fill; a chance to use for some aim; an aim that we can pursue in a mortal life no less than in an immortal one. Immortality cannot give value to a life that is not valuable in its mortal form. Just as biological reproduction escapes Sisyphean absurdity only if the individual life without its reproduction is valuable, immortality escapes absurdity only if a mortal life has meaning. Technology is in need of values that make meaningful the life it makes easier or longer. So it is never more than a serving sphere.

---

[6]   At least we may thus understand Heidegger's remarks on the wholeness of life in *Being and Time*.
[7]   Freeman Dyson, *Infinite in All Directions*, New York (Harper), 1988.

Nevertheless, presupposing there are aims that give meaning to a mortal life, immortality is an immensely attractive aim. As we did not find a serious objection, I conclude it should not be excluded from the aims of technology. Yet even if it were ever realizable, it would not devalue Arendt's aim of "immortalization," the immortality in memory;[8] for this is the aim of fame that the ambition of extraordinariness craves, whether our life is mortal or immortal.

The ordinary response of men to their mortality is resignation blended with a tendency to kick against the unavoidable. That all men are mortal and therefore Socrates, because he is a man, is mortal, this paradigm of a syllogism has not accidentally been taught for centuries in the schools. Judging people was considered to be in need of a repeated reminder of mortality, because such creatures are particularly reluctant to recognize it.

Immortality is also a paradigm for the grapes we declare sour because they are out of reach. It was left to the poets to complain of mortality. Philosophers do not cry over the milk of immortality they think has been spilt out to the gods. But it is again no accident that philosophers who defended free will against the determinism of nature showed signs of rebellion against the fate of mortality. Descartes mentioned death as something we might push back, and Kant shows similar expectations when he described reason:

> Reason in a creature is a faculty of widening the rules and purposes of the use of all its powers far beyond natural instinct; it acknowledges no limits to its projects.[9]

Surprisingly, Kant here, like Descartes, is ready to recognize reason as a power of breaking all rules and widening the use of all our other capacities.[10] Such reason cannot acknowledge any limits, whether of convention or of nature. Technology is the expression of this power; it cannot acknowledge limits either. Society can and needs to set to it the limits described in the five legitimacy conditions we have listed, but no limits beyond that.

---

[8] Cp., among other writings, Arendt, *Men in Dark Times*, 9.

[9] Kant, *Idea for a Universal History* from *A Cosmopolitan Point of View*, Second Thesis. Transl. L. W. Beck. ("Die Vernunft in einem Geschöpfe ist ein Vermögen, die Regeln und Absichten des Gebrauchs aller seiner Kräfte weit über den Naturinstinkt zu erweitern und kennt keine Grenzen ihrer Entwürfe.")

[10] Cp. my paper: *Reason and Will in the Idea for a Universal History and the Groundwork*.

Chapter 15

The Media and the Professions

THERE IS ANOTHER SERVING VALUE SPHERE THAT HAS NOT BEEN recognized by Hegel and Weber, the sphere of the media. The main argument for recognizing a value sphere of information or the media is that there cannot be a flourishing society or a set of effective checks against abuse of power without strong and independent media that inform citizens about public affairs and what pertains to deciding on them. The sphere of the media today is the place for public affairs that some theorists think the state is necessary for. If modernity can be saved only by institutionalizing life orders in a way that they turn the ambition of extraordinariness into support for society, the present institution of the state is to be reduced to a sphere of justice enforcement, and control of the spheres by themselves is to be maximized. This warrants special importance to the sphere that provides citizens not with all possible but all relevant knowledge – relevant, that is, for public affairs, the things that concern everyone. In stating this task of the media, I abstract from aims they also pursue, in particular from entertainment and advertisement. Though both the media and science aim at truth, their aims are different. Science, as we'll see, pursues truth in describing and explaining the world; the media pursue truth that is relevant for deciding on public affairs. They do not, like science, aim at truth for truth's sake, but truth for the sake of information about and discussion of public affairs. Both aims are often pursued for their own sake, and some heroes die for them. Still, the media, unlike science, are a serving sphere. They secure a society that is free for doing useless but significant things.

By informing about and discussing public affairs, the media pursue a value that is not reducible to another sphere. They also meet the other conditions of our definition of a value sphere: Their activity can be that of a profession and allow schooling.[1] Yet if we recognize the media as a sphere of their own,

[1] Cp. Chapter 11.

are we not to recognize more professions as value spheres? How about bakers, watchmakers, or doctors? If we assign the first to economy and the second to technology, they may insist that they do not aim at contributing to the wealth of the nation or to mastering nature, but at the irreducible quality of fine bakery or watches. In this case, however, we shall assign them to the sphere of the arts, as like artists they intend to produce a perceivable work whose sense or meaning does not consist in being useful. Actually, watchmakers have been artisans, who often justly have not been distinguished from artists, and bakers have not been regarded as artisans only because of the perishableness of their product.

The medical profession starts with the treatment of disease by methods not known to everyone. From its very beginning, medicine is a practice of acquiring and using knowledge for mastering nature. Therefore, we ought to assign it to technology. But certainly there may be more value spheres than we have listed. However, as long as we do not find more, we cannot list more.

The practice of the media is relatively new. In less complex societies there is little need to inform about public affairs, and in closed societies, which may be very complex, the media are used for spreading false or irrelevant information. In many early societies, priests had the function of releasing information about public affairs, like meteorological data important for agriculture and river regulation. In Rome from 131 BC to 330 AD, when the emperor moved to Constantinople, administrators regularly informed the public on legal proceedings, later also on other public events, using *acta diurna,* daily news, written in public places on stone or metal boards.[2] In China the Tang dynasty (618–906) published government news, the Di Bao, that in the eighth century were handwritten on silk and mostly read by government officials.[3] Yet a profession of information about public affairs could not develop as long as reading and writing were a privilege of the clergy. When this privilege fell and printing was introduced in Europe, independent individuals started publishing magazines in the beginning of the seventeenth century. As far as newspapers and other periodicals are commercial products, their publication is one of the many activities of the sphere of economy. But as far as they aim at the specific task of informing on public affairs, they aim at the specific value of the media sphere. The same is true of the mass media that more recently have been added to the print media.

The spread of print media in the preceding centuries and other mass media in more recent times bears witness to people's interest in affairs that concern everyone because everyone's life can be changed by them. As it is not easy to distinguish this interest from a more general curiosity in human affairs, it is regulated by the right to privacy. This right should protect, not only individuals

---

[2] Cp. *Encyclopedia Britannica*, 1911.

[3] Cp. Chunming Li, Microfilming and digitization of newspapers in China, http://www.ndl. go.jp/en/iflapac/preconference/pdf/LiChunming.pdf.

from that curiosity, but also the interest in public affairs from distraction. The interest in public affairs is a power feared by the powerful, as it aims at judgments on public affairs that favor or disfavor states and other institutions that claim to serve the public good.

Therefore, control of the media is no less important a source of power than control of the means of coercion and of investment, the sources of political and economic power. The better-known state powers of political theory, executive, legislative, and judicative have never alone been capable of checking each other, as theory expected them to. What rather brought about the balance of powers necessary for any flourishing society was the competition of the state, economy, and public opinion. The means of coercion, of investment and of information, are the most important sources of social power. Therefore, the media are a hot object of power-seeking people and in danger of losing its specific task of informing about public affairs.

Public opinion was for a long time determined by the priests, in the Enlightenment by independent authors, and since the nineteenth century increasingly by editors of magazines. Today, the mass media are controlled by a few individuals. According to both utilitarian and Cartesian rationality criteria, with Arendt we must again say, "Surely, nothing could be worse." Yet the sphere of information also is a challenge to extraordinariness that is borne by an amazingly great number of engaged journalists. Without them, the American war in Vietnam would have lasted still longer and many cases of corruption would never have been detected. Moreover, it is a challenge also to scientists, historians, and philosophers.[4] Natural scientists, in particular, have responded to the challenge by informing the world about the threat of environmental catastrophes furthered by man-made factors.

The media sphere can exemplify what sphere autonomy means. It develops its own standards of perfection. Engaged journalists know best what perfect information about public affairs consists of. They do not need lessons from the moralist or philosopher, just as the experienced lawyer knows best how justly to adjudicate conflicting claims, and the business manager knows best how to make a firm profitable. The problem, though, in the sphere of the media as well as in justice and other spheres, is that their agents are exposed to the pressures of the most powerful spheres, economy and the state. The inroads of economy and the state that the media are exposed to have become particularly strong today, because technology has made control of information possible

---

[4]   Arendt points out the role of truth in politics in her *Truth and Politics*, in *Between Past and Future*, 227–64. She herself was as much an engaged journalist as a historian and philosopher. Other theorists, like Noam Chomsky, use their scientific reputation for pointing to obvious crimes of the powerful that would not be believed if stated by normal journalists, and to the systematic disinformation by the media; cp. Edward Herman, N. Chomsky, *Manufacturing Consent*.

to an unprecedented extent. Information is increasingly mediated by electronic technology that can be centralized and controlled, as publication by speech, the press, and even broadcasting could not. Big business and states have an interest in such control; business for protecting what they consider their intellectual property; states for muzzling critics. They combine in an unholy alliance to transform the Internet from a medium of liberty to its very contrary.[5]

Independence and plurality of information obviously need protection. Technology that allows control of the media, in particular in the Internet, should be forestalled and counteracted; concentration of the media is to be reversed; juries that pillory pressures, instituted; independent journalists, privileged by reduced taxation and broadcasting times. The public has become aware of the danger of the present situation, but has not yet stopped the trend to media concentration. It will be difficult to break the unholy alliance of state and big business. But the aim of spreading relevant knowledge, most times described as the aim of spreading the truth, has a peculiarly strong attraction that is independent of civilizations, philosophies, and moralities.[6] Moreover, the media today have an effect even their concentration in a few media czars can hardly stop: They make visible to a world public the incredible contrast between the luxury of some classes and the shameful misery of many more people. This instigates a fury at the prevailing injustice that we can feel everywhere today. It can become both destructive and constructive, depending not least on our ideas and the media.

[5] Michael Hardt and Antonio Negri, *Empire*, 298–300: "... the global information infrastructure might be characterised as the combination of a democratic mechanism and an *oligopolistic* mechanism. ... The original design of the Internet was intended to withstand military attack. ... The oligopolistic network model is characterised by broadcast systems.... The entire culture industry – from the distribution of newspapers and books to films and videocassettes – has traditionally operated along this model. A relatively small number of corporations ... can effectively dominate all these networks. The networks of the new information infrastructure are a hybrid of these two models.... The new communication technologies, which hold out the promise of a new democracy and a new social equality, have in fact created new lines of inequality and exclusion, both within the dominant countries and especially without them." Cp. ibid. 33. On the possible and actual controls of computer users, cp. Richard Stallman's publications; for a brief introduction http://www.gnu.org/philosophy/right-to-read.html; for a more comprehensive view *Free Software, Free Society*, Boston, GNU Press, 2002; http://www.gnu.org/philosophy/fsfs/rms-essays.pdf. On the more general dangers of the Internet, cp. Cass Sunstein *republic.com*, 2002.

[6] Its attraction has been convincingly described by Vaclav Havel; cp. his *Power of the Powerless* (1978), reprinted in *Or Living in Truth*.

Chapter 16

Science

S CIENCE IS A CANDIDATE FOR A NONSERVING SPHERE, BUT IS IT different from technology at all? Isn't it but a form of technology that has not yet become conscious of its true task? In fact, it is difficult today to distinguish them, because much work done under the title of science is in fact technology. Traditionally, they have been thus distinguished: Natural science explains the processes of nature; other sciences explain other parts or aspects of the world. Technology does not explain but uses the knowledge of science for controlling nature without asking why it is able to control. Natural science explains natural processes in a way that allows controlling them but gives an understanding of nature that technology lacks. I'll argue that this distinction is right.

The prevailing view of what scientific explanation is has been expounded by Hempel, Oppenheim, Popper, and other philosophers of science.[1] We explain an event (an *explanandum*) if we deduce it (more exactly its description) from, first, one or more laws of nature and, second, the (description of the) "antecedent" conditions – that is, the conditions that preceded the explanandum. This view takes account of the fact that explanations often consist of no more than deductions of the explananda from laws and antecedent conditions. Yet it neglects that very often knowledge of laws and of antecedent conditions allows exact predictions but gives no understanding at all. Richard Feynman, one of the best experts on quantum mechanics, asserted: "I can safely say that nobody understands quantum mechanics." Predictions in quantum mechanics are unequalled, yet if we want to understand the behavior of nature in this area and ask "But how can it be like that?" we will "get 'down the drain,' into a blind alley from which nobody has yet escaped. Nobody knows how it can be like that."[2]

[1]   Carl Gustav Hempel and Paul Oppenheim, "Studies in the Logic of Explanation."
[2]   Richard Feynman, *The Character of Physical Law*, 129.

Nonetheless, Feynman does not conclude that physics is technology and can only state laws that allow predictions but no understanding. He accepts neither pragmatism nor the kind of subjectivism once in vogue that declared that in science "man encounters only himself"[3] nor the kind of skepticism that believed that "scientific truth not only need not be eternal, it need not even be comprehensible or adequate to human reason."[4] He rather points to "one of the amazing characteristics of nature," namely, "the variety of interpretational schemes which is possible"; "the correct laws of physics seem to be expressible in such a tremendous variety of ways."[5] Scientific understanding depends on *interpreting* the laws. Different interpretations of the same laws give different pictures of the whole of nature. "As long as physics is incomplete, and we are trying to understand the other laws," interpretations "may give clues about what might happen in other circumstances."[6] What the physicist's understanding aims at, and what requires of him a choice between different interpretations, is "to see the connections of the hierarchies,"[7] of different levels of nature in which known laws hold. Scientific understanding, unlike scientific explanation, consists in comprehending the connections between the different levels of nature. Let me quote Feynman more extensively:

> For example, at one end we have the fundamental laws of physics. Then we invent other terms for concepts which ... have, we believe, their ultimate explanation in terms of the fundamental laws. For instance, "heat." Heat is supposed to be jiggling, and the word for a hot thing is just the word for a mass of atoms which are jiggling. But for a while, if we are talking about heat, we sometimes forget about the atoms jiggling – just as when we talk about the glacier we do not always think of the hexagonal ice and the snowflakes which originally fell. ... Now if we go higher up from this, in another level we have properties of substances – like "refractive index," how light is bent when it goes through something; or "surface tension," the fact that water tends to pull itself together, both of which are described by numbers. ... On, up in the hierarchy. With water we have waves, and we have a thing like storm, the word "storm" which represents an enormous mass of phenomena, ... And it is not worthwhile always to think of it way back. ... As we go up in this hierarchy of complexity, we get to things like muscle twitch, or nerve impulse, which is an enormously complicated thing in the physical world. ... Then come things

---

3   Werner Heisenberg, *Das Naturbild der heutigen Physik*, 1955, 17f; quoted from Arendt, *The Human Condition*, 261, who expresses agreement with Heisenberg.

4   Arendt, *The Human Condition*, 290. Arendt refers to Whitehead, *Science and the Modern World*, Penguin 1926, 116: "Heaven knows what seeming nonsense may not to-morrow be demonstrated truth."

5   Feynman, *The Character of Physical Law*, 54f.

6   Ibid. 53.

7   Ibid. 125.

like "frog." And then ... we come to words and concepts like "man," and "history," or "political expediency." ... And going on, we come to things like evil, and beauty, and hope. ... It is not sensible for the ones who specialize at one end, and the ones who specialize at the other end, to have ... disregard for each other. (They don't actually, but people say they do.) The great mass of workers in between, connecting one step to another, are improving all the time our understanding of the world ... and in that way we are gradually understanding this tremendous world of interconnecting hierarchies.[8]

According to Feynman scientific understanding aims at grasping the connections between the different levels of nature. It is an aim not so very different from that pursued by Renaissance figures like Doctor Faustus, who, in Goethe's description, wanted to know "was die Welt im Innersten zusammenhält": what in its inmost core keeps the world together?[9] What does the understanding of the "tremendous world of interconnecting hierarchies" consist of? When is one of the competing interpretations of a law chosen? We understand the interconnecting hierarchies when we do not only understand the dependence of the properties of heat, water surface-tension, frogs, and men on the levels "down" in the hierarchy, on the atoms and other particles but also learn the character of atoms and other particles by the properties of the upper hierarchies, the heat and frogs. An interpretation of a law is chosen when it contributes more to the understanding of the interconnecting hierarchies than its competitors do. Crucial in this interpretation of the laws is the knowledge of properties, not only of the particles but also of phenomena like heat and frogs.

Such an understanding presupposes the ontology of substances, which are agents or bodies, and properties; for we cannot think of properties without agents or bodies that have them. This ontology must be specified to take account of the special dependence of particles on each other and on the condition of the universe.[10] By contrast, if scientific understanding consisted only in referring to laws and not also to properties, it would not differ from technological understanding; technological understanding can do without bodies or agents and their properties. One may prefer an ontology that does without substances. But then we would be unable to connect the world of heat and frogs, which presupposes substances and properties, with forces and particles.

Considering its ontological presupposition, scientific understanding is not so much different from ordinary understanding. Scientific understanding points out the interconnection of a heat phenomenon and a particle phenomenon; ordinary understanding points out the interconnection of the phenomenon to be explained and a property of something we did not know or think of before the explanation. We understand why Peter became furious when we learn that

---

[8] Ibid. 124–6.
[9] Goethe, *Faust* I, Nacht lines 382–4.
[10] I owe this point to a conversation with Orly Shenker from Tel Aviv.

he is hot-tempered and Paul provoked him; or why the glass broke when we know that it fell on the floor and glass is fragile. In ordinary explanations, the properties interconnected like hot-temper and fury are not described in a mathematical and lawlike form, whereas in scientific explanations they are. But this difference does not change the ontology presupposed in both ordinary and scientific explanation. Only because ordinary and scientific explanations presuppose the same or a comparable ontology can scientists aim at a comprehensive understanding of the whole of the world. Otherwise they would miss the aim most of them think they pursue – namely, to explain events of the ordinary world.

Although agents in quantum physics are very different from agents in the ordinary world, still if there is only one world (with however many dimensions), quantum agents must somehow reappear in or develop to ordinary agents, and ordinary agents must somehow depend on and come from quantum agents, just as the gravity of stars and gravitons reappears in the property of our ordinary bodies to be more or less heavy. Science explains the properties and agents of the ordinary world by giving us a deeper knowledge of them. The Australian philosopher of science Brian Ellis has sketched a line of development from the layers of the world explored by natural science to the layer of the ordinary world that is similar to Feynman's picture of the interconnections between the levels of his hierarchy:

> "Fixed agents, like atoms and molecules, have fixed causal powers. Variable agents, like lumps of copper, have variable causal powers, because they can become charged or fatigued. Free agents, such as ourselves, have meta-causal powers, powers, that is, by which we can deliberately take steps to increase our causal powers in some respects, change our attitudes, revise our priorities, and so on."[11] Such meta-causal powers are the powers of deliberation and judgment that might even follow the reason to prove the agent's independence of any antecedent factor.

Now, if scientific explanation, like ordinary explanation, explains by referring events to properties, powers, and forces and not to laws only, it may seem not to be radically different from religious and mythical explanations either. For religious and mythical explanations also explain events by referring them to properties and forces of agents. However, there is an important difference. Only scientific explanations can be tested and refuted and confirmed by observation. That is why laws are necessary for scientific explanations; we need laws to deduce predictions from theories. This difference excludes normative elements from scientific explanations, whereas religious and mythical explanations often include such elements. It is this difference that prevents natural science from

[11] Brian Ellis, *The Philosophy of Nature.*

playing the social role of imposing a moral order on society that the utilitarian rationality of closed societies once played.

If indeed it is the Feinbergian and not the Hempelian view of explanation that science looks for, then science is different from technology, as the technician does not aim at a kind of Faustian understanding of nature. In fact, history confirms the Feinbergian view. It shows that science undermined salvation religion. If science followed the Hempelian view, it could not have done so, as Hempelian science is compatible with salvation religion. Such compatibility is often argued for today. Indeed, also Feinbergian science is not logically incompatible with salvation religion. It is logically possible both that the universe is the product of impersonal forces and that we shall be judged at the end of the day by an almighty and omniscient god. But psychologically it's incompatible.

The quality of the world the salvation idea presupposes is that of a creation that shows the traits of its creator. The creator of salvation religion shows interest in the well-being of men; otherwise he would not offer them salvation. But the world science has detected up to now does not show signs of such interest. This is not a moral judgment on which one might differ; it is a descriptive judgment for which one needs only to know the meaning of the words used and the world science shows us. If, however, theologians declare that we cannot know the character of the creator, then science is indeed compatible with religion. But in this case they do no longer defend a salvation religion. How can salvation be expected of a god whose character is unknowable?

Compatibilists of science and religion will argue that it was not science that made the salvation idea unconvincing but the experience of natural evils, like the earthquake of Lisbon in 1755, and that such experience, though shaking faith, is insufficient for rejecting it. Yet natural disasters have accompanied mankind since their beginnings without provoking religious doubts. It is only against the background of a scientific world view that disasters shook faith. Before modern science was generally accepted, disasters were considered divine punishments for human sins.

It is true, modern science excludes not belief in an almighty and good god, but explanation of events by divine intervention. Many a great scientist has been a pious believer and considered the laws of nature he helped detect a proof of God's inexhaustible wisdom. That did not prevent his strict rejecting of explanations by divine intervention. However, though by excluding divine intervention science does not exclude God's existence, it allows assuming his nonexistence. It is open for both confirming belief if empirical data are of a kind that suggests the existing of a god and refuting it if they are not. Once this openness was accepted, as it was when science was accepted, the Lisbon earthquake and a lot of other ordinary experiences and scientific experiments led to the judgment that there is not the God salvation religion believes in. The physicist Steven Weinberg has described this process:

> "All our experience throughout the history of science has tended in the opposite direction" (than to find "any sign of the workings of an interested God"), "toward

a chilling impersonality in the laws of nature. The first great step along this path was the demystification of the heavens. ... Life, too, has been demystified ... The process of demystification has accelerated in this century, in the continued success of biochemistry and molecular biology in explaining the workings of living things."[12]

The technician is not interested in whether the world shows signs of God or is "demystified" (or "disenchanted" or transformed "into a causal mechanism," as Weber said);[13] he is interested in controlling the processes of nature, with or without a god. Yet Weinberg thinks the scientist unavoidably has an interest in God's existence, because the world would be different if he did exist. He states that it is hardly possible "not to wonder whether we will find any answer to our deepest questions, any sign of the workings of an interested God, in a final theory." He does not hesitate to ask: "Will we find an interested God in the final laws of nature?,"[14] nor to argue: "If ... we found some special role for intelligent life in the final laws at the point of convergence of the arrows of explanation, we might well conclude that the creator who established these laws was in some way specially interested in us."[15] He even says we must conclude so if when defending his thesis "a bolt of lightning were to strike me down at the podium."[16] Similarly, he admits that "sometimes nature seems more beautiful than strictly necessary" – more beautiful than nature should be if there is no "special status for life and intelligence" and no "standards of value or morality" in nature.[17] Along with the fact that "the arrows of explanation" do not converge where "a bolt of lightning" striking him down would point to it is by the brute fact that "the God of birds and trees would have to be also the God of birth defects and cancer,"[18] that he finds "impersonality in the laws of nature."[19] We might add, in Weinberg's spirit: what physics tells us about nature does not fit the idea of a loving and redeeming god but at best that of a god who cannot

---

[12]   Steven Weinberg, *Dreams of a Final Theory*, 245f.

[13]   Weber, *Zwischenbetrachtung*, 564, ed. Kröner, 472.

[14]   Weinberg, *Dreams of a Final Theory*, 245.

[15]   Ibid. 251.

[16]   Weinberg, *New York Review of Books*, Jan. 20, 2000, in a letter referring to his article "A Designer's Universe," ibid. Oct. 21, 1999.

[17]   *Dreams of a Final Theory*, 250.

[18]   Ibid. 250.

[19]   Ibid. 245f. Weinberg also has practical reasons for rejecting religions that refer to a life after death to influence this life: "Unlike science, religious experience can suggest a meaning for our lives, a part for us to play in a great cosmic drama of sin and redemption, and it holds out to us a promise of some continuation after death. For just these reasons, the lessons of religious experience seem to me indelibly marked with the stamp of wishful thinking." Because of its sobering effect on religious fanaticism, the skepticism of science becomes an ideological force. "Across Asia and Africa the dark forces of religious enthusiasm are gathering strength, and reason and tolerance are not safe even in the secular states of the West. ... We may need to rely again on the influence of science to preserve a sane world. It is not the certainty of scientific knowledge that fits it for this role, but its *uncertainty*." (Ibid. 255 and 259.)

be understood in terms of love or interest in humans (a tale supported by what history can tell us).

Unfortunately, in his argument for God's non-existence Weinberg does not explicitly distinguish the hard facts of physics from his interpretation of them. Scientists agree on the facts, but can diverge in their interpretation, as became clear when Weinberg's theses raised furious protests. The facts of physics do not prove whether God exists or does not; yet they imply knowledge that is relevant for answering metaphysical questions. The distinction between scientific and metaphysical theory is blurred in Weinberg's assertions. It has been better observed by another physicist, Freeman Dyson, who shows the same interest in metaphysics, though argues for a different interpretation of scientific facts. Dyson found an opportunity to expound his views when Weinberg summarized his view in a pithy remark: "... the more the universe seems comprehensible, the more it seems pointless."[20]

Weinberg seems to have identified "demystified" and "pointless." He is completely right that science has "demystified" (or "disenchanted," as Weber said) nature. But demystified nature is not necessarily pointless. For understanding the specific goal of science it is important to distinguish the notions. We can detect a "point" also in a disenchanted world. Such detection would not be scientific, but science, just because it has disenchanted nature, cannot exclude it either and can even favor it. What science has given us to know about nature until now does not fit in with salvation religion but it may fit in with a metaphysical view on the "point" of nature.

Actually, this is what Dyson claims. He argues that, first, science shows that natural evolution has produced life and intelligence in the form of men and second, not science but "meta-science," the metaphysical reflection on science, shows us that the point of the universe is to produce and spread life and mind in the universe.[21] Recognition that spreading life and mind in the universe is the point of nature implies that it is our task and obligation to spread life and mind over the universe. Such recognition is not scientific knowledge but faith; it does not raise a claim to truth but to moral or metaphysical rightness, a rightness that concerns the meaning of the world.

Dyson's "meta-science" even explicitly identifies life and mind with God. This may seem a relapse into traditional religion. But in fact the religion he commits himself to is incompatible with salvation religion. For the task of spreading mind is the task of humans. It is no longer God who helps people, but people who are to help God in attaining an aim he may have set but needs people to achieve. Dyson is explicit in drawing this conclusion. He calls his theology Socinianism, in reverence to the two Italian heretics Laelius and

---

[20] Weinberg, *The First Three Minutes*, 131f, 154.
[21] Dyson, *Infinite in All Directions*, 1988.

Faustus Socinus who defended the view that God needs the help of men.[22] The difference of this idea from the salvation idea could not be greater. The physicists Weinberg and Dyson show in different ways the incompatibility of science and salvation religion. Ironically it is not Weinberg the agnostic who makes the death of the salvation idea by science most visible, but Dyson the believer. The substitute he offers reverses the roles of God and man. It is man who has to save God from misery.[23]

Yet doesn't the fact that not science but meta-science is incompatible with salvation religion show that science it is not different from technology? Technology can be described as the attitude that trusts in the power of humans to help themselves rather than in the power of prayers and similar religious activities. Isn't it this very attitude that reappears in science and explains its undermining of salvation religion? I think there is a difference. The technician's attitude that we can and should help ourselves does not disfavor salvation religion. The pious love adages like: "God helps those that help themselves," and "Do your best, God will do the rest."[24] They do not see any incoherence in betting on two horses, the human and the divine one. The technician does not either. The scientist does because she wants to know the nature of the world; whether it does or does not contain a divine power that helps us. She cannot get an answer directly from science; science, like technology, aims at a knowledge that needs to be accepted by everyone. But unlike technology, it aims at a knowledge that can be relevant for finding an answer to metaphysical questions. If science could not be used for meta-science, and physics for metaphysics, they would no longer be science.

So far I have only discussed natural science. How about disciplines that either are not empirical, like philosophy, mathematics, logic, formal linguistics,

---

[22] Ibid. 119. Laelius Socinus (1525–62) was the uncle of Faustus Socinus (1539–1604). Similar ideas of a developing god dependent on human support have been developed in the 20th century by Max Scheler, *Die Stellung des Menschen im Kosmos*, especially 54ff and 67ff; *Die Formen des Wissens und die Bildung*, ibid. 85–119, esp. 101–4, and by Hans Jonas, *Organismus und Freiheit*. esp. chap. 1 and 3; *Der Gottesbegriff nach Auschwitz. Eine jüdische Stimme* (1984), 190–208 (with remarkable similarities to Scheler, who yet is not mentioned).

[23] Of course, this idea is not absolutely new, as Bernard Lewis, "The Roots of Muslim Rage," 47–60, 7th paragraph, aptly reminds us: "The idea that God has enemies, and needs human help in order to identify and dispose of them, is a little difficult to assimilate. It is not, however, all that alien. The concept of the enemies of God is familiar in preclassical and classical antiquity, and in both the Old and New Testaments, as well as in the Koran. A particularly relevant version of the idea occurs in the dualist religions of ancient Iran, whose cosmogony assumed not one but two supreme powers. The Zoroastrian devil, unlike the Christian or Muslim or Jewish devil, is not one of God's creatures performing some of God's more mysterious tasks but an independent power, a supreme force of evil engaged in a cosmic struggle against God. This belief influenced a number of Christian, Muslim, and Jewish sects, through Manichaeism and other routes."

[24] In German the adage expresses the sense still sharper: "*Hilf dir selbst, so hilft dir Gott*": Help yourself, and God will help you. There are similar adages in other languages; in Italian, it is "*Aiutati che il ciel t'aiuta.*"

informatics, and game theory, or that investigate man and human societies? What is common to the very different sciences there are, is, first, the idea that they look for truth or demonstrability for the sake of truth or demonstrability. This is why they belong to the same value sphere. Truth is not the meaning of the world, which is aimed at by metaphysics or philosophy, religion and, as we'll see, art. Truth in empirical science is correspondence of a theory with facts. So an empirical theory must be falsifiable by them. We can never be sure that they will not be revised; hence, they can provide us only with fallible knowledge. Scientists can passionately fight for them, not because they can be sure of their truth but because they are the theories that they think they have the best reasons for. Still, as science has an idea of truth, that of complete correspondence of theory and facts, it aims at truth for truth's sake. But it knows we can never completely know the facts empirical theories are to correspond with. Nonetheless, empirical science progresses if the scope of reasons by which we can check the theories widens.

It is not easy to define what truth in nonempirical sciences consists of. In mathematics, it is based on mathematical proofs, in theology and jurisprudence, on arguments that lean on and interpret presuppositions of faith and of law that constitute theology and jurisprudence; in others, on arguments about the consistency of the conceptual systems they develop. It seems it is demonstrability rather than truth that is aimed at by the nonempirical sciences. However, demonstrability shares with the idea of truth its independence of practical interests. Such independence, though, does not exclude application of theories in technology; on the contrary, it is this property that makes them applicable.

Second, all sciences aim at truth (or demonstrability) by systematically registering their theses, theories, and criticisms of them, making them public to anyone who is interested, and transmitting them to the following generations. This distinguishes them from the bodies of knowledge that do not pursue truth for truth's sake. Their common aim made possible their institutionalization in academies and universities that united all of them. Its institutionalization belongs to the most revolutionary properties of science. It rejects the prescientific expectation that transmission of knowledge from parents to children, and in secret ways, is how knowledge should be transmitted. In particular it rejects the idea that discoveries must be kept secret in order to exclude others from taking advantage of them. It emancipates knowledge from the tutelage of society.

Today, the institutionalization of science as an independent sphere has been undermined; the idea of pursuing truth for its own sake has gone out of fashion.[25] As an institution of its own, science has had a moral influence on

---

[25] M. Hardt, A. Negri, *Empire*, 155f, favor "clinging to the primary concept of truth" if it is "a powerful and necessary form of resistance," and refer "the real revolutionary practice" not to truth but "to the level of production," arguing: "Truth will not make us free, but taking control of the production of truth will." This is worse than fashion.

society, as it enjoys respect for its following truth for truth's sake. Yet its moral authority has a falsifying function only, for though it can reject false pretensions it cannot establish positive aims and values. Its moral influence presupposes agreement on moral values or principles. This applies also to disciplines that, like jurisprudence and theology, examine, criticize, and justify norms. In doing so, they presuppose moral standards that they cannot justify.

Only practical philosophy aims at justifying norms without presupposing a norm (just as this book aims at justifying the Cartesian approach). It might impose an order upon society. But it is because of this ambition of practical philosophy that it cannot be considered a pure science, even though in its ambition for the rightness of its principles it claims the same impartiality and universality that pure science claims for its truth. Its impartiality and universality make it a member of academies but exclude it from the narrower circle of disciplines that claim only to describe, explain, and understand, and it is this claim that the moral authority of science is due to.

Actually, practical philosophy, like religion, metaphysics, and other disciplines of philosophy, does not raise claims on truth but on moral rightness and on what kinds of life are meaningful. Like in science, there are reasons for and against accepting a theory. Still the reasons are different not only from those in empirical science but also from those in nonempirical sciences, as they do not presuppose the disciplinary presuppositions of the sciences. Of course, philosophers cannot write anything without presupposing at least as many assumptions as scientists do. Yet in distinction to them, no presupposition defines their theories. Every one can be replaced by another if reasons are given for doing so. However, philosophy shares with science the idea of demonstrability, which makes them admissible to the sphere of science.

Social and human sciences merit a special consideration. I'll understand by them only disciplines that investigate human actions and behavior, and exclude those parts of sociology and psychology that investigate natural processes in humans that are not subject to our will. The way human sciences explain their objects, that is, actions, is necessarily different from the explanation of the natural sciences. If, as I have argued in criticizing Kant,[26] people have free will and its recognition does not contradict the methodology of science, there can be a science of human behavior in spite of free will, but it cannot aim at detecting laws of human behavior that exclude free will.

The understanding of natural science, as I have tried to expose, depends on their detection not only of laws but also of basic properties and forces of the bodies and particles of nature. So the fact that human sciences cannot aim at detecting laws does not make them radically different from natural sciences. But there *is* a radical difference between them, because their theories cannot be

[26] In Chapter 3.

tested by deducing predictions from them. The reason is that such predictions, like any other assumption about human powers or properties, can and often do affect human behavior. Belief in an economic or psychological or any other theory of human science can be sufficient to make their predictions true, and disbelief in them can be sufficient to make them false. Just as a prediction of a brain scientist about my future actions can codetermine my decisions, a prediction deduced from a theory of human science about men's behavior can codetermine their decisions. George Soros has called this property of human science theories their unavoidable reflectivity.[27]

Does this reflectivity imply that theories of human science cannot be tested empirically at all? Postmodern philosophers have drawn this consequence. If they are right, there is no difference between an ideology and a scientific theory about man. In fact, there can be a difference between them only if there are empirical elements by which a human science theory can be tested. It is history that can deliver to human science such elements. If a theory of human science is incompatible with a historical fact, it is disconfirmed, though not necessarily falsified: What we think is a historical fact may be also disconfirmed by a theory of human science, just as the use of experimental and prediction data in natural science does not exclude that a theory of natural science can disconfirm experimental data. In fact, what is called falsification in science is better called disconfirmation. Anyway, often enough experimental and historical data can serve as an empirical test. Historical facts are on the same observational level as are empirical data; and they are equally fallible. They also are theory-impregnated. Yet most often, they are not impregnated by the theory they are to check, and are therefore capable of functioning as a potential falsifier of human science theories.

There is another difference of human science from natural science. If its theories cannot be tested by predictions deducible from them, then their explanations cannot diverge from ordinary explanations as far as the explanations of natural sciences can. These can deviate very far from ordinary explanations because even the assumption of the most fantastic properties of agents (as we

---

[27] George Soros, *The Alchemy of Finance*. Cp. also Soros, "Introduction to W.H. Newton-Smith," 1–10, 7, saying, "It is a pity that Popper failed to recognize the difference" between natural science and social theory; and John Gray, "The Moving Target," *New York Review of Books*, Oct. 5, 2006 (on Soros). Reflexivity of social theory was already known as the Thomas theorem that "the situations that men define as true, become true for them" (W. I. Thomas, *The Unadjusted Girl*, Boston (Little, Brown) 1923; W. I. Thomas and D. S. Thomas, *The Child in America*, New York (Knopf) 1928; by Robert Merton's use of the notion of self-fulfilling prophesy (R. K. Merton, 'The Self-Fulfilling Prophecy,' *Antioch Review* 8, 1948, pp. 193–210; Merton, *Social Theory and Social Structure*, Glencoe (The Free Press), 1949, rev. ed. 1957); and by its discussion in the philosophy of science (in particular by Ernest Nagel, *The Structure of Science*, New York (Harcourt) 1961; but even by Popper under the name of *Oedipal effect* in his *The Poverty of Historicism*, New York (Harper and Row) 1957). Curiously, most theorists think only of predictions becoming a reason for making them true, not of their becoming a reason to refute them. Spite seems to be little developed among them.

find them in quantum physics indeed) can be tested by risky predictions, and are to be accepted if they prove successful. Because in contrast human science theories can only be tested by historical facts, they will not deviate very far from ordinary explanations, as historical facts will not be far from what is acceptable to ordinary explanations. Hence, if a theory in human science deviates far from ordinary explanation, then it is likely to be false.

As little as natural science, human science can impose a moral or political order on society. A science of economy will criticize the ideology of economists who teach that self-regard is the cement of society and the deregulation of markets the panacea of all social problems. It can tell how aims can be attained and how they cannot. Yet it cannot scientifically prove the rightness of aims. Discussion and justification of aims and values that claim universal consent is possible only in practical philosophy.

By its specific aim of pursuing truth for truth's sake, natural science did not only exert a moral and political influence on society. It also bore witness to the fact that there is a way of life that recognizes impractical truth for its god, not the truth of relevant information but of a correspondence that might be completely irrelevant for practical life. By pursuing such an aim, science devalues the aims of the serving spheres. It sends a message to the world comparable to the message sent formerly by salvation religion: People can detach themselves from the ends of the ordinary world in favor of an end that is more adequate to human capacities. Truth for truth's sake is alien to the ordinary world. In pursuit of this aim, science cannot be but extraordinary. Science is one of the few aims worth living and dying for that any politics that sticks to the ideal of autonomy must protect.

Science once had a puzzling result for our need of extraordinariness. It had, as Weber said, disenchanted the world and presented it as a huge causal mechanism that excludes not only extraordinariness but even action.[28] But once we understand the world not as a huge causal mechanism but a tremendous system of interconnecting hierarchies, it leaves room for the ambition of extraordinariness and the other specific properties of man. So science is not only a challenge for extraordinariness because the problems it raises will never be exhausted and will always require extraordinariness for their solution. Rather, the interconnecting hierarchies including the "meta-causal powers" of "free agents, such as ourselves"[29] that scientists and philosophers of science today ascribe to the world fit in with the idea of extraordinariness and the Cartesian conception of the self.

---

[28] Weber, *Zwischenbetrachtung* 564; ed. Kröner ed. 472 (cp. fn. 113 and 114).
[29] Ellis, *The Philosophy of Nature*, 31.

Chapter 17

Art and Religion

HEGEL RECOGNIZED ART AND RELIGION, LIKE SCIENCE, AS ACTIVITIES that belong not to "objective" but "absolute" spirit. What he wanted to imply, as I understand him, is that first, they have their objective meaning in themselves and not, as the activities of the serving spheres, in an aim outside the activity; second, that their meaning saves life from Sisyphean absurdity.[1] We can explain that science has such a meaning by its special significance for us. "All men by nature desire to know," Aristotle said, "as is indicated by the love we have for our senses, even apart from their practical uses."[2] Whatever we learn about the world is delightful just because it gives knowledge, whether it is useful or even is bad news or not. We just prefer knowledge to ignorance, as we prefer seeing to being blind, even if what we have to see is bad. If also art and religion are absolute spirit, their significance needs to be absolute, that is, independent of their utility as well. Yet what does this mean?

According to some traditional theologians, religion serves the salvation of our souls, hence, has no absolute significance, as it serves an aim outside its activity. If we follow Hegel and our own distinctions, this is a mistake. Yet what is the special utility-independent delight of religious activities? According to Hegel, in both religion and art it is again the delight of knowledge. The knowledge of religion and art is more intuitive, metaphorical, and embedded in practice and less articulate than that of science (that Hegel understands as philosophy, in particular his own) but it is knowledge too.

If we admit sexuality and sport to the nonserving spheres, it is implausible that we can arrange all of them in a hierarchy of the kind Hegel assumed. If sexuality

---

[1]   My interpretation does not do justice to the many aspects of Hegel's philosophy; I only take up aspects that fit in with my consideration of value spheres. The texts I rely on are the concluding sections of Hegel's *Encyclopedia*.

[2]   In the very first sentence of his *Metaphysics* I, 980a1. Transl. David Ross.

and sport can save life from Sisyphean absurdity, we should expect it of art and religion as well without understanding them as undeveloped forms of science or philosophy. We may well assume that the absolute significance of art and religion includes a kind of knowledge but need not conclude that it is inferior to that of science. It may be just different and on a par with philosophical knowledge.

Let's first ask if art and religion are nonserving spheres at all. Trusting the slogan *l'art pour l'art*, art for art's sake, at least art is. This slogan expresses the view that a work of art, a poem for instance, is "written solely for the poem's sake," as one of its adherents, Edgar Allan Poe, formulated.[3] It clearly marks out that art does not serve an aim outside its own activity, but neither explains why such activity has absolute significance nor what the poem's sake is for which a poem is said to be solely written. The more common view (though no longer called *l'art pour l'art*) that still accords art absolute significance is rather that a poem is written for the sake of something it refers to and that what it refers to is not the poem itself but a realm attainable only by art works. Such a realm is thought to be different from the realm that scientific sentences refer to. Even though a poem may describe the same events scientific sentences describe, the poem is thought to refer to something different from what the scientific sentences refer to. Yet what is the realm art works refer to, if there is such a realm?

Science refers to the world in space and time that it tries to explain. So, if art refers to something different from what science refers to, works of art must refer to something beyond space and time. This is in fact what Plato maintained, conceiving the beyond as ideas. They shine through the beautiful things as a reminder of a timeless beauty beyond the perishable world of destructibility and destruction.[4] Plato's view fits the fact that art and beauty are of absolute significance for many people. No wonder then that it was immensely influential. But attractive though it is for everyone who is discontented with this world (and who is not?), it produces more problems than it solves. Why can reference to a world that is not ours be absolutely significant? What is it that shines through into our world? Does beauty give us a hint that the evil of this world will be compensated in the world beyond? If so, does not art serve justice or religion and thus cannot be considered a nonserving sphere? It is improbable that if we get answers to these questions they will not raise new questions.

Today, anyway, most artists do not like to say their aim is the presentation of beauty or sublimity. Some rather prefer the idea that the task of art is making us perceive something we did not perceive before. This idea does not necessarily contradict the Platonic view, but avoids reference to a Platonic world of ideas. If we follow this line, the problem is: What do the arts make us perceive – possible worlds, action possibilities, true reality? Why or when is it, or what in it is, absolutely significant? And how can it be something that all works of art, a

---

[3] E.A. Poe (1850), "The Poetic Principle," in *Works* vol. III, New York (Redfield) 1850, pp. 1–20, 5.
[4] Plato, *Phaedrus,* 245–50.

piece of music, a sculpture, a novel, despite their differences, make us perceive? The simplest answer would be just to say that they all make us perceive a meaning we did not perceive before, and that it is such a perceiving that is delightful and absolutely significant, even if what we perceive is bad news.[5]

If we try this answer, we'll have to be more specific on what the perceiving of meaning is. What can a work of art make us perceive that a scientific discourse cannot? There is certainly this difference: A scientific discourse makes us understand something by words with a more or less fixed conventional meaning; the work of art presents something by the matter and form or the sounds and lights it consists of or, in the case of literature, by the actions and states it presents by the words it consists of. The scientific discourse signifies by signs that have meaning by linguistic convention; the work of art signifies by its matter and form that lack a conventional meaning. Literature, though like a discourse it uses words, still does not signify by their conventional meaning but by the stories and scenes, ideas, and impressions raised by the use of the words. Like the other art works, it signifies by its matter and form, which are words, yet using them in a way that cancels or restricts their conventional meaning. So works of art signify or represent by nonconventional meaning.

How can works of art signify by nonconventional meaning? How can they tell us something just by their own matter and form? Can't only the signs of our ordinary language have meaning? Perhaps we can say that people mean something when they are intending something, but though artists can intend something, their works certainly cannot. So how can we talk of meaning that is not the meaning of the signs of our ordinary language, nor an intention?

The signs of an ordinary language can only possess meaning because there are signs or events that have meaning for us, whether we want it or not. The most important of such signs are the gestures, utterances, and movements of human beings and animals: laughing and crying and actions like the caress of my hand and a punch in my face. We know them by nature or instinctively. We need them for teaching the meaning of ordinary words. We cannot prevent a cry of pain having meaning and importance for us; we cannot but react to it with pity or *Schadenfreude*. Even if we react with indifference, this has again a specific meaning, because it presupposes the suppression of a more spontaneous reaction like pity. Nor can we prevent ourselves from reacting to a punch in a face with wrath or fear or indignation or malice or the suppression of feeling. Only because children understand the meaning of such actions can they learn a language.[6] Arendt presupposes this immediate knowledge of the meaning of actions when she says that actions open up a common world to the participants. The common world they open up is the world of the shared meaning of the action.[7]

---

5 This is what Aristotle thought, as he regards art as a form of imitation that we enjoy as far as we detect a resemblance between a presentation and what it presents. Cp. Aristotle, *Poetics*, 47a.

6 Wittgenstein made much use of this fact in his later philosophy; cp. my references to him in Chapter 2.

7 See Chapter 9, text to note 13.

Like the movements on which all verbal meaning depends, art works present nonverbal meanings. They include the meanings of sounds, colors, forms, and movements and their combinations, which music and fine arts present. Though not conventional, such meanings are not necessarily natural either. Often they can be understood only in the context of a tradition. In particular the actions presented in literature often have a meaning we can know only if we know their social context. Yet also the patterns of sounds and colors used in music and fine arts can be understandable only if we understand the tradition of music and fine arts. Such a tradition is an evolution from the use of naturally meaningful forms and movements comparable to the evolution of ordinary languages.

Probably, when Hegel suggested art is an imperfect form of science, he had in mind that both of them signify the one by conventional words and concepts that are dependent on conventional meanings and the other by nonconventional signs that may raise images, intuitions, and ideas. Probably he ranked science before art and religion because the propositions it produces by its concepts can be checked for truth, while the products of art and religion cannot. But we neither can nor need to assign superiority to the conceptual and discursive way of presentation. It is more convincing to assume that science and art are two complementary ways of signification; by nonconventional signs we express what cannot be expressed by conventional signs, and vice versa. To take up and modify a little a distinction Wittgenstein made in his theory of logic, in the one way we *show* something that cannot be said and in the other we *say* something that cannot be shown.[8] We may add that only what can be said can be true or false, while what can be shown can only have meaning with more or less importance.

The meanings of art works have been described by Kant as aesthetic ideas that, unlike the meanings of ordinary language, are not concepts but intuitions.[9] Speaking of aesthetic ideas has the advantage of suggesting a criterion of the quality of an art work: It is the better, the richer the ideas are that it produces in the recipient. Talking of meanings has the advantage of suggesting what is common to science or conceptual knowledge and art and how they differ. We should use both the notion of an aesthetic idea and that of a nonconventional meaning and take advantage of both aspects. We may then provisionally define the specific aim of the arts as the presentation of nonconventional meanings or of aesthetic, intuitive ideas and explain that they can have absolute significance if what they present has absolute meaning for the recipient.

But what is this significance? Let us here distinguish between the significance of art in premodern and modern societies. In premodern societies the arts, similarly to the markets, are embedded in tasks and institutions that did

---

[8] Wittgenstein, *Tractatus logico-philosophicus*, Preface and 6.11, 6.12, 6.124, 6.522. He pointed not only to the first side. He even tried to present his *Tractatus* as a work of art that in addition to what it *says* in discursive meaning presents a nonverbal meaning that can only be *shown*. As any nonconceptual meaning, also this meaning is oracular.

[9] Kant, *Kritik der Urteilskraft*, Anmerkung I to §57; 1793, 239f; ed. Vorländer, Hamburg (Meiner) 1959, 200f.

not belong to their sphere. Their role was to praise the powerful and to help produce the emotional effects religion and politics ordered the artists to produce. Alongside the slow and imperfect transformation of the life orders of closed societies into autonomous value spheres, the arts also searched for their specific goal and value. Weber conceived of this process as "rationalization" that "on the territory of the Occident, and only there," brought to their sphere-specific perfection science, the state, the market, and also the arts. He gives examples of what this perfection in the arts consisted of – rational harmonic music, symphonies, operas, the use of the Gothic vault and, more generally, the "rationalization of the entire art."[10]

But this is not yet the emancipation of art from aims that are external to it. Economy was emancipated by Mandeville's and Adam Smith's claim it should follow its own market morality; science, by its claim to pursue truth independently of the dogmas of religion; the state in most parts of Europe never had to be emancipated because since the times of ancient Rome it never stopped considering itself entitled to follow its aim (the value of a pseudo-sphere) of increasing its power.[11] Artists expressed a claim to autonomy when, at the end of the eighteenth century, they proclaimed that art is not to serve society and its expectations but only its own aims. There have been similar demands before, but only in the nineteenth century did they find recognition.

What had changed to favor the autonomy of the arts? As mentioned, Plato ascribed to beauty a special relation to the divine. The Platonic tradition conceived of what art refers to as a timeless, divine realm of ideas. Yet before the end of the eighteenth century, neither philosophers nor artists inferred that the arts were a sphere with specific privileges, for up to this time competence for contact with the divine was assigned to religion; the arts (and philosophy) were allowed to participate in this role only as a servant. Moreover, this competence was considered to be one that proclaimed the truth about the divine in words with conceptual meaning, in the discourse of science and philosophy. However, when religion lost its power over the intellectuals, the arts could claim a privileged role in the presentation of the divine, even though the divine was no longer called so.

When religion lost its power, old problems were felt anew: What are people to do with their lives if they can no longer trust the Holy Scripture or its interpretation by the churches? Does life have meaning at all, if there is, perhaps, no God? As religion lost authority, art won autonomy. Because art presents nonconventional meanings, it became the more important the more the discursive meaning presented by salvation religion, that is, its truth, lost credibility.

---

[10] On the first pages of his Introduction to his *Collected Essays to the Sociology of Religion*.

[11] This shows in the fact that the church had to struggle for its emancipation from the state, not the other way round, when it claimed the right to nominate popes and bishops. Cp. Harold Berman, *Law and Revolution*.

It claimed competence for the realm religion had maintained competence for, though art did not aim at expressing ideas in conceptual discourse but only in nonconventional meaning. Notwithstanding this difference, art and religion became competitors, as both of them claim the same competence. This does not exclude that an artist presents his meanings as complements to the salvation idea, but it makes it rare. And even then the artist will understand the message of religion as something that cannot be expressed in conceptual discourse, but only metaphorically or allegorically. By this view she will reject the former claim of religion to express a truth about the divine in conceptual language that might compete with science.

This claim of religion was even more challenged by science. Science, as I've tried to show, has made it impossible to accept the nonmetaphorical claim of religion that there is a salvation from our troubles by immortal life either in bliss and eternal punishment for those who miss the chance of salvation. Liberal theologians have recognized this fact and withdrawn to the position that the tales of salvation and resurrection have to be understood metaphorically, in a deeper nonconceptual meaning. They assigned to religion the same sphere that art expresses its messages in. According to liberal theologians, religion can be distinguished from art only by the specific message of promise and consolation but not by the nonconceptual way that excludes truth claims.

Therefore, the competition of religion and autonomous art is not only a competition for the attention of the public. Such vying, as Weber has remarked,[12] is implied by the fact that the value spheres offer alternative ways of living among which modern individuals have to choose. Rather, religion and the arts raise competing *validity* claims, either in different modes of expression or the same nonconceptual mode. The only thing religion might claim to be capable of that art is not is that it promises men their salvation in an ordinary, nonmetaphorical sense. But this is just what is incompatible with science.

The meaning art presents can concern very different things while salvation religion only turns around salvation. But it always deals with how to see or feel or be in the world, and this can, though need not, have absolute meaning in the sense of freeing life from absurdity. So it competes with religion in its claims on the meaning of life, but is superior to it, both because of the broader scope of meanings it offers and in its clarity as to the mode of expression, which it knows to be necessarily in nonconceptual signs. It shares this property with prerevelation religions they too express what they express in the nonconceptual mode that implies validity claims but excludes truth claims. This means that art is necessarily oracular. Because it is nonconceptual, it raises a lot of ideas and intuitions that stimulate but cannot be fixed in concepts; hence, like the ancient oracles its meaning has many dimensions. Its oracularity radicalizes its nonconceptuality and probably has been another reason for Hegel's giving superiority

---

[12] E.g., Weber, *Wissenschaft als Beruf*, ed. Kröner, 330; *Zwischenbetrachtung* 441f.

to philosophy. But this preference sprang from the prejudice that life has an unambiguous meaning. (Maybe Hegel would reply that his concepts are not fixed but dialectical and therefore can even express ambiguity.)

I conclude that just as the state is only a historical way to help adjudicate conflicting claims, so salvation religion is only a historical way to present meaning in life. Just as the state has arrogated tasks of administration and justice that are better performed and perfected on the one hand by the sphere of justice and on the other by the media and other spheres that can deal with the tasks of administration themselves, so salvation religion has arrogated the intellectual task of presenting and exploring meaning, but also the communal task of celebrating crucial events in life like birth, death, marriage, and remembering the past. Yet again these tasks might be better performed by activities that are not biased by their commitment to historical prejudice, as salvation religions are. On the one hand they are better performed by the arts; on the other hand by communities that may use the transmitted religious forms, but without understanding the forms conceptually.

However, if what salvation religions perform today were performed by the arts and by committed communities without the beliefs, ceremonies, and hierarchies for which religions are known, this would not be the death of religion. For religion is not exhausted by these functions. First, there are people, called religious virtuosi by Weber,[13] who are capable of feeling at one with, or close to, the universe or its essence or creator, and finding and spreading deep satisfaction and peace by such feeling. For them the forms that religious institutions impose on religious activities and states are negligible crutches for those who lack religious virtuosity. It is highly improbable, and not desirable, that such virtuosity will ever die out. It is an activity one can show extraordinariness in, even though it may require a kind of modesty that at first sight can seem incompatible with any ambition.

Second, there are certainly a greater number of people who lack both religious and artistic virtuosity and still wonder at and admire the universe, in spite of all its horrors produced by nature and humans. Their admiration can be free of consent to the facts of the universe but still deep and mixed with an oracular hope that guides their life. It is difficult to ascribe them religious activities or states, as their attitude to the world that might be called religious does not consist in separate states or activities but accompanies their ordinary states and activities. Hence, it is difficult to consider their religion as a value sphere, much less to think of its activities as ones that can become a profession. Yet it is something for which there can and need to be schooling and learning, and the passage from the religious nonvirtuosi to the virtuosi is smooth. Though it is a little misleading to consider the virtuosi a profession, as they stop being virtuosi

---

[13] Weber, *Einleitung in die Wirtschaftsethik der Weltreligionen*, in *Gesammelte Aufsätze zur Religionssoziologie*, 237–75, ed. Kröner, 411.

when they earn money by it, it is not false either, considering the original meaning of the term (which means avowing of one's being called).

So we should recognize religion as a value sphere aiming at an irreducible value. A society that aims at autonomy and equal liberty needs to protect and respect this sphere no less than those of science and art. Nonetheless, religion in the institutional forms that prevail today, which claims infallibility and maintains that religious attitudes and beliefs can be formulated and prescribed in conceptual language, cannot be respected. Its death would be the renaissance of true religion.

Chapter 18

Sport

HEGEL WANTED TO ADMIT ONLY SUCH NONSERVING ACTIVITIES AS enact reason or judgment, recognizing only religion, art, and science. This is probably also true of Weber, but he rightly presumed that human sexual activities often differ enough from animal ones by their inclusion of judgment. Yet there is another class of activities that both have a significance that saves life from Sisyphean absurdity and meet the definition of a value sphere. They require judgment, offer schooling, and can become a profession with perfection standards. These are the activities of sport. They have been performed in many premodern societies, in ancient China, Persia, Egypt, Greece, Rome, Mexico, and other ones. They have often been embedded in religious rituals, but today we can see that they aim at an irreducible value not aimed at another sphere. Sport emancipated itself from political and religious dependency only in the nineteenth century, though no less than science and art (and the media and justice enforcement in the serving spheres), it is in great danger of subjection to stronger spheres.

Today, sport has become a field for enacting extraordinariness, perhaps the field for extraordinariness par excellence. Like the value of religion, art, science, and eroticism, the value of sport is clear for the adherents and remains closed for the value-blind. It attracts a community who develop standards of excellence that do not depend on the will of the majority but spring from the nature of the sport activity, just as the communities of scientists and artists develop standards of excellence that do not depend on the will of the majority but spring from the nature of science and art. It unites a spectrum of different sports, from chase to chess, just as science, art, religion, and eroticism unite a spectrum of sciences, arts, religions, and (as we'll see) forms of eroticism. The different sports are as different from each other as the different sciences and arts are, but they are united by a family resemblance that unambiguously marks them off from art and science and other value spheres.

What distinguishes sport from other value spheres and prevented its rec-ognition as an irreducible value is its cultivation of activities that depend on the strength of the body, nerves and brain included. This fact has been taken for proof that sport is not a specifically human activity. The premise was that bodily activity is animal and the specifically human coincides with actions and passions of the mind rather than the body. If this were true, we should not recognize excellence in sport as extraordinariness, because extraordinari-ness is enacted by judgment or the trinity of reason, free will, and self, which animals are incapable of enacting. But though sport is the cultivation of bodily activities, they still are specifically human. They are cultivated in a specifically human form inaccessible for animals, namely, as activities that are performed and enjoyed for their own sake, independent of their contribution to the goals of everyday life or to the aims of other value spheres. Kant describes the essence of beauty as "purposiveness without purpose."[1] His idea is that things are beau-tiful if their parts are well organized though not organized for some use. The idea fits the way sport cultivates bodily activity: purposively, because they aim at victory, but in this purposiveness for no use.

Playfulness or detachment from the ordinary life is a necessary condition of all sport. Another is that it is competitive. Individuals or teams fight against one another or against nature to prove their superiority in a particular field of mastering one's own body, nerves and brain, yet only for play. These properties belong to the specific attraction of sport that is exploited and undermined by the profit and prestige interest of business and politics. Originally, to be a sport champion is attractive because sport is attractive, not because it brings money to the champion.

For our interest in extraordinariness the fact that mankind has produced sportive activities is a marvelous confirmation of the Cartesian conception of the self. Why should maximizers of happiness subject themselves to the pain of training? How short (if it comes at all) is the moment of victory and how long the hardship of exercises! Why should rational beings whose rationality is not imbued with the arbitrariness of free will open up a dimension so obvi-ously detached from ordinary life? How can people sacrifice their lives for what is but a play, not "really" to be taken seriously, though the sport fan may die for it? It is the point of sport not to be taken seriously by the established standards of seriousness. It is this very character by which sport escaped the attention of theorists classifying value and analyzing society. Yet by this char-acter, sport testifies the power and existential importance of men's craving for self-assertion and extraordinariness. If sport did not exist, the Cartesian could invent it.

Success in most kinds of sport does not only depend on effort, but also on luck. Therefore, sport champions challenge not only the opponent, but also fate.

---

[1] Kant, *Critique of Judgment*, trans. J. H. Bernard, New York (Macmillan), 1951, §§V–VIII, §17.

In competition, individuals or teams pit their individual or group selves against each other. In challenging fate, they pit their selves against an imagined power of fate. We need not presuppose a Cartesian self to explain how individuals and groups challenge each other. But it is difficult to explain how they can challenge fate if we do not presuppose a self that distances itself from anything that does not belong to its capacity of deciding on whether to say no or yes to any kind of possibility. The attraction of gambling is often blamed for its irrationality, and it is irrational to bet against the odds. But it is one of the rare moments when we feel our selves in its pure form of the power of judgment that distances itself from everything that might influence it and exerts its absolute freedom to say no or yes to possibilities, even to possibilities that are unlikely to come true. Sport shares an element of gambling, and this enhances its attraction, in particular for the many who are not active in sport but participate in it as fans.

The worldwide enthusiasm for sport is one of the contemporary phenomena we may pin our hopes on. Sport adds to the most recognized fields of excellence in science, politics, and arts a very broad and easily accessible field that unites competitiveness and mutual recognition. It might even replace competition by weapons for a competition that is much more appropriate to the human mind. Yet it would be a disaster if it was subordinated to this aim of politics, just as it is alarming that it has been so strongly subordinated to the aims of economy. Sport will lose its attraction if it is not exerted for its own sake.

Chapter 19

Latin and Absolute Love

L OVE CAN BE DIFFERENT IN QUALITY AND POWER OF SAVING LIFE
from Sisyphean absurdity. There is the perfection of a flirt and of a life-
long passion, as there are the different perfections of different sports.
Nonetheless, they aim at the same value of devotion to a person. In the "organic
cycle of rural existence," as Weber says, sexuality is something "naturally given."[1]
Yet the naturally given is neither a life order nor a value sphere. For sexuality to
become a value sphere, it needs to be understood as something worth living for.
Weber seems to assume that sooner or later the specific value of sexuality will be
detected. But most of the time, most people enjoy sexuality without recognizing
in it a specific value with specific perfection standards. Prostitution belongs to
the oldest professions, but this warrants recognition as a value, neither to sex nor
to prostitution. For sexuality to become a value sphere with a recognized value
a culture of eroticism needs to arise. Such a culture requires conditions that can
vary and produce different cultures depending on historical conditions.

Some conditions are required for any culture of eroticism to arise. There can
be no culture of eroticism if a society shows no attention to the quality of passions or teaches its members to respond to them as to a purely physical affection,
as if the body was occupied by a virus or demon to be eliminated by pills or rituals. The culture also will be hindered or restricted if society favors attitudes and
characters that do not well fit in with cultivating love. A society that cultivates
sobriety, as the Romans did, will not give much importance to love. Nor can a
culture of passion arise unless at least tacitly a power of freely responding to a
passion is ascribed to humans, even though on a theoretical level freedom of the
will is denied. Only then is there room for the idea of a perfectibility of responses
to passions. Moreover, lover and beloved one need to be morally equal.

---

[1]   Weber, *Zwischenbetrachtung*, 558; ed. Kröner, 466.

Even though in ancient Rome a culture of eroticism developed that is documented in wonderful love poems, it never presented love as a value one might sacrifice one's life for. This happened in the culture that developed in eighteenth- and nineteenth-century Europe and at some other times at courts and in social circles in other high civilizations. As documented in literature, songs, and operas, actions and passions ridiculous from a sober point of view have been celebrated as the only possible thing to do and feel. Men and women sacrifice to their love all that to the sober seems valuable. Women, and sometimes also men, are presented as the objects of a love that raises the lover beyond the ordinary. Love is presented as an absolute value superior to the values of spheres like the family, the state, religion, or business. Let us call this kind of love absolute love, and the love or sexuality cultivated in ancient Rome and other civilizations that did not celebrate absolute love, Latin love.

Today, we have a culture of Latin love rather than absolute love. We need not ask whether there will or should be the sphere of sexuality in a modern society that realizes sphere autonomy. There will, because sex under nearly any form is too attractive as to be eliminable, and there should be, because eliminating it by medical or any other intervention would be a human rights violation. Nor need we to ask if there will or should be a sphere of sexuality that includes Latin love. If the standard of living does not drop too low, there will be Latin love, and there is no reason why it shouldn't. There is even a positive reason that it should. Latin love knows its perfection standards and thus offers another opportunity for extraordinariness. Will there be a profession of Latin love? Certainly not in the usual sense of a profession, but people can and do specialize in Latin love.

What we need to ask is if there can and should be a sphere of sexuality that includes absolute love. We may well doubt if there should be. In the nineteenth and the beginning of the twentieth centuries, absolute love was part of a culture that had lost trust in the meaning offered by salvation religion. Love, along with art and political ideas like nationalism and communism, promised an alternative. Absolute love became a new evangel. It was considered the hub of life, the inexhaustible spring that gives meaning to life. But its news is somewhat less good news than that of the salvation evangel, as it does not free human life from suffering. Absolute love gives unshakeable meaning at the price of an absolute sacrifice, the sacrifice of one's life and the willingness to suffer. The stories of absolute love are tragedies. Happy endings play it down. But is a passion, and that is what absolute love has been, really worth sacrificing our life? True, the evangel of absolute love is superior to that of salvation as far as it frees the religious answer to the meaning of life from its self-centered obsession with one's own salvation. But are there not causes that have a more legitimate title to claiming our life?

I think there are. The world is so full of injustice that the fight for justice has a greater claim to sacrifices than the passion of absolute love. Adorno said that "it is barbaric to write a poem after Auschwitz."[2] This I think is wrong, but it is true that after Auschwitz the passion of absolute love once celebrated in poems can and should no longer have its former meaning.

But before concluding that the sphere of sexuality should not include absolute love, let us ask whether it could rise from its ashes. This seems improbable. It is not just a moral postulate today that justice is a cause worthier of claiming sacrifice than love. Rather, it is a feeling steeped in the passion of anger at the injustice done by the powerful. The excitement of erotic love, if taken for a cause worth sacrificing a life, is incompatible with the sentiments aroused by the knowledge of contemporary moral disasters. Formerly, such sentiments have often been aroused in the observers of injustice done to other people; the victims had been so much crushed that they were incapable of responding with rebellion. Today, they are also aroused in the victims. This warrants that they will not be ineffective.

Moreover, for love between man and woman to become absolute, it is necessary that women are both recognized as morally equivalent to men and less involved in the affairs of the ordinary world than men. If they are involved, they are partners and competitors, but not objects of veneration. Correspondingly, men can be objects of female veneration only as long as they are felt to be on the same level as women and not competitors in the ordinary world. These conditions seem absent in contemporary modern society.

But we do not only find conditions that exclude absolute love. There are also facts that favor it, although in a form that is very different from that of nineteenth-century absolute love. People need active and passive love; they want to love and be loved. The love they need is not only sexual excitation and satisfaction but also a recognition that encompasses the whole undivided individual and does not distinguish between activities we are good at and those we are not. Yet the importance of value spheres in modernity reduces the chance of receiving undivided and unconditional recognition.[3] Undivided unconditional recognition is received in love and close friendship. Because the family is losing importance as the place of sexual love, it also is losing importance as the place of giving and receiving unconditional recognition. Close friendship is impeded by the separation of spheres as well. Therefore, love becomes the most important sphere for undivided recognition. But to receive unconditional recognition one must give unconditionally. We recognize someone as a person that merits undivided recognition as a whole person irrespective of the specific capabilities she can excel

---

[2] Adorno, "Kulturkritik und Gesellschaft," in *Gesammelte Schriften*, Bd. 10.1. Frankfurt (Suhrkamp) 1980, 11–30, 30. Engl. transl. Samuel and Shierry Weber, *Prisms*, 19.

[3] Carl Schmitt rejected liberalism and sphere autonomy for this reason. Cp. Chapter 23. We may describe his response to the problem by the inversion of a later popular slogan: "Make war not love!" because he looked for undivided recognition, not in love but in politics that he defined as the sphere of irreconcilable opposition of friend and foe.

or fail in only if she does something that proves that she can give others her own undivided and unconditional help.

This condition has a paradoxical result. We do not give unconditionally if we expect to receive unconditional recognition. Giving unconditionally excludes this expectation, because reciprocity would be a condition for giving. Hence, the desire for receiving unconditional recognition cannot be satisfied unless it turns into the will to give unconditionally, even though it may be that we give unconditionally and still retain some hope of receiving unconditional recognition. Yet the will to give unconditionally is no passive love, nor a passion of love. It is the love of saints and heroes.

So, if it is true that people look for unconditional recognition and the former places for receiving it have lost significance, we can infer that if love becomes important as the place for undivided recognition, it needs to change its character. To take on the new role, it can no longer be a sexual passion but needs to be active love, an activity of giving love without expecting sexual or any other reciprocity. It will be the overflowing goodness of saints rather than the love of nineteenth-century opera heroes.

Can we empirically confirm this inference? We can. Look at Janusz Korczak, the Polish pedagogue who followed his Jewish orphans to Treblinka to be murdered with them. He acted for justice, but not only for justice. Justice did not demand of him to follow his orphans into the extermination camp. Korczak's action is an act of absolute love. Probably he did not even intend to receive undivided recognition as a person. The justly unconditional admiration and public praise of him can be understood as preparing or creating an unnoticed culture of absolute love.

Another example are the actions of Rüdiger Nehberg, a baker from Hamburg, who risked his life for spectacular adventures that stirred the international public to take notice of the genocide threatening the Yanomami Indians in Brazil and of the female genital mutilation practiced in some African Muslim societies. Again, he acted for the cause of justice, but justice did not demand his actions. Unlike Janusz Korczak, Nehberg could enjoy his actions as adventures, although his actions were extremely risky and might easily have killed him (and did kill a companion of his); perhaps even the expectation of receiving recognition for his whole person was not unimportant for him. Yet common to Korczak and Nehberg is that their actions were a sacrifice to particular individuals. It was not justice but the attachment to particular individuals that they felt made their actions necessary. This attachment is not sexual love, but a form of absolute love. Like Korczak, Nehberg is justly unconditionally admired not only for what he did in a specific sphere but as an undivided person.

Probably quite a few of the self-sacrificing actions of dissidents in totalitarian and fundamentalist regimes, and of defenders of the rights of minorities, are not only done for the sake of justice, but also for absolute love, for the will to give unconditionally, and if so, the agents must be unconditionally recognized as the admirable persons they are. What enables them to their deeds is not their dedication to the values of justice or liberty, which is only a necessary condition, but an unconditional passion caused, like the absolute love of former times, by the experience of particular events. The passion is motivated by the love for persons. It springs not only from moral considerations but from the will to do, for those one likes, what is best for them. Absolute love retains the arbitrariness of sexual love in the choice of its objects. Even though it does not spring from a sexual interest, it springs from an emotion that cannot motivate to do good to people or projects one does not like. Although its actions must not transgress the rules of justice, it is not directed by principles of justice. The gratification of acts of absolute love is not sexual but it still is a sensual pleasure.

Because of the lack of a sexual motivation we may doubt if we can or should recognize self-sacrificing actions like that of Korczak or of human-rights fighters as acts of absolute love. But even the eroticism Weber described is an irreducible value not because of "erotic intoxication" or ecstasy[4] but of what he called the "infinitude of devotion."[5] Absolute love, like other forms of love, is an irreducible value because it is a devotion to a person; it differs from them not only by its nonsexual form but also by the infinitude of its devotion. If this is true, there is today a form of absolute love and a culture that celebrates it, though with insufficient understanding of its own nature.

Unlike the absolute love of the nineteenth century, the actions of absolute love or devotion we can observe in contemporary society are not abated but abetted by the prevailing indignation at injustice. This sentiment spurs to giving unconditionally. We may even say that commitment to particular people who are hindered from defending themselves against injustice is the prevailing contemporary form of absolute love, though there certainly are also actions of absolute love today that are not spurred by indignation at injustice. It is, moreover, a consciously political form of love that can be reciprocated and is not restricted to the West at all.[6]

It is amazing and admirable that today's society has developed a sphere in which absolute love can flourish, even though it has remained unnoticed. Its demands cannot be met by many people, yet the demands of former absolutes have also been an option only for the few. What is necessary for a culture of

---

4   Weber, *Zwischenbetrachtung*, 562; ed. Kröner, 471.
5   Ibid. 560; ed. Kröner, 468 ("Grenzenlosigkeit der Hingabe").
6   It has been described by V. S. Naipaul, *India*, 333–5, in his presentation of the ex-communist Debu's "almost mystical experience of receiving the love of the people" (335). Naipaul also is aware of the rage that spreads in non-Western civilizations at the injustice done them by Western colonization, a phenomenon connected, as he says, with a "general awakening" to history (ibid. 420, cp. 444, 459, and 461). Bernard Lewis, in his paper on the "Roots of Muslim Rage," finds the same rage at injustice in Muslim countries, though he argues that it should not be addressed to the West but to those politicians in Muslim countries who misapplied Western models without regard to their own traditions.

absolute love to flourish is not that everyone can follow its demands, but that many recognize it as an activity that gives meaning to life, a meaning as absolute as this love is. By contrast, if society lacks a sphere of absolute love, it lacks the means to solve the problem of how and where to give unconditionally. Paradoxically enough, frustration of even the will to give unconditionally can turn into hatred and destruction.

Part V

A Self-Understanding
Not Only
for the West

Don't trust truth if it's trivial.
Xun ze, 250 BC

I have discussed value spheres, as they are the institutions modernity centers on. The prevailing Lockean conception of the self and the allied utilitarian approach fails to take account of both their destructive and constructive potential. Thus, they have contributed to the decline of the West, while following the Cartesian conception might give it new life. Theorists can overrate the social effects of conceptions, as concepts are their medium, but they also can underrate them, as they are eager not to fall victim to the prejudices of their profession. Conceptions are a factor in social dynamics; moreover, they are a factor we can change. The advertising industry exploits this possibility without regard to truth and moral rightness. Philosophy should do with regard.

We have found a list of value spheres that form a fairly broad spectrum of possibilities for enacting the ambition of extraordinariness inextricably connected with the self. Establishing such a system would strengthen constructive powers. It also would realize the idea of sphere autonomy that includes and is included by the idea of individual autonomy, since autonomous spheres presuppose autonomous individuals and individual autonomy needs spheres for individuals to develop their capabilities. It would redeem the promise of modernity, everyone's equal right to liberty, as the spectrum is broad enough to offer everyone an opportunity for choosing a life they think suits them. Yet of course, there are a lot of objections to the project. I'll consider what I think are the most important among them.

Chapter 20

Is the Core Idea of Modernity
Realizable At All?

THE CORE IDEA OF MODERNITY, UNIVERSAL LIBERTY, ACCORDS everyone an equal right to use their capabilities the way they want to. It has always raised doubts if it is realizable. For no society can survive without tuning the intentions and interests of its members. The traditional idea, realized in all pre- and post-modern societies, is that tuning requires masters and morality. The revolutionary idea of the economists was that the market replaces them. Meanwhile we know that markets do not suffice; so, are we not to return to the masters and drop the idea of universal liberty?

Actually, universal or equal liberty is often understood in an illusionary way as a right of self-determination, namely, as a right to decide on one's life without regard to other people. Yet though it includes the individual's right to her private affairs, most parts of our lives are interwoven with public affairs. So to understand the right to self-determination as the right to choose one's life in an isolation in which one might be unmolested by other people would be an illusion. Rather, in the first place, it is the equal right of everyone to participate in the process by which the conditions of society are fixed and transformed from a development individuals are dependent on to one they rule in cooperation. Such a process does not only comprehend political decisions but includes those in all serving value spheres. Hence, equal liberty implies the right to equal participation in any serving sphere.

Yet we meet another objection when we consider how participation in the spheres is performed. People are different in their capabilities and interests; so some will put more ambition and talent in, say, economic or political activities and be luckier than others and will dominate the sphere and, possibly, society. Liberty gives them a right to do so, but the result will be inequality, and inequality will reduce liberty for those who have become poor or weak. Hence, equal or universal liberty is inconsistent. Its equality causes inequality and its liberty suppression. The idea of value spheres radicalizes equal liberty by stimulating everyone to use their special talents, and this even in the most extraordinary way possible. Hence, it is equally inconsistent, and so is modernity.

The answer to the objection is that the institution of value spheres projected here allows a clear distinction between spheres of liberty and spheres of equality. The serving spheres are those of equality, though not of a strict one; the nonserving ones are the spheres of liberty and inequality. If you are better in physics or singing, I may envy you but have no right to complain. But if you are superior in economy, politics, the media, technology, or biological reproduction, then you have a power I may complain of. Despite familiar liberal ideas of liberty, the serving spheres need to restrict liberty.

Let's start with the sphere of technology. Everyone should have the right to excel as a technician, but as soon as some technicians use their superior power to manipulate or coerce the rest, this is illegitimate because it restricts their equal liberty. But may we also prevent the concentration of technological power in a few technicians to protect equal liberty, or prevent the use of genetic engineering for enhancing capabilities if it is not open to everyone? May we forbid the rich to enhance the capabilities of their children even though they have never done injustice? I think we ought to, but it is not easy to find reasons for this intuition of justice. Let's first turn to politics and economy.

Inherited privilege or privilege attained by immoral means is obviously unjust. Yet what is wrong with political superiority, that is, superiority in deciding on public affairs that is not based on inheritance or crime but superior talent and ambition? There is agreement that the equal human right of everyone to equally participate in deciding on public affairs does not exclude someone's right to command, provided everyone has an equal chance to be trusted with such a right. So if political inequality springs from unequal talent or ambition, what's wrong with it?

A first answer will depend on two variables; first, on what the greater political power is used for, and second, on why the politically less ambitious are less ambitious. If unequal political power is used to enhance the political interests and capabilities of the politically less ambitious, it is legitimate, as it is used for abolishing political inequality. The more it is used for maintaining existing political inequality, the less it is legitimate. Similarly, if the politically less ambitious are less ambitious for lack of information, education, or other social factors that make them apathetic, then political inequality, even though not based on privilege, will be illegitimate. But political inequality is legitimate if it is based on the deliberate and informed choice of the politically less ambitious. The presumption is that individuals need urgent reasons for renouncing their right to equally participate in deciding on public affairs. As politics is the realm of public affairs and public affairs are what concern everyone, everyone ought to participate unless they have been well informed when they decided against their equal participation. Only then may political equality, required by the nature of public affairs, be lessened.

Inequality in information is unavoidable; we even expect some to become better informed so they may inform us. Yet it is an obvious offense of equality if unequal information is used for manipulating people's beliefs, as happens today. Therefore, the media must not be left to the powers of the market. Independence of concerned journalists and competition of the media must be understood as the basis of both liberty and equality and promoted by measures of the kind suggested previously.[1] This is a grave restriction of the liberty of businessmen and publishers, but it is necessary for realizing political equality.

If this is true, equal liberty, the ideal of modernity, and, hence, modernity itself, cannot be realized if equality is conceived as equality before the law only, which has been understood as formal equality. Rather, it requires a kind of material equality that includes the right of everyone to education and financial security that allows them to articulate and defend their views and interests with equal force. But is this right not incompatible with liberty? In fact, it has been rejected by the classical liberal theorists, and it restricts the liberty of the strong. How can such material equality be justified? If the rich have acquired their riches only by honest means; if they do not meddle with politics and suppress no one; if they just enjoy and use their riches for buying what they can buy, perhaps looking down upon the poor – what's wrong with that?

Let me first point out why markets can easily become an object of hate and why it would nevertheless be unjust to abolish them for realizing the necessary material equality. In market societies, the poor are as much dependent on those who rule the market as the politically powerless are dependent on the politically powerful. Nobody loves dependence. Yet economic dependence is often felt to be even more humiliating than political dependence, because economic inequality can sometimes be explained by greater effort, whereas political inequality is often inherited. Some people start life in similar conditions and end the one rich and the other poor. Even though the poor might say the rich were luckier, they will often blame themselves for having failed. At the same time they will suspect the rich of using unfair means that the poor have been too virtuous to use. Consequently they will feel entitled to hate them. Yet are they?

Not all rich people use unfair means. If the economic difference is not extreme, economic superiority unblemished by unfair means is not illegitimate. Declaring any economic difference illegitimate commits us to the abolition of markets. With them a sphere of activities would be abolished which, as any other one, is a sphere of moral ambivalence, but at the same time a sphere that offers opportunities for exerting one's reason, will, and self. Abolishing it even though it is subordinated to the rules of justice is an illegitimate restriction of men's liberty.

[1] In Chapter 15.

One might argue that it is a negligible restriction, as men will still find opportunity enough for asserting their self in other value spheres. But if markets are subjected to a just embedding, they are just, and their prohibition is unjust. Further, to the extent that individuals are free to decide on the allocation of resources and the evaluation of work, market decisions take over part of the political decision making in a more immediate and democratic form. The abolition of markets would funnel decisions on public affairs into channels that do not admit the currents that spring from individuals' views and wants concerning what should be produced and how work should be rewarded. Yet such views and wants are an invaluable source for finding the best means to produce a flourishing and just society. Abolishing the market rather than taming it would be a mistake for reasons of both efficiency and justice. It would be stupid and unjust.

So let's consider it settled that economic inequality that is neither extreme nor blemished by unfair means is legitimate. But when is inequality extreme? And how can extreme inequality be illegitimate if it is legitimate when it is not extreme? There is no puzzle here. Inequality is extreme if the poor or weak cannot participate in deciding on how to use natural resources like land and fresh water, while the rich possess or consume them abundantly. Such inequality is illegitimate because natural resources are the common property of mankind. No one has produced them; they are the things men find in nature; hence, no one has a privilege to exclude others from their use and the decisions on how to use them. If economic differences are called extreme, what is meant is that the extremely rich, whether blemished by unfair means or not, consume land and fresh water and other natural resources abundantly and thereby exclude the very poor from equally participating in decisions on the use of the common property of mankind.[2] We may define a society of extreme inequality as one that excludes the very poor from the equal right to participate in the decisions on the use of natural resources.

Some philosophers have argued that those who are the first to use natural resources have the right to appropriate and bequeath them to whom they like. Yet this argument serves too obviously the interest of the *beati possidentes* to be taken seriously. There should be a better reason for according someone the privilege of appropriating a common property. Most medieval philosophers considered natural resources goods that can never become private property and may be left to someone only as a trust to a custodian. John Locke asserted that individuals may appropriate natural resources, but only by "mixing" their labor with it. His idea was that only if one enhances the value of the resource is she entitled to appropriate it. He explicated this condition by the proviso that appropriation is legitimate only "where there is enough, and as good left in common

---

[2]   For statistics on the relations between the rich and the poor see Shaohua Chen and Martin Ravallion, "How Have the World's Poorest Fared since the Early 1980s?," S. 153.

for others."³ This proviso is offended when economic differences are "extreme": They present a distribution that does not leave "enough, and as good" natural resources for the poor.

Still today, even neo-liberals uphold Locke's proviso. One of them, Nozick, argued,

> a person may not appropriate the only water hole in a desert and charge what he will. Nor may he charge what he will if he possesses one, and unfortunately it happens that all the water holes in the desert dry up, except for his. This unfortunate circumstance, admittedly no fault of his, brings into operation the Lockean proviso and limits his property rights. Similarly, an owner's property right in the only island in an area does not allow him to order a castaway from a shipwreck off his island as a trespasser, for this would violate the Lockean proviso.⁴

One would expect from this argument the conclusion that, because without political intervention water will soon be as scarce as in a desert and life for the poor worse than that of a castaway, political intervention will be necessary. But Nozick, rather, confessed to "believe that the free operation of the market system will not actually run afoul of the Lockean proviso ... the proviso will not ... provide a significant opportunity for future state action."⁵ Maybe *state* action will not be necessary, but political action will. In any case, Nozick confirms our answer to when economic inequality is extreme: when the rich, by their possession of land and other natural resources, exclude the poor from equal participation in deciding on the use of natural resources. Hence, it is an imperative of justice to impose restrictions on the rich that secure to the poor an equal right in the decisions on the use of natural resources. Only such a right secures equal access to the use of natural resources.

So although economic superiority, if unblemished by unfair means, is in principle legitimate, there is the restriction not to exclude the poor from equal access to the natural resources. The restriction is grave, since it requires from the institutions for the enforcement of justice radical redistributive actions. Equal access to natural resources cannot be secured to everyone by giving them a piece of land or a sum of money that represents their part in the common property of natural resources, although some authors think this possible.⁶ It can only be secured by the material conditions that enable everyone to participate in the decisions on the use of common resources (even though they may refuse participation). To such conditions belongs an education that enables them to stand up for their views and interests. This requires more than teaching them

---

³   Locke, *Two Treatises of Government* I, §27.
⁴   Robert Nozick, *Anarchy, State, and Utopia*, 180f.
⁵   Ibid. 182.
⁶   For arguments, see Hillel Steiner, *An Essay on Rights*, 270–3. See my comments in *Gleiche Freiheit*, 125–32.

reading, writing, and arithmetic, though many of the poor are even excluded from learning these basics. It requires schools that are expensive and must be financed by those who up to now have enjoyed the advantage of a privileged access to natural resources. Therefore, attacking extreme economic inequality will lead to a considerable reduction of economic inequality.

Consideration of scarce natural resources that gives us the criterion of when economic differences are extreme and why they are illegitimate explains as well when and why concentration of technological power is illegitimate. Such concentration allows the specialist to exclude laypersons from deciding on the use of the natural resources, hence is a case of extreme inequality that justice enforcement has to prevent. The same criterion shows why the use of biotech for enhancing capabilities is illegitimate as long as it is not equally open to everyone. It would exacerbate existing inequalities to a degree that would enable the powerful to exclude the rest from deciding on the use of the natural resources. We may well infer that, since most people today are excluded from participating in decisions on the use of natural resources, we are all living in extreme inequality. This is true, though we should still further distinguish between societies where, in addition to such violation of participation rights, people are even excluded from consuming most of the natural resources necessary for life.

The criterion also shows why and when differences in natural reproduction are illegitimate. It is possible for both families and more comprehensive collectives, like nations, religions, or civilizations, to put their efforts in natural reproduction rather than in developing capabilities. At least for some time, they will not starve because of overpopulation. That time can suffice for rendering life conditions difficult for groups that do not neglect the cultivation of capabilities, when their use of natural resources is restricted by the swelling numbers of those more active in reproduction. Yet for the same reasons that it is unjust that the rich appropriate an overproportional part of the common property of natural resources, it is unjust if those rich with children do.

Most individuals and families lack the inclination to reproduce for the sake of reproduction; rather, it is the fear of lacking support in old age or leaving nothing behind when dying that pushes them to procreating many children; this source will dry out if inequality is no longer extreme. But ideologies and states, for increasing their power, can have an interest in high reproduction rates among their subjects; so it is important to recognize the illegitimacy of this interest.

Inequality is particularly dangerous, though difficult to declare illegitimate, if it springs from unequal efforts that are allied with equal ethnicity. Any ambition of extraordinariness makes visible the differences between men. On the market, this ambition makes also visible the differences between groups and ethnicities and reinforces or creates aggressions against the more successful. People living outside their original countries, like the Jews, Chinese, Indians, Koreans, and a bunch of ethnicities less well known for their economic self-assertion have proved their particular economic gifts and the role of culture in economic development.[7] They attract hate rather than admiration.[8] Differences in economic self-assertion divide all existing societies into classes and produce deep conflicts everywhere. If such divisions combine with ethnic ones, somber fates are programmed. How can such economic inequality be illegitimate if it is clearly based on proportionate unequal efforts?

It is not only envy that enrages the economically disadvantaged against the successful. It is also the idea that they are deprived of their part in the use of natural resources. Economic success grants privileged access to natural resources, but these are rightly considered to be the common property of mankind. Economically successful minorities whose success is due to their greater efforts still commit injustice if they attain privileged access to the common resources. This they do if they control the economy. Moreover, they control access not only to the natural resources but also to the cultural ones that also are common property. Therefore, those who are economically inferior are justified to demand change, though of course this does not justify pogroms. One way to secure them equal access to the common property of natural and intellectual resources is by special programs of affirmative action and economic promotion.[9]

There is no demand for material equality in the nonserving value spheres. Such equality has no point where other individuals cannot be threatened in their claims to be free to assert themselves and strive for extraordinariness. Attaining values of the nonserving spheres does not threaten less-excellent people in their access to the natural resources and other conditions for survival. Formal equality, equality before the law, of course is to be observed in any sphere. But this is less difficult to realize and to justify than the material equality that has to be respected in the serving spheres.

---

7   Underlined by Gunnar Myrdal, *Asian Drama*, New York (Pantheon) 1968, and Lawrence Harrison, "Promoting progressive cultural change," in Harrison & Huntington, 296–307.

8   Cp. Amy Chua, *World on Fire*.

9   Cp. Chua, ibid. 270f, on the success of affirmative action policies in Quebec and Malaysia and the disastrous consequences in Indonesia where such policies have not been tried.

Chapter 21

Harnessing Extraordinariness

VALUE SPHERES ARE THE SOCIAL HARNESS FOR TURNING AN ambivalent into a creative power. Without value spheres, extraordinariness ends in destruction. Arendt implied this when she remarked: "One, if not the chief, reason for the incredible development of gift and genius in Athens, as well as for the hardly less surprising swift decline...was precisely that from beginning to end its foremost aim was to make the extraordinary an ordinary occurrence of everyday life."[1] The rise of gift and genius would not have been possible without conditions that unfettered the ambition of extraordinariness. But if such conditions are not accompanied by standards, a civilization will decline. Without standards to measure what is extraordinary, what is often done becomes ordinary and the ambition of extraordinariness is satisfied only by sensational and scandalous actions that end in destruction. Yet the standards are detected, learned, and transmitted in the value spheres.

Providing us with standards to discern the extraordinary from the sensational and the unusual is but one function of value spheres. Another and perhaps still more important one is to attract individuals to constructive activities by which they can enact their ambition. True, value spheres can only decrease the probability that extraordinariness is evil; they cannot guarantee that it is good. But we cannot expect more from creatures with free will. To understand how extraordinariness can be harnessed by value spheres, let us clarify what the kinds of extraordinariness are that need harnessing.

First there is quantitative and qualitative extraordinariness. *Quantitatively* extraordinary are the actions recorded in the *Guinness Books of Records*; they

---

[1]   Arendt, *The Human Condition,* 197. Arendt shows understanding of the disciplining role of the value sphere of science when in ibid. 324, she marks out that scientists in "their early organizations, which they founded in the 17th century...developed their own moral standards and their own code of behavior"; cp. 271.

are more extreme than what we are used to. When I have danced for fifty hours without a break, this is extraordinary. But if there is no context that makes this action meaningful, as a sporting event might do, then we may well ask what it is good for, except for being recorded in a Guinness book. There is no intrinsic value in the action. It testifies to the power of our ambition of extraordinariness but does not satisfy it. Nor can its extremeness be moral or immoral. It lacks the meaning to have moral significance. It is *amoral*. It does not need a harness. But it does need an alternative that allows individuals to enact their ambition of extraordinariness in meaningful activities.

There are several kinds of *qualitatively* extraordinary actions. The first kind aims at an undisciplined extraordinariness that enjoys its coming closer to an ideal than the others are able to. The ideal, though, is not a value of the value spheres. Hegel's struggle for recognition belongs to this kind, but also the great conquests of war heroes like Alexander, Caesar, and Genghis Khan, and any activity that enjoys itself for the admiration it receives. Although actions of this kind are done for the sake of fame, they are also done for the sake of the activity, because the agent feels them worth doing and admiring. They are considered by the agents to be great and not morally bad, but not necessarily morally good either. Obviously, their extraordinariness can easily become one of atrocity. We may call them *pre-moral*. They need harnessing by value spheres.

The second and *moral* kind aims at extraordinariness by aiming at values that one must have learned to appreciate. These are the values of the value spheres. They are known in closed societies, yet pursued for their own sake only in open ones. In learning to appreciate them one learns their standards of excellence and becomes incapable of not wanting to excel in their pursuit if one performs them. As we have seen, activities of this kind are virtuous in Aristotle's sense.[2] They aim at excellence, give meaning to life, are enjoyed in their doing, allow enacting one's specific capacities, and contribute to the flourishing of society, which consists in everyone's enacting their specific capacities. Though the spheres compete for men's dedication, they coexist in harmony and even promote each other, if only one of them, the sphere of justice, secures the order of their harmony. In that case, they need no harness. But if some spheres dominate the other ones, these spheres need a harness.

The third kind aims at extraordinariness by rejecting the choice of the activities of the second kind. Activities of this kind are purely destructive and *immoral*, but nevertheless pursue an objective value, the value of negation. It can give meaning to life and be pursued for its own sake because we always enjoy the enactment of our powers, and the power of choosing destruction belongs to the greatest human powers, as Descartes was bold enough to argue by referring to Medea. This kind of extraordinariness can never be eliminated without eliminating judgment and reason. Nor can a harness turn it into a constructive

---

2   Chapter 11.

power. But the clearer the values of the value spheres can be seen, the less probable it becomes that people will act against them to prove their liberty or greatness.

There is a fourth form of extraordinariness that requires self-denial of the agent and pretends to be especially virtuous by aiming at values without an individual's interest. Extraordinary actions of this kind are offered by totalitarian movements that dissolve the individual selves. It's not impossible that they produce something good, but more probable that they are especially destructive, because the individuals participating in them feel freed – not only from their interest, but also their responsibility. They are particularly attractive when people feel that they are superfluous, as they do today; hence, they are inclined to deny their selves and their responsibility.[3] Let's call such extraordinary activities *irresponsible*, though its agents are responsible for them. They cannot be harnessed either, but will be the less probable the more individuals find opportunities for self-assertion.

Agents will find these activities easier, the less ambiguous the specific value of a sphere is. For most spheres it has taken some time to find out what their value is; for quite a few, like the state, the family, and religion, it has not become clear even today. However, rather than lack of clarity of a sphere's value, it is the tendency of some spheres to dictate to the rest their sphere-immanent rationality that hinders people from finding opportunity for their ambition. This tendency is particularly strong in the state and the economic sphere, as they control the means of investment, of coercion, and often also of information and corset thinking in the categories of profit and power maximization. They blind the eye against the riches of meaning in activities of other spheres, in particular, as Arendt pointed out, in action and work.

So the most urgent task today in harnessing extraordinariness is to find out how economic and political imperialism can be stopped. Because the state, as I have argued, is no value sphere proper and therefore to be dissolved or reduced to the sphere of justice enforcement, we need not consider its harnessing. Market economy, by contrast, should not be abolished and therefore is in greatest need of harnessing. However, economy is often considered a sphere that cannot be judged by moral or justice standards. Moreover, it is looked up to as the process by which the rest of society is to be adapted. Liberals and Marxists unite in this view. For Marx, as we have already seen,[4] the communist revolution is the adaptation of society to economy. "Modern Industry," he said,

> indeed, compels society, under penalty of death, to replace the detail-worker of to-day, crippled by life-long repetition of one and the same trivial operation, and thus reduced to the mere fragment of a man, by the fully developed individual, fit for a variety of labours, ready to face any change of production, and to whom

---

[3]   This is perhaps the most urgent consequence Arendt drew from her studies of totalitarianism.
[4]   In Chapter 13.

the different social functions he performs, are but so many modes of giving free
scope to his own natural and acquired powers.[5]

Though the adaptation of society to economy allows the rise of "the fully developed individual," this is just a fortunate accident. Men are incapable of, and hence
ought not to try, changing economy. In economy there is no place for politics, let
alone for imposing justice on it.

Marx has bequeathed his view to contemporary social scientists, politicians,
and corporation leaders. Five hundred of them, declared to be a "global brain
trust" by former and last Soviet Union president Mikhail Gorbachev when
meeting under his chairmanship, predicted in unison that only 20 percent of
the population will be needed in jobs; the rest will be appeased by "tittytainment," as former U.S. National Security Advisor Zbigniew Brzezinski formulated.[6] Not only did no one dare to ask how long the 20 percent would be willing
to sustain the rest, but no one thought it worth discussing that one might take
influence on the economic tendencies. One has to adapt to them.

This is an extreme example. There are also examples of efforts to change and
to impose justice on economy.[7] But the trend to looking up to economy as to fate
is unbroken. Yet modern industry does not only replace the detail worker, as
Marx predicted; it replaces most workers of any kind. In abstract principle, we
should not fear but hope for this, as it makes the old dream of mankind true that
automata will free them from the labor of life.[8] But today, adaptation will not
change any condition that renders unemployment a disaster and a source of further disasters. Economy has to be adapted to the standards of justice. Because it
is a public affair, it must respect everyone's right to contribute with equal voice
to the decisions on public affairs, if we follow democratic ideas.

How can this right be realized? Can everyone have a right to have a say in any
economic decision? That would do injustice to those who have initiated economic activities. It rather consists in at least two participation rights. The first
one is to participate in the decisions on the embedding conditions of the market.
Such conditions can be very different, depending on circumstances, the kind of
commodities and goals. The point is to see that the "*root* of the evil (of markets)
lies not in how corporations do business, but in how *we* regulate and incentivize

---

5   Marx, *Capital*, vol. 1, transl. Moore and Aveling; chap. 15, sec. 9.
6   Hans-Peter Martin, and Harald Schumann, *Die Globalisierungsfalle*, 10, 12f. The conference
    took place in a Fairmont Hotel in California.
7   Even they are rarely free from appeals to economic trends one has to adapt to; else one "will
    be left behind as the global economy moves forward," as a well-meaning Japanese tycoon
    said, when he, like so many others, admonished his co-citizens to their "own efforts" (Isao
    Nakauchi, head of the Daiei company, in Peter F. Drucker, *Isao Nakauchi, Drucker on Asia*,
    151f). Nakauchi demands also "self-less" efforts (153).
8   Marx, in footnotes 73 and 74 to his fifteenth chapter of the first volume of his *Capital* in the
    English edition, refers to Aristotle and quotes a Greek poem that expresses this dream. In the
    German edition (MEW 23) ch. 13, p. 430.

them." For instance, pharmaceutical firms can earn billions by acquiring patents by which they can recoup their research costs and exclude the poor from access to their products. But they can earn (and compete) no less by acquiring premiums disbursed by a health fund (that might be instituted by the industry rather than the state) to the degree they reduce global disease.[9] In this case the pharmaceutics market would be embedded in a global health system. The way markets are embedded has to be decided in a process open to everyone.

The second right is the common property right of equal access to the use of natural and cultural resources. Such access is impeded for everyone who against her will is without a job, as employment is today the access to the common property of natural and cultural resources. Involuntary unemployment violates this right; the jobless are excluded from actively using those resources.

How can these participation rights be realized? The first one is realized when everyone is included in proposing, discussing, and voting for or against schemes of market embeddings. But how can everyone have the right to a job, perhaps even an adequate one, if society just cannot offer everyone a job that suits them? Now, many who are working today would like to stop working or to work less. It is only the fact that if they did they would have no money to live on that makes them cling to labor. Though the dole is often a bribe to seduce the unemployed into renouncing their right to participate in economic life, it is legitimate if it enables the jobless to gain an equal access to the common resources outside employment. If the dole is replaced with a basic income[10] and the basic income is complemented by actions that promote activities in the noneconomic value spheres, the jobless are not excluded from their common property.

The basic income would be paid out of a fund raised from producers and paid unconditionally, in order to give everyone an equal chance of deciding which sphere to choose for their activity. But it is paid in a relatively low amount, so that it allows leading just a thrifty life while work in economy remains attractive enough for the economically talented, the workaholics, and those who prefer a more comfortable life. Let us look at some objections.

The first objection is that it would be unjust to tax the industrious to finance the lazy. The answer is that technology has made the moral predications of industriousness and laziness obsolete. The industrious are today the people who arrogate the natural resources. They exclude the rest of mankind (80 percent,

---

9 Thomas Pogge, "Intellectual Property Rights and Access to Essential Medicines," unpubl. manuscript. A more general condition for embedding corporations is to subject them to the same rules of punishment natural persons are subjected to. In Germany and other countries juridical persons, corporations included, cannot be sued by penal law. Many theorists argue corporations can neither decide nor act. This is another bad consequence of the Lockean conception of the self that defines it by consciousness rather than by the power of deliberate judgment, which can well be collective.

10 Cp. Philippe van Parijs, *Real Freedom for All.* For an argument that is closer to the Cartesian approach, see Philip Pettit, "A Republican Right to Basic Income?"

if we believe the Gorbachev conference) from common property. Natural resources have not been produced by those who exploit them; they are not their private property. So it is just to tax the industrious for their privileged use. True, it would be both unjust and stupid to tax them so severely that they would stop producing; the wealth they produce is only to a part the result of their use of common property. Another part is their due. They have a right to be rewarded for their social function to make the economically most productive use of social resources and to be rewarded in proportion to the degree of their productivity. But society has also a right to siphon off from their product the value that is due to the resources that are common property. The amount of this value cannot be measured by fixing the value of natural resources; for natural resources do no longer exist in their original form when no labor had been added to them.[11] It can only be measured by the costs necessary for keeping them in a state in which everyone has equal access to them. To these costs belong on one hand the costs for enabling the jobless to have equal access to them and on the other hand the costs for sustaining natural resources, including a healthy environment. Hence, it is just to tax the economically successful for these costs.

A second objection presupposes that modern society is irreparably rotten as long as its economy is capitalist, and that basic income presupposes capitalism rather than abolishes it. It presupposes it indeed, as it exploits it for filling the basic income fund. Traditionally, the sphere of economy is the sphere of activities that provide a society with the goods and services it thinks it needs. This aim is pursued by any kind of economy. But modern economy is characterized by a specific way to attain this general aim, namely, by the agents' pursuit of their individual maximal profit.[12] Marx claimed, as did Aristotle and many others, that such an aim is destructive for society.[13] But as Karl Polanyi has pointed out, the aim is destructive only if it is not embedded in noneconomic conditions that have often been religious and political but today need to be justice conditions.[14]

---

[11] Hillel Steiner (in: "Liberty and Equality, An Essay on Rights," 271; "Three Just Taxes") proposes that the "over-appropriators" of natural resources, in proportion to their over-appropriation, compensate the "under-appropriators." I think it is just impossible to evaluate over- and under-appropriation in any currency. Cp. my *Gleiche Freiheit*, Berlin, 123–38, and my paper, "Zwei Wurzeln der Allmendebewegungen, eine Politik."

[12] Cp. Weber, *Zwischenbetrachtung*, 545, Kröner ed., 450, who calls the aim of the sphere of economy wealth, measured in "money prices."

[13] Described and complained about already by Aristotle, *Politics* I, 3 1256b27–58a19, at a time when economy probably was not yet completely dominated by this form, and by Marx, *Capital* vol. I, pt. 1, chap. 1, sec. 3, subsec. D. Marx describes the traditional aim of trade by the scheme $C - M - C$, the modern one by $M - C - M'$; C stands for a commodity, M for money and M' for an increased amount of money. Aristotle argued that only if "wealth-getting has a limit" (and thus is not *chrematistic*) will it not seduce men into "employing each of their faculties in an unnatural way" and lead to the corruption of society. Marx quotes Aristotle on *chrematistics* approvingly in *Capital* vol. I, pt.2, ch. 4.

[14] Polanyi, *The Great Transformation*.

Basic income would subject capitalist economy to such an embedding. It is a harness that does not forbid profit making and extraordinariness in it but uses it for freeing as many people as possible from the drudgery of labor and for activities in other value spheres where they can find meaning. Of course not all economic agents can be expected to love such a harness. It is obviously a question not only of insight but also of power, if they can be coerced to bear it. Fighting for a basic income will be no less necessary than fighting for the abolishment of capitalism would be.

A third objection is that the basic income would make work in the economic sphere so unattractive that too few people would remain in it. The proponents of basic income presume it is possible to balance out how low basic income and how high net salaries in business should be for having the desired effect of an economy that both flourishes and allows people to move from the economic to other spheres, even an economy that flourishes because it allows this moving. Only if even the lowest basic income that just ensures a decent life would leave too few people in economy would it be necessary to reject basic income. But this is implausible, as the problems of unemployment arise just because the economy can produce what society wants with ever less workers. Experts agree neither on how much can be paid as a basic income nor on the best way to institute it. But many agree that a basic income is possible that ensures a decent life and does not reduce production.[15]

A fourth objection is that basic income will not make people active in the noneconomic value spheres but rather restrict their lives to fighting for increases of basic income. This danger[16] can be prevented if activities in other spheres are rewarded by their sphere-specific forms of gratification and individuals learn to esteem such gratifications. To the extent people esteem them, money loses its present attraction of a measure of excellence. In fact, for the powerful and the aristocrats, measuring a person's value by her money is the mark of inferiority and the nouveau-riche. The greatest veneration for money comes from those who badly need it. The high esteem it is held in reflects how badly people need it as they struggle against poverty. Once basic income makes such struggling superfluous, the danger that life centers on increasing basic income will decrease.

Now let us see if the harness of basic income can be put on modern economy. Probably it cannot be introduced without coercion, and hence, without the state, as the state has concentrated the means of coercion in its hands. But the state is not necessary for its introduction. Rather than lobbying the state for introducing basic income, its adherents can argue with and put pressure on business associations on which its introduction depends anyway. What is crucial is the creation of a fund that finances basic income, and this can only be filled by levies

---

[15]   Cp., among many others, Thomas Straubhaar, "Grundeinkommen."

[16]   This is the reason I criticized basic income in my *Gleiche Freiheit*, 161ff.

from the economically productive. The chances of such a fund are the better the more people unite to pressure the economy into accepting basic income. Yet many people will only unite in this goal if their more immediate concerns are involved. Their most immediate concern is not to get a basic income that will be anyway modest, but to get a job that conforms to their formation and talents. Therefore, the fight for basic income has the better chance the more it is connected with the fight against unemployment.

Chances for such a fight may be low, but they are better than some decades ago. Totalitarian movements and terrorism are responses of individuals to their economic superfluity and the lack of meaning they find in their life. The responses have come from classes and traditions with little esteem for individual autonomy and a tendency to subordinate individuals to communal or religious values. Yet today unemployment and economic superfluity threaten also individuals from classes and traditions that have been proud of their autonomy and individuality. The protesting youth of the 1960s and 1970s came from these classes and traditions or identified with them. But at that time, they had not yet been threatened by economic superfluity; at least, they did not feel superfluous. Their theorists did not seriously accuse established society of threatening the masses with exclusion or even extinction. Though it was phrased in Marxist vocabulary, their complaint was not different from Weber's complaint that society had become a house of bondage. Like Weber, they criticized it for reducing not the money but the capabilities of the masses, in particular for stunting their initiative and imagination. Like Weber, they understood the house of bondage as a golden cage.

Such impoverishing is reason enough for rejecting a society. Yet the argument that it impoverishes the masses in their capabilities is not likely to be accepted by the masses, as they do not feel stunted. Therefore, the revolutionary efforts of the neo-Marxists were condemned to failure. But today the classes that felt secure from poverty forty years ago have lost their economic security. What Western societies today threaten their once-privileged individuals with is the very contrary of what Weber and Marcuse feared. It's not inclusion and submersion in a job; it is joblessness and exclusion. As one of the participants of the Gorbachev conference said, because only 20 percent of today's jobs will be left, the crucial question everywhere will be "to have lunch or be lunch."[17]

The threat of exclusion and unemployment cannot be measured by numbers. The number of unemployed can be relatively low, as in the United States, but the threat can be felt more intensely than in countries with a high unemployment number. The sentiment that we have no alternative but "to have lunch or be lunch" is widespread. The solution cannot to be to create more jobs; it is to secure access to deciding on public affairs for everyone and to adapt economy to the variety of human capabilities. Yet this is the long-term aim. It is also

[17] Martin and Schumann, 10.

necessary to respond to the pressure exerted now on nearly everyone that makes them feel they have to struggle for either having or being lunch. The demand for basic income is such a response, as an unconditional income for everyone frees them from the fear of being lunch. But there will be no money to be levied from firms if the economy is declining, as it tends to do today. Even if the economy is not on a long-term vicious circle of shrinkage that robs basic income of its financial basis, firms can always threaten to stop investing. Therefore, the demand of basic income needs to be supplemented by means to prevent economic shrinkage.

Most former movements for radical change considered the economy rather than the state their object of change. The state was to become the tool for enforcing the interests of mankind or the masses on an unwilling minority. Market economy was to be replaced by an economy immediately producing for the desires of everyone. The market, though, has kept its promise to produce wealth; what it failed in was a just distribution, but justice has been considered the aim of the state. It was the state that proved impotent to secure everyone's liberty and equality, which alone would justify its existence. So the conclusion should be to keep the market but, first, to secure that it works for what it is good for, namely continual wealth production, and to prevent a vicious cycle; second, to control the distribution of the wealth it produces, and third, to entrust the control of the market to a justice enforcement institution that is not necessarily the state.[18]

Let's sketch how joblessness might be fought against and basic income be introduced. Capitalist firms are not fond of a strong market position of employees, as this raises wages and lowers their profits. They dislike both full employment and basic income that frees individuals from the necessity of selling their labor power to them. Yet the decrease of wages they fight for has a disadvantage also for capitalist firms. Falling wages entail falling demand for the firms' products, and falling demand raises again unemployment, decreasing still more wages and demand, until production breaks down in a great economic crisis. Vicious cycles and crises are inherent in the capitalist system. But they can be stopped, even to the advantage of capitalist firms, if firms are coerced to raise wages and pay levies for specified tasks like that of financing basic income and improving education.[19]

---

[18] As Locke already stated (*Two Treatises* II, §143), the concentration of the means of coercion that distinguishes the state from other justice-enforcement institutions, is "too great a temptation to human frailty apt to grasp at Power." Neither has his requirement of putting legislative and executive in separate hands been met, nor is it sufficient today when the number of state tasks has immensely increased. A board of economic experts and laypersons vested with democratic legitimacy and specified executive power would probably do a better job than the state in controlling the market. It is more rational to entrust the many public tasks performed today by the state to separate institutions that are vested with democratic legitimacy and a narrowly specified executive power.

[19] Cp. the similar thesis, related to globalization, by Robert Goodin, "Globalising Justice."

Such coercion would lower profits but not do injustice to the firms, provided they are all equally coerced. For first, if profit becomes too small for a firm to survive, it has to withdraw from the market. Though this does harm to it, it is no injustice. It is the effect of the competition rules of the market embedded in justice conditions. Second, to repeat, by the levies they are coerced to pay, they pay back to the public sphere what they have pulled out of it when they used the common property of natural and cultural resources. Finally, no one is prohibited from aiming at profit maximization if only they pay the levies imposed on them. A profit ceiling does not exclude extraordinariness in gaining profit. It even fosters the capitalist system. It results in a virtuous cycle of increasing demand and improved education, work motivation, and inventiveness. Higher wages raise demand, improved education raises inventiveness; higher inventiveness raises the capacity of meeting the demand, and rising demand and production capacity raise again production and employment.

A crucial condition of the virtuous cycle is that governments or other justice enforcement institutions are strong enough to impose their regulations equally on all firms worldwide. Otherwise countries that impose regulations will suffer economically and be conquered by the corporations residing in the countries that do not impose the regulations. Because the strongest states are those with the strongest corporations, they would lose their strength if they acted against the interests of their corporations. The weak states are dependent on the decisions of the strong corporations and their states. Hence, it is highly improbable that states will impose the necessary regulations on the firms.

We might expect corporation leaders to learn that in the end, vicious cycles also damage the corporations. The consequences of a vicious cycle today are devastating indeed. It will be spiraling down to more and more unemployment until in the end a small part of the population, perhaps the 20 percent predicted, is left to do the work they think is necessary for them. Formerly, the workers replaced by machines were needed for work at new generations of machines and for the colonial and imperialist expansion of the most industrialized nations,[20] though already then millions of workers overseas, made superfluous by European machine products, have become economically superfluous. Yet in the West, need for workers motivated governmental work programs that put some money in the hand of workers and triggered off a virtuous cycle. In contrast, today's generations of computers and robots need extremely few workers to serve them, and imperialist expansion, once a job machine, has been stopped or restricted. Governmental work programs will conserve a production that keeps firms dependent on workers. So corporation leaders will prefer a shrinking economy that nevertheless does not reduce their profits. This will be bad for most employees, as well as for most firms, but good for the most powerful of them. They will look forward to a small community

---

[20] For the latter, cp. Arendt, *The Origins of Totalitarianism*, 156f.

of users of a technology that exploits the resources of the earth and its inter-planetary surroundings.[21]

The experts of the Gorbachev conference still talked of feeding the expected 80 percent populations of unemployed, even if it is only tittytainment they thought of offering them. Yet, people without a work that gives meaning to their lives and without an education that activates their selves will be irritable and explosive. It is only a question of time when the readiness to care for them will yield to disgust, and the ruling classes will observe with loud moral indignation the wretched poor killing each other, as they do in parts of Africa and Asia and in many suburbs. The prospect of a world with falling numbers of employed and, in the end, much smaller numbers of human inhabitants on Earth, is appealing not only to corporation leaders. Some environmentalists are no less attracted. Yet looking closer, the prospect is horrible. The vicious economic cycle would reduce the number of men on Earth by wars and terrorism with all the atrocities we are already watching on television. Even if a world with fewer people were preferable to one with more, which is not evident at all, there should be less cruel ways to arrive there than vicious economic cycles.

So, though not probable, there is hope that there will be enough people to grasp the fatal consequences of vicious cycles and to unite to oppose them. It was not probable either that the small minority in the United States that started the fight against the Vietnam War succeeded. Arendt has pointed out that one of the peculiarities of the antiwar movement was that its initiators detected "that acting is fun." They rediscovered the specific joy of what was lost with the ancient polis, political action. They "discovered what the eighteenth century had called 'public happiness,' which means that when man takes part in public life he opens up for himself a dimension of human experience that other-wise remains closed to him and that in some way constitutes a part of complete 'happiness.'"[22] This discovery is certainly not forgotten.

Harnessing economy and its specific extraordinariness in profit maximization is probably today the most important challenge for extraordinary actions in favor of public affairs. Once economy furthers rather than fetters the other value spheres, a crucial step to realizing modernity will have been done.

---

[21] Hardt and Negri, 158, still indulge in thinking "the poor have . . . become ever more important: the life of the poor invests the planet and envelops it with its desire for creativity and freedom. The poor is the condition of every production." A paradigm of wishful thinking.

[22] Arendt, "Thoughts on Politics and Revolution," in *Crises of the Republic*, 203. She also expected in, ibid. 230f, and in *The Human Condition* 216, that such political fights will radically change politics and produce more flexible political institutions like councils that can better express the will of the people.

Chapter 22

Cartesian Modernity

A SOCIETY THAT REALIZES SPHERE AUTONOMY AND HINGES AROUND the nonserving value spheres can be called Cartesian modernity, as it follows Cartesian rationality. If it is a utopia, at least it escapes the reproach of being another effort of bestowing happiness on mankind, because unlike the classic utopias it does not aim at happiness. If we are Cartesian selfs, a broad spectrum of autonomous value spheres is just what people tend to produce. If it presents our nature rather than a utopia, we can expect it to already exist somehow. Actually, this is the case, because modern society is differentiated into the spheres I have described, even though in an imperfect form.

Are there chances that it can be more perfectly realized? Popper hoped the victory of the Allies against Hitler would be the victory of the open against the closed society, but it was not. The closed society threatens modernity more than ever before. It appears today in two forms: as religious fundamentalism and as the authoritarian power state. Both forms are symptoms of the sickness of the liberal state. The liberal state is a conceptual contradiction. The liberal core idea of equal liberty demands to shrink the state to a justice enforcement institution, which the state has never been; even the liberals have expected it to promote the interests of the inhabitants of its territory.

The power state removes, on the one hand, the liberal checks against the enormously increased means of control; on the other hand, the ideology that once was to justify the removal of liberal checks. It makes do with appeals to national pride and dignity. It is represented by states outside the West that look back to an empire, as China, Russia, and some more do, but is a tacit guiding idea also in the West. Some liberals believe that authoritarianism is incompatible with the intelligence required of people in high-tech industry and their intelligence will open their closed societies. But intelligence, as Popper had pointed out, is not reason or the capacity to argue and criticize.[1] Of reason we might expect the opening of closed societies; of intelligence, not.

Fundamentalism claims to be capable of giving people what it says modernity cannot give them: meaning to life and ideas of how to justly organize our capabilities. One of its attractions is that it rejects the state and replaces it with a social form based on revelation or other doctrines exempt from criticism or revision. In this it meets a demand that the West, as long as it follows the utilitarian approach, fails to meet indeed.

But if we understand the West as Cartesian modernity, it is not without hope. When we looked at history, the Cartesian conception gave us some help in understanding it. It also helps understand some conspicuous phenomena of our time as efforts at enacting capabilities that today are neglected or suppressed but would be still more suppressed by the power state and fundamentalism. Even though some of them are destructive, we must not overlook their significance in testifying the indelibility of the self's effort at self-assertion and extraordinariness. Rather than condemning them as irrational, we need to understand their rationality and their support for Cartesian modernity.

There are first the so-called protest phenomena. Youth refuse to dress and dance and do as their parents do. Why? Do they want to distance themselves from their parents so as to find their own identity? But former generations did not think it necessary to thus distance themselves from their parents. More particularly, we may wonder why, in the 1960s and 1970s, a wave of youth protest swept the West, in spite of huge differences between Western countries. The paradigmatic German parents were Nazis, but the paradigmatic American ones were far from being that. What the youth still rightly felt as the same enemy was the diminution of capabilities, the restriction of activities and joys to a spectrum much narrower than necessary. Maybe the rebellious generations in the end did not prove less crippled than their parents, as critics like Allan Bloom imply;[2] still they felt their parents' stuntedness. They protested against a crippling life of modern Sisyphean absurdity of producing for production's sake.

Related to the protest phenomena, though as different in its appearance as a smiling face from one foaming with rage, are the totalitarian movements. The individuals who follow them renounce their selves for despair of their superfluity and restrict their ambition to the extraordinariness of their movement. In their resignation they are the extreme contrast to the protest youth of 1968. Still, they share the feeling that established capitalist society does not allow them

---

[1] Popper, *Objective Knowledge*, 120.

[2] Allan Bloom, *The Closing of the American Mind*, in particular, 99. Hardt and Negri, 274 interpret the youth revolution as "the refusal of the disciplinary regime" of capitalism and convincingly assign it a crucial role in changing conditions of capitalism. But, as they say themselves, it was also "the experimentation with new forms of productivity," and this is close to the recognition of extraordinariness.

to enact what is most important to them: their capability of doing something that proves their extraordinariness. Yet, we should also see the moral progress from the totalitarian to the protest movement. The 1968 youth did not renounce their self.

Another response to the insight of being unbearably crippled by society is terrorism, in particular in its suicidal form. Some observers claim terrorism is a consequence of poverty. As far as poverty causes misery, this is true. But poverty need not be misery at all. Misery is lack of recognition of one's value. It is suffered by people who find they are not needed. It can be more intensely suffered by youth from well-to-do families. Terrorists respond to misery not by renouncing the self, as do the adherents of totalitarian movements; therefore it is a mistake to equate them. They respond to it by enacting the full potential of the self, if only for the suicidal attack, under the condition of being recognized as a hero or martyr for doing so. Crucial for this state is not belief in a heavenly reward, though this may further it, but trust in a public that will admire them as extraordinary. For the same reason, irreligious Japanese Kamikaze and German Stuka pilots performed similar suicidal attacks. What all of them demonstrate and wanted to demonstrate is their power of rising above the passivity of a subject and becoming a self, even by an extraordinary feat.[3]

Terrorism is not only different from totalitarianism; it is even a progress from renouncing the self to using it in an uncrippled form. It also dramatically shows the urgency of channeling the ambition of extraordinariness into constructive waters. Much as we need to condemn and fight its immorality of killing the innocent, it testifies the power of the ambition of enacting capabilities that do not find recognition in the established society.

Another and more agreeable response to the lack of opportunities for enacting human capacities is involvement in political movements outside the state sphere that aim at protecting values not sufficiently protected by the states, even though the states justify their existence by claiming to protect them. Most important among them are NGOs constituted to protect the environment and human rights. They do what the states claim is their task; they protect justice and life conditions. They do so by enacting capabilities, often in extraordinary actions that the representatives of the states seem incapable of. Their success confirms that the states lack lasting reasons for their existence that are independent of historical particularities.

It is not only the protest movements and other oppositions to liberalism and the established West that witness to the realizability of Cartesian modernity.

---

[3] Cp. Roy, *Globalised Islam*, 43: "The real genesis of Al-Qaeda violence has more to do with a Western tradition of individual and pessimistic revolt for an elusive ideal world than with the Koranic conception of martyrdom." Roy, in ibid. 38f aptly calls contemporary fundamentalist movements "the triumph of the self," Robert Pape, *Dying to Win*, University of Chicago Press, 2005, gives more examples that suicide attacks are independent of religious beliefs.

So do its main competitors if we listen to their arguments. One of them is utilitarianism, though we should not forget that unlike the adherents of the power state and fundamentalism it shares with the Cartesian approach belief in the Enlightenment. When confronted with the fact, unknown to classical utilitarians, that happiness can be maximized by euphoriant drugs and "pleasure machines"[4] or even by transforming men into ever-happy animals, its less dogmatic defenders retreat to "complex utilitarianism." This is a position that differs from the former one-dimensional utilitarianism proclaiming only the pleasure/pain dimension as a standard of goodness by adding the dimensions of self-activity, self-development, and communication with reality and other people.[5] It obviously dilutes, if not abandons, utilitarianism in favor of the Cartesian approach. Also utilitarians, when confronted with the short way to happiness technology offers, rather than trusting their principle, trust the moral intuition that this would be a nightmare and aim at a cultivation of activities that is close to Cartesian modernity.

The adherents of the power state do not rely on arguments; hence, they can hardly witness the realizability of Cartesian modernity by their arguments. The attraction of the power state is the attraction of the power and prestige enjoyed, curiously enough, not only by the few who rule but also by the ruled. Its satisfaction presupposes the authoritarian childhood form of the self whose attraction also shows in the willingness to identify with sport clubs. Yet identification with a club can be chosen for reasons while the identification with a state most times is the result of pressures accompanying citizens' life from their birth. Nonetheless, as everyone is born with the capacity to judge, the transformation of the authoritarian self into an authentic one, difficult though it is, becomes a general tendency under favorable conditions. And the conditions today are not unfavorable.

This is shown by the attraction of fundamentalism, probably the hardest competitor to Cartesian modernity. Fundamentalism requires of its adherents the sacrifice of their own judgment, but only in the end. It attracts because it appeals to and requires independent judgment. That it attracts in this way gives hope that the power state's appeal to the authoritarian self will cede to the demands of the authentic self. But fundamentalism is based on belief in an infallible authority. To win adherents it needs arguments, but to keep them it needs their subjection. Whether it can keep them is not independent of the response of the West.

---

[4] Olds and Milner (1954) proved the existence of a center in rat brains that when stimulated made rats desire to repeat the stimulation. Their detection led to the idea of pleasure machines. Nozick, *Anarchy*, 42, described them as "an experience machine that would give you any experience you desired."

[5] Jonathan Glover, *What Sort of People Should There Be?*, 133–67.

The need of fundamentalism to appeal to the individual's judgment, and in the end to replace it with trust in infallible revelation and dogma, shows paradigmatically in an Encyclical letter by former Pope John Paul II on faith and reason. It is full of assertions that faith requires reason, though also that reason requires faith. It recognizes "philosophy's valid aspiration to be an *autonomous* enterprise, obeying its own rules and employing the powers of reason alone,"[6] concedes that the former description of philosophy as an "ancilla theologiae," a servant to theology, "can scarcely be used today, given the principle of autonomy to which we have referred" and defends "the grounding principles of autonomy which every science rightly wants guaranteed."[7] It pays homage to what once seemed an enemy, natural science: "So far has science come, especially in this century, that its achievements never cease to amaze us," expressing "admiration and ... offering encouragement to these brave pioneers of scientific research, to whom humanity owes so much of its current development."[8] It affirms the moral autonomy of the individual, asserting that "There is no morality without freedom ... each individual has a right to be respected in his own journey in search of the truth," although it adds that "there exists a prior moral obligation, and a grave one at that, to seek the truth and to adhere to it once it is known," referring to the truth as taught by the Church.[9]

However, reason has to be abandoned at some point. Rightly calling scientific theories for their fallibility "hypotheses," Pope John Paul II argues:

> People seek an absolute which might give to all their searching a meaning and an answer – something ultimate, which might serve as the ground of all things. In other words, they seek a final explanation, a supreme value, which refers to nothing beyond itself and which puts an end to all questioning. Hypotheses may fascinate, but they do not satisfy. Whether we admit it or not, there comes for everyone the moment when personal existence must be anchored to a truth recognized as final, a truth which confers a certitude no longer open to doubt.[10]

The assertion that only "a certitude no longer open to doubt" can "satisfy" men implies that we need infallibility for satisfaction. But faith is too cheap if we

---

6 John Paul II, *Encyclical letter Fides et ratio*, September 14, 1998, § 75. I have commented on this letter in an article, "Ist die Enzyclika *Fides et Ratio* eine Herausforderung an die Philosophie."

7 Ibid., loc. cit. §77.

8 Ibid. § 106. John Paul II initiated the rehabilitation of Galileo by a commission of Catholic scholars and declared in a speech to the Pontifical Academy of Sciences "the validity of Galileo's position in the debate," though specifying that "In Galileo's time, to depict the world as lacking an absolute physical reference point was, so to speak, inconceivable. And since the cosmos, as it was then known, was contained within the solar system alone, this reference point could only be situated in the earth or in the sun. Today, after Einstein and within the perspective of contemporary cosmology neither of these two reference points has the importance they once had." (§11 in the edition of *L'Osservatore Romano* N. 44 (1264) – November 4, 1992).

9 John Paul II, *Encyclical letter Fides et ratio*, loc. cit. §25.

10 Ibid. § 27.

accept it as infallible to be satisfied. Moreover, even if a believer can gain a certitude no longer open to doubt, it needs to be one she finds after painful experience and never one that is taught her by an institution that claims infallibility. John Paul's II appeal to satisfaction, even if he did not mean it thus, implies the argument that the infallibility of the Church is justified by the satisfaction it gives people. So we need only to explicate the implication to make the argument unacceptable both for believers, as it corrupts faith, and for nonutilitarians, as it downgrades faith to a means for satisfaction. Amazingly, utilitarianism has conquered Rome and lays the ground for a conservatism that prefers the peace of a closed society to the unrest of modernity.

Compared with this comfortable conservatism, the contemporary interpretations of Islam that are aptly called political Islam impress for the stringency of their identifying faith with the fight for human rights and their rejection of any expectation that faith might be cozy. They appeal both to the ambition of extraordinariness and to the indignation at the injustice that modern media make obvious to everyone. Sayyid Qutb, one of the most influential thinkers of political Islam, represents this interpretation: "Islam urges men to fight for their rights";[11] it is "the movement for freeing mankind and demolishing the obstacles which prevented mankind from attaining this freedom."[12] Religious duties contract to this fight; salvation consists in freedom "from servitude to anyone except God,"[13] and God demands nothing but fighting for men's rights. Even the idea of a world beyond is subordinated to this fight: "This world and the next world are not two separate entities, but are stages complementary to each other";[14] "the essential spirit of this religion is found in this – that practical work is religious work, for religion is inextricably bound up with life and can never exist in the isolation of idealism in some world of the conscience alone."[15]

Attractive though this interpretation is, the freedom and justice it promises are conditioned by the same proviso the Pope has formulated. Like the Pope, it "constructs its foundation of belief and action on the principle of total submission to God alone." Though God demands nothing but fighting for justice, submission to him in the end means submission to the "principles and values" of the shariah, for they are immunized to criticism by being declared "eternal and unchangeable."[16] Therefore, despite its promoting individual capabilities, political Islam can lead to their restriction, as it did under the Taliban in

---

[11]   Sayyid Qutb, *Social Justice in Islam*, 33.

[12]   Qutb, *Milestones*, 65.

[13]   Qutb, *Social Justice*, 55; cp. Qutb, *Milestones*, 130. I use the word *God* for *Allah*.

[14]   Qutb, *Milestones*. 91.

[15]   Qutb, *Social Justice*. 29. As Olivier Roy, *Globalised Islam*, shows, contemporary Islam develops properties and experiences similar to those of early Protestantism (cp., e.g., ibid. 61).

[16]   Qutb, *Milestones*, 87, 104, 60.

Afghanistan. But it is not necessary.[17] Christianity once demanded the same total submission to revelation and yet triggered modernity. Two further points have to be considered. First, Islam's claim to infallibility is raised not by one central authority like in Catholicism but, like in Protestantism, by a plurality of voices. Second, political Islam is only part of a renaissance of Islam that comprehends both ascetic and mystic aspects, just as Protestantism did.[18] It is stirring up the authentic self no less than Protestantism did.[19] So it may well lead to a strengthening of the core idea of modernity, universal or equal liberty.

The renaissance of Islam and similar revival movements in other religions demonstrate the weakening attraction of the West. The West is haunted today by the same specter of Sisyphean absurdity that haunted the closed society, replacing its aim of biological reproduction and expansion with the aim of economic production and expansion. This is the reason why perhaps the main reproach of the intellectuals who articulate criticism of the West is that it lacks spirituality. One of the first to do so has been Muhammad Asad, who inspired many Muslim thinkers and was a convert to Islam, born Leopold Weiss in 1900 in what at that time was Austrian Lemberg.[20] The West can learn from his critique, even if it is only part of the West (though the prevailing one) he describes:

> The true philosophical basis of the Western system is to be sought in the ancient Roman view of life as a matter of advantage, quite independent of absolute values. It is a view which can be summarized thus: Because we have no specific knowledge, either in the way of practical experience, or in that of proof, about the origins of human life, or about its destiny after physical death; therefore it is best for us to confine our powers to those material and intellectual fields which are accessible to us, rather than let ourselves be tied down to metaphysical and moral questions arising from claims which can have no scientific proofs.[21]

[17] As Roy (87f) reports, once the Islamic state was established in Iran, Khomeini, "for the higher interest of the Islamic state," in conflict with the Council of Guardians, declared "that it might ignore or alter some *sharia* requirements." As he also reports, religious rule under the Taliban "let the free market work and interfered hardly at all with the economy except by collecting *zakat*," the Islam tithing of 2.5% of one's wealth (98).

[18] Roy, informing about the immense variety of often contradictory tendencies in contemporary Islam, points to the differences between "Islamists" and "neofundamentalists," in particular that "the aim of action" of the latter "is salvation, not revolution" (248), but also to their similarity in emphasizing religiosity rather than religion and the role of the individual self. As he says, they are "a product and a tool of globalisation" (270), which makes both of them modern *malgré eux*.

[19] Cp. Tariq Ramadan, *Western Muslims*, vii: "Even the most distant pathways always lead us inward, completely inward, into intimacy, solitude between our self and our self – in the place where there is no longer anyone but God and our self."

[20] Ukrainian Lviv, Polish Lvov.

[21] Muhammad Asad, *Islam at the Crossroads*, 1934, Arab transl. 1941, quoted from Qutb, *Justice in Islam*, 281f.

Asad's view of the West is not very different from the interpretation given by Weber. Both agree that the West is characterized by its rejection of metaphysical speculation and mystic contemplation. Weber found the origin of this character not in ancient Rome but Judaism's preference of mundane ascesis, but this is not the crucial difference in their interpretation. What is crucial is their different evaluation. What for Asad is weakness and vice is strength and virtue for Weber. Yet Weber is not free of Asad's doubts about the strength of the West when he considers its present state. It is a cage of bondage, because the "spirit" of ascesis that alone made possible the splendid rise of the West "escaped."[22] So he might consent to Asad 's description of the West:

> The average European, whether he is a democrat or a fascist, a capitalist or a Bolshevik, a worker or an intellectual, knows only one necessary religion – the worship of material progress; the only belief he holds is that there is but one goal in life – the making of that life easier and easier. ... The shrines of such a culture are huge factories and cinemas, chemical laboratories and dance-halls and power stations. The priests of such a worship are bankers and engineers, cinema stars and industrialists and aviators.[23]

Asad is right in ascribing to the West a high esteem for material progress but he is wrong in reducing it to this esteem. What is essential to the West is that, first, it distrusts metaphysical speculation and prefers mundane ascesis; second, it has a higher regard of the individual than of society; third, it favors a plurality of value spheres with sphere-immanent standards. In these properties there is no less spirituality than in the properties of Islam. But there is a fourth property Asad rejects, though it is shared with Islam (and Judaism). It is what he calls its "escape from 'the tyranny of nature.'"[24] The West aims at escaping from the tyranny of nature indeed. For the Muslims no less than for the Christians, kowtowing to nature as a divine power is paganism or what the Muslim tradition, including Qutb, calls *Jahiliyyah*.[25]

Muslims no less than Westerners share the idea that man is to fight against the tyranny of nature, which even obliges them to unite in this fight. Yet what allows Asad to understand this fight as a vice is the historical fact that in this fight the West has become a power of suppression rather than liberation, of organizing men's capabilities in a way that replaces Sisyphean reproduction for reproduction's sake with an even more Sisyphean production for production's sake. This development of the West is justly criticized and called a lack of spirituality. But Asad was not alone in his critique; rather, it was shared by Western contemporaries, by Heidegger, Arendt, and Adorno, to mention only a few.

---

[22]   Weber, *Gesammelte Aufsätze zur Religionssoziologie* I, 204.
[23]   Asad, loc. cit., quoted from Qutb, *Social Justice*, loc. cit. 282.
[24]   Ibid.
[25]   E.g., Qutb, *Milestones*, 55f.

Once we grasp that men aim not at making "life easier and easier" but at self-assertion and extraordinariness, we can understand that we shall never escape from the tyranny of nature as long as we do not aim at institutions that offer everyone with their different talents as broad a spectrum of activities as possible. Such a set of value spheres will be futile unless in addition to the spheres that directly serve the fight against the tyranny of nature – economy and technology – they include nonserving spheres that enable individuals to explore the realms of truth and sense and give spirit to life. Western societies belong to the few that have developed such nonserving spheres. They are far from realizing their autonomy but have produced its idea as a realizable aim. What they can learn from Asad's critique is that they suffer from their insufficient understanding of their own specific potential.

In his philosophy of history, Hegel discerned as the turning point of history the detection of a kind of "inner world" (*Innerlichkeit*) that opens up to man the riches and powers of the mind and reconciles him to the imperfections of the "outer" world. The limits of what formerly passed for the paramount value became evident when the expansion of Rome found an end and the ambition of man was forced to turn inside, which Hegel said happened paradigmatically in Christianity.[26] We do not overrate our time if we find in it a similar possible turning point. We have to turn from the spheres that attract most attention to the nonserving spheres. They pass for a luxury that one might abandon. A luxury they are, but rather than dispensable, they are the hub of society. Without them, modernity would lack its point and worth. If there were no nonserving spheres, the serving spheres – even justice – would not escape Sisyphean absurdity. The nonserving spheres are the unrecognized sanctuary of modernity. Its existence is the greatest strength of the West; its lack of recognition, its greatest weakness. As they are neither recognized nor felt to exist, even defenders of the West feel "emptiness at the core of liberalism."[27]

So why do they lack sufficient recognition? In fact, they attract and give meaning to most people, but public recognition and, more generally, the way to think of society, utilitarian rationality, and the Lockean conception of the self, do not fit this fact. Absolute love, as we have seen, is performed and celebrated, though not recognized for what it is. Sport is still more performed and celebrated, but considered an entertainment and object of economic exploitation rather than an activity having its own value. Science and religion attract people for their pursuit of useless truth and metaphysical questions but are esteemed rather for their contribution to either technology or social stability.

The most interesting case is art. The less it is expected to express ideas that can be discussed in the discourse of society on what is important, the better it flourishes. Music, including pop and rock but also music classified as serious,

---

[26] Hegel, *The Philosophy of History*, part III, sec. III, ch. II (Christianity); transl. J. Sibree, 337–53.
[27] Fukuyama, *The End of History*, sec. III.

is in a marvelous state; without it, life for most people would be immensely impoverished. By contrast, literature looks languid. Comparing it with what it meant in ancient Athens, Elizabethan England, or Goethe's Weimar, its power of giving meaning to life is not exhausted. It suffers from the expectation to deliver discursive ideas and to be useful for society. It rejects prevalent rationality and conceptions, but in its opposition remains in the categories of the opponent. It lacks the trust of music in the power of nondiscursive ideas. If it regains it, it will be oracular, not easy to place in the political and ideological locations, but as important as music again.

Many authors complain of the predominance of rock music and its commercialization. It produces in the young, Allan Bloom says, "premature ecstasy," making "life into a non-stop, commercially prepackaged masturbational fantasy."[28] Involuntarily they confirm the power of music to shoot its message through the prevailing utilitarian ideology. Because music is not considered to transport important ideas, it was not exposed to a crippling discipline. Bloom, like Plato, is aware that music does transport ideas, though oracular ones, and like Plato wants to discipline it. The problem is not so much that the result would be similarly spoiling as it has been in literature, but how little they understand the value and the potential of autonomous spheres. Cartesian modernity is no less incompatible with Platonism than with utilitarianism.

[28]   Bloom, *The Closing of the American Mind*, 80 and 75.

Chapter 23

The Undivided, Universally Developed Individual

I F AUTONOMOUS VALUE SPHERES AND CARTESIAN MODERNITY ARE AIMED at, two closely connected ideas are rejected that have been rarely absent in utopias and criticisms of liberalism. The first is the idea that individuals find perfection not by specializing in an activity but by developing all their capabilities. It is the ideal of the universally developed individual. The second is the idea that our life should not be torn apart by incompatible tasks; that we should be one and whole in all our activities and should have a chance of being recognized as a whole person rather than for our extraordinariness in a value sphere. It is the ideal of the whole individual. Both ideals react against the painful experience of being torn up by incompatible demands: of economy and the family, of political and justice considerations, of scientific and religious attitudes. In absolute love, as we have seen, the individual can act as a whole person and receive undivided and unconditional recognition. But this is a way that, though in principle open to everyone, in fact will be open only to a minority. So is it true that Cartesian modernity will not give us a fair chance of acting as whole persons?

No doubt there are tensions between the spheres. But looking closer at them we can see that if they tear individuals up, they do not because the spheres are incompatible but misunderstood. To take the example of the tension between science and religion, it arises only if religion is understood as a salvation religion that asserts views on the universe in a conceptual language that contradicts the views of science. This incompatibility is dissolved once we see that such assertions have to be abandoned. Similarly, the tension between politics and justice spring from claims of politics that need to be rejected. Any clash between politics and justice has to be solved in favor of justice.

Another example is the tension between economy and family. Economy demands of the agent to pursue her own profit, family forbids it. This is a tension that cannot be abolished. The family is the sphere of friendship and love (at least to the children); when we choose it, we commit ourselves to abandon the egoism of economic activities. But the economic activities, though they pursue the agent's profit, in the end are not egoistic if they produce wealth part of which is siphoned off by taxes to fund the public institutions of regenerating natural resources, education, and a basic income. If people can be sure that economic activities produce public wealth, the unavoidable tension between self-directed and other-directed attitudes in economy and the family can be well borne.

But it is true that Cartesian modernity offers opportunities for enacting extraordinariness in value spheres; hence, apart from absolute love, does not give everyone a fair chance of acting as a universally developed individual. However, the double ideal of the universally developed and the whole individual who acts independently of the spheres remains attractive. Where does its attraction come from? If we look at Marx, who followed the first ideal, we find that he hoped future society would "replace the detail-worker of to-day, crippled by life-long repetition of one and the same trivial operation, and thus reduced to the mere fragment of a man, by the fully developed individual."[1] He even proclaimed that until now, man,

> is a hunter, a fisherman, a herdsman, or a critical critic, and must remain so if he does not want to lose his means of livelihood; while in communist society ... each can become accomplished in any branch he wishes, society regulates the general production and thus makes it possible for me to do one thing today and another tomorrow, to hunt in the morning, fish in the afternoon, rear cattle in the eve-ning, criticise after dinner, just as I have a mind, without ever becoming hunter, fisherman, herdsman or critic.[2]

For Marx an individual is "fully developed" if he is "fit for a variety of labours, ready to face any change of production"; the "different social functions he performs, are but so many modes of giving free scope to his own natural and acquired powers."[3] The attraction of this ideal arises from the delight indi-viduals take in choosing any activity that suits their capabilities. But if we choose to be a hunter, a herdsman, a critic at the same time, we shall be imper-fect everywhere. The delight in the free choice will be outweighed by the dis-pleasure at the poor quality of our performance. So we have a reason to prefer specialization as the means fpr perfection. But shall we not be crippled, one-dimensional creatures by becoming specialists?

Marx was right that most of the activities open for choice today narrow our perspective on life and the world. But he was wrong in expecting that the

---

[1]   Marx, *Capital*, vol. 1, transl. Moore and Aveling; chap. 15, sec. 9 (The Factory Acts). (MEW 23, 512).

[2]   Marx, *The German Ideology*, transl. C. Dutt and C. P. Magill, Pt. 1, A, sec. *Private Property and Communism*. Fukuyama, *The End of History and the Last Man*, 355, says this "vision ... was (not) meant seriously."

[3]   Marx, *Capital*, vol. 1, transl. Moore and Aveling; chap. 15, sec. 9 (The Factory Acts). (MEW 23, 512).

more activities we perform, the less crippled we become. Activities cripple not because they are performed exclusively but because they fetter our attention in one direction only. They are performed, as Marx says, as a "social function." As long as they are thus understood, they prevent acting for the sake of a cause that is beyond a social function. It is only when we act beyond a social function that our activities become liberating rather than crippling. We do so in the value spheres, in particular of the nonserving spheres. They are inexhaustible and exclude crippling. The deeper we enter into them, the richer we become.

How about the attraction of the ideal of the whole and wholly recognized individual? It was for this ideal that Carl Schmitt became an intransigent critic of liberalism. "Liberalism," he claims, "not only recognizes with self-evident logic the autonomy of different human realms[4] but drives them toward specialization and even toward complete isolation."[5] Such isolation he regards as the easiest way to the universal subjection of life to economy. As he says, not much different from what Arendt taught later, it "is the surest and most comfortable way to the general economization of intellectual life and to a state of mind which finds the core categories of human existence in production and consumption."[6] Yet unlike Arendt, to escape it, he defines the political as a sphere ruled by the opposition of friend and foe rather than by reference to public affairs or a common good.

Schmitt's definition allows using politics as a means to trump sphere autonomy. Political actions are the only ones that require recognition of a person, not for some particular capability or perfection but as a whole person – as nothing but a friend or a foe. The political becomes the sphere of an opposition between enemies that are divided by an "existential" difference. The opposition "denotes the utmost degree of intensity of a union or separation," but is neither economic nor moral. Its content is only that the other is "the stranger; and it is sufficient for his nature that he is, in a specially intense way, existentially something different and alien." Whether someone is a stranger cannot be decided by any objective criteria; rather, "Only the actual participants can correctly recognize, understand, and judge the concrete situation and settle the extreme case of conflict. Each participant is in a position to judge whether the adversary intends to negate his opponent's way of life and therefore must be repulsed or fought in order to preserve one's own form of existence."[7]

It is sufficient for me to declare you someone who threatens my "own form of existence," even though there are no moral, political or any other differences,

4   Schmitt uses the term *Sphären* (spheres); it is improbable that he did not want to allude to and criticize Max Weber's idea of "Wertsphären" and his liberalism, which were well known when Schmitt wrote his article.
5   Carl Schmitt, *The Concept of the Political*, 72. For "drives," Schmitt uses the term *übertreibt* (exaggerates).
6   Ibid. 84.
7   Ibid. 26f.

to be justified in "repulsing" you with "the utmost degree of intensity." Schmitt most probably thought of the Jews as such existential foes; in any case, the Nazis proceeded in the very way Schmitt had proposed. They killed the Jews not for some objective difference but because they had declared them foes in Schmitt's sense.

True, the use Schmitt made of the idea of the whole, undivided individual shows not that the idea is corrupt but that it is corruptible. However, it shows that, first, sphere autonomy protects individuals from attacks motivated by reasons – economic competition and differences of background, in the case of the Jews – that the attackers are ashamed of avowing; second, that, as Schmitt claims, acting and being recognized as a whole, undivided individual requires a situation of an "extreme case" indeed, because the whole individual is challenged in extreme situations. The extreme case, though, need not be one "of conflict," as Schmitt thought. Obviously it can also be one of absolute love when individuals risk their life no less than in war.[8] But absolute love and war are only the most conspicuous cases of sacrifices for a cause. In fact, we act as undivided individuals whenever we act for a cause we are ready to sacrifice our life for. That is what we are whenever we live for a value sphere.

However, though Schmitt's attack on sphere autonomy turns into its defense if only we look a little closer at it, isn't it true that sphere autonomy promotes a departmentalization of life, the recognition of experts and specialists but not of personalities, so that, as Nietzsche and Weber complained, people become "experts without spirit and epicures without heart"?[9] This is again a misunderstanding of the nature of value spheres. Commitment to a sphere does not abate spirit and heart, it raises them. Only if sphere activities remain superficial, as they often do in contemporary society because people are forced to be active in spheres they are not talented for nor interested in, do experts without spirit and epicures without heart abound.

But the suspicion against sphere autonomy is perhaps not sufficiently expressed by the Weber citation, because it is too abstract. Let us take up the more concrete concern that modernity is ruining the family. This is a disaster for the children, but by implication for our civilization. I have proposed the reduction of the family to the aim of child rearing and its separation from the sphere of sexuality. Isn't this intolerable? Isn't it a scandalous splitting of men and women into fragmented personalities? Allan Bloom argued that if families are not recognized as the home of both sexual love between the parents and nonsexual love between parents and children, they will break up and children will be the victims. Isn't this obvious? Let's look at his argument.

---

[8] Cp. note 3 in Chapter 19 on Schmitt.

[9] Weber, *Die protestantische Ethik*, Gesamm. Aufs. zur Religionssoziologie vol. 1, 204; ed. Kröner, 380: "Fachmenschen ohne Geist, Genußmenschen ohne Herz." Weber alludes to similar remarks in Friedrich Nietzsche, *Thus Spake Zarathustra*, Preface, sec. 5.

Bloom agrees that sexual freedom, and by consequence the separation of the two traditional functions of the family, belongs to the "promise of modernity" but argues that "previously children at least had the unqualified dedication of one person, the woman, for whom their care was the most important thing in life. Is half the attention of two" – when parents split – "the same as the whole attention of one? Is this not a formula for neglecting the children?" He even finds "special handicaps, a slight deformity of the spirit, in the students, ever more numerous, whose parents are divorced ... I would guess this is because they are less eager to look into the meaning of their lives, or to risk shaking their received opinions."[10]

If this is true, the cause of such deformity is not the divorce but, as Bloom himself asserts, "the chaos of their experience" in their families that made them "tend to have rigid frameworks about what is right and wrong and how they ought to live."[11] But such a chaos will not arise if parents do not understand the end of their sexual love as the end of their duty to care for the children. Bloom overlooks that children also under "the unqualified dedication of one person, the woman" as well as under the unqualified dedication of both parents can get spoiled. Children do need love, but they also need models of adults they may strive after. It is sheer nostalgia or naiveté to suppose girls might strive after the model of a woman who sacrifices her life for "the unqualified dedication" of the next generation, so that again the female part of this generation will repeat the Sisyphean work.

If we stick to the idea that society is to be adapted to human capabilities, the family must be organized so as to meet as best as possible the task of child rearing. Assigning to the family the additional task of being the home for sexual life either overburdens it or deforms sexuality. Neither way is compatible with modernity. We may envy couples who are happy enough to retain their love over the years of their child rearing or longer. But lasting love cannot be the norm to build families on. Nor does it guarantee the best possible rearing of children. Parents who love each other do not necessarily care for their children with equal intensity.

For the best possible rearing, both social and ideological conditions must be met. To the social conditions belong institutions that help parents, whether they are couples, singles, or other constellations of adults, to perform their enforceable duty of caring for the children with joy. Children need to have the unconditional security of not only knowing that they are loved, but also that they are no burden to their families. They need to feel that they are welcome, a cause of joy, not of duty. For this, the best will of the parents is not enough. Parents need

[10] Bloom, *The Closing of the American Mind*, 114f, 128. He adds (128), "Under such arrangements the family is not a unity, and marriage is an unattractive struggle that is easy to get out of, especially for men."

[11] Ibid. 113.

the help of society. It is in child rearing that the dependence of the individual on society crops up most urgently. In fact, as Durkheim has pointed out, individuality presupposes socialization. If parents are relieved of some of their former tasks by individuals better talented and specialized in these tasks, they will perform their duties not as duties but as joys.

Already today daycares, kindergartens, and schools take over considerable parts of what formerly was a task of parents or their servants. If such institutions are staffed by the right persons and are easily accessible, they perform better than parents and their servants. Whether they do depends on the esteem, education, and salary a society grants them. Their easy access depends on their number and their locality. There should be no work places without crèches. Children who have always felt welcome will rarely show the deformity Bloom complains of. However, they may still be discontent and rebellious, as are many young despite all the love their milieu gave them. Bloom is mistaken in his presumption that "unconditional love" is all children need. What they need as badly is certainty about what they are needed for. This is why, for rearing the young, a society needs ideas, not only on how to rear them, but on what they are reared for.

As Hannah Arendt remarked, in education, parents "assume responsibility... both for the life and development of the child and for the continuance of the world," that is, their civilization. The "child requires special protection and care.... But the world, too, needs protection to keep it from being overrun and destroyed by the onslaught of the new that bursts upon it with each generation." It "is the peculiarity of modern society" – as understood by the utilitarian approach – "that it regards life... as the highest good; and for this reason, in contrast to all previous centuries, emancipated this life and all the activities that have to do with its preservation."[12] Yet the young, as every individual whose self is not corrupted, demand not life but extraordinariness. They crave for activities they can prove their selves in. If society does not offer them opportunities for their ambition, they "can't get no satisfaction." And even such offering is not enough. The opportunities need to be offered in the right spirit. The youth must grasp that they and their ambition of extraordinariness are needed for continuing this idea. They must understand that what is passed to them has "passed on as their most precious heritage from generation to generation," as Braudel describes a civilization.[13]

Far from proving the inner inconsistency or tragedy that Bloom, Nietzsche, and Weber before him, ascribe to modernity, the family proves the sphere that

---

[12] Arendt, "The Crisis in Education," in *Between Past and Future*, loc. cit. 185f, 187.

[13] Fernand Braudel, *A History of Civilisations*, 35. When I here argue that without opportunities for extraordinariness people "can't get no satisfaction," I do not imply utilitarianism (as did the Pope, cp. Chapter 22), but quote Mick Jagger, whose use of the words is far from a utilitarian argument.

shows the very strength and virtue of modernity. The West sprang from the rebellion against Sisyphean absurdity that consisted in a family life submerging the individual in the chain of generations. Though Bloom does not intend to restore the closed society, his critique implies this intention and, hence, the restoration of the Sisyphean absurdity, at least for the female part of mankind.

But Bloom's critique perfectly conforms to the utilitarian approach and the Lockean conception of the self as a subject constituted by consciousness and craving for happiness rather than extraordinariness. His nostalgia is dangerously infectious because the West did not emancipate itself from the utilitarian approach. Although in fact and deed its members act as Cartesian selfs act, the West still lacks the understanding of both the self and itself. Reflecting about how to solve what is called the family problem shows how badly we need clarity about the Cartesian nature of the self.

No one can guarantee that individuals will not be torn up by the challenges life presents them. Modern society is perhaps more complicated than closed societies are, but people shrink without challenges. What can be shown is that sphere autonomy tears individuals apart neither necessarily nor very probably.

Chapter 24

The End of History?

BY ITS PREVAILING UTILITARIAN SELF-UNDERSTANDING, THE WEST IS bound to judge that the end of history is reached when the institutional means to enable everyone to pursue their happiness are secured worldwide. The prevailing self-understanding is no longer utilitarian in the sense of equating happiness with a state of passive pleasures; it even includes liberty of action in the state it considers the highest good. But it is still utilitarian, as it understands life as the pursuit of (multidimensional) happiness rather than as the search for extraordinariness. Moreover, it is oriented to the serving value spheres and neglecting the nonserving ones. No wonder therefore that, when it became obvious that the Soviet empire would collapse, the end of history was declared in the West. Capitalist economy does provide the means to produce a society that satisfies utilitarian standards, if only by "tittytainment." Already two years before the collapse, Francis Fukuyama produced an interesting argument for the end but at the same time realized that something is wrong with the kind of liberalism that he too conceives in the utilitarian way.[1] He starts with rhetorical questions:

> Have we in fact reached the end of history? Are there, in other words, any fundamental 'contradictions' in human life that cannot be resolved in the context of modern liberalism, that would be resolvable by an alternative political-economic structure?

Showing that fascism and communism failed and the cravings of religious fundamentalism can be "successfully satisfied within the sphere of personal life

---

[1] Inspired by Alexandre Kojève and other critics of liberalism. Cp. my *The End of History or of Politics?* In Fukuyama and Huntington, forthcoming.

that is permitted in liberal societies," his answer is in the positive. But then surprisingly he states:

> The end of history will be a very sad time. The struggle for recognition, the willingness to risk one's life for a purely abstract goal, the worldwide ideological struggle that called forth daring, courage, imagination, and idealism, will be replaced by economic calculation, the endless solving of technical problems, environmental concerns, and the satisfaction of sophisticated consumer demands. In the post-historical period there will be neither art nor philosophy, just the perpetual caretaking of the museum of human history. I can feel in myself, and see in others around me, a powerful nostalgia for the time when history existed. Such nostalgia, in fact, will continue to fuel competition and conflict even in the post-historical world for some time to come. Even though I recognize its inevitability, I have the most ambivalent feelings for the civilization that has been created in Europe since 1945, with its north Atlantic and Asian offshoots. Perhaps this very prospect of centuries of boredom at the end of history will serve to get history started once again.[2]

How can we accept a state as the end of history that will give us so little satisfaction, in particular, no opportunity for the "struggle for recognition" that we analyzed as a form of the ambition of extraordinariness? Only one year later, Bernard Lewis, in an analysis of the contemporary state of the "the religious culture of Islam," came to the conclusion that in this culture "we are facing ... no less than a clash of civilizations – the perhaps irrational but surely historic reaction of an ancient rival against our Judeo-Christian heritage, our secular present, and the worldwide expansion of both."[3] What he called the "Muslim rage" cannot be "resolved in the context of modern liberalism." Thus, Lewis criticized Fukuyama. Three years later Samuel Huntington confirmed Lewis's thesis.[4] Though by their thesis both of them warned against the very politics of military intervention that actually was pursued by the American government, in the end their thesis seemed to justify the politics, as in a clash of civilizations every Westerner has to stand up for the West.

At the same time, John Rawls, on a still more abstract level, was sketching a version of modern liberalism that implies the end of history, but without allowing for Fukuyama's nostalgia. He defends an "idea of a liberal democratic peace" that includes nonliberal but "decent" or "well-ordered" hierarchical peoples that, unlike "outlaw" or "rogue" states, respect law and order.

---

[2] Fukuyama, *The End of History?* sec. III and V. Note that he also finds "emptiness at the core of liberalism." In his book *The End of History and the Last Man*, his doubts become even stronger.

[3] B. Lewis, "The Roots of Muslim Rage." All quotations are from the section titled The Clash of Civilizations.

[4] Huntington, "The Clash of Civilizations?"

He imagines them to be "an idealized Islamic people named 'Kazanistan.'" Kazanistan is not "as reasonable and just as a liberal society." But as it is in some respects "enlightened," such peoples "should have the opportunity to decide their future for themselves."[5] The idea of a liberal democratic peace excluding "outlaws" and including "decent" nonliberals is based on what Rawls, following Raymond Aron, calls "satisfied peoples," peoples who are "satisfied and happy," "not swayed by the passion for power and glory, or the intoxicating pride of ruling." "Domination and striving for glory, the excitement of conquest and the pleasure of exercising power over others, do not move them against other peoples. All being satisfied in this way, liberal peoples have nothing to go to war about."[6]

Using the term *Augustan threshold* for describing an empire's transition from the phase of expansion to that of consolidation,[7] we might interpret both Fukuyama and Rawls on one side and Lewis and Huntington on the other as attempts to inspire a U.S.-led empire of the West to cross the Augustan threshold. While Fukuyama does not hide insight into less attractive aspects of the phase of consolidation but rejects the idea that there are serious dangers outside Western civilization, Lewis and Huntington point to such dangers but plead for a soft and chary consolidation. Rawls comes close to the idea of the Roman emperor Augustus, who succeeded in making the Roman society cross the threshold by assigning its empire the mission of securing peace to the world, the famous *Pax Romana* that justified and even sacralized Rome's ruling of the world.[8] Interesting though these efforts are, they do not sufficiently take account of the ambition of extraordinariness.

Rawls, and also Fukuyama, as far as he allows himself to think that the struggle for recognition can be abandoned, are wrong in believing that rational people will stop striving for glory and the excitement of conquest and that "the struggle for recognition, the willingness to risk one's life for a purely abstract goal" and "daring, courage, imagination, and idealism," will and can "be replaced by economic calculation, the endless solving of technical problems, environmental concerns, and the satisfaction of sophisticated consumer demands." This striving can only be stopped by drugs or genetic engineering. "What makes peace among liberal democratic peoples possible is the internal nature of peoples as constitutional democracies and the resulting change of the motives of citizens," says Rawls.[9] He understands the change as the end of "passions for power and glory" that only "move a nobility and lesser aristocracy to

[5] J. Rawls, *The Law of Peoples*, 75, 83, 78, and 85.

[6] Ibid. 46f. The book is the rewriting of the Oxford Amnesty Lecture Rawls held in February 1993.

[7] Introduced by Michael Doyle, *Empires*, Cornell University Press 1986, and amply used by Münkler, 2007.

[8] As pointed out by Münkler, *Empires*, 84ff.

[9] Rawls, *The Law of Peoples*, 29 n.

earn their social standing and place in the sun."[10] What a pious wish. Power and glory are not passions of a "lesser aristocracy" but of everyone. The life of satisfied peoples Rawls envisions is indeed a "prospect of centuries of boredom." Rather than produce peace it "will serve to get history started once again," with all its wars and atrocities.

Only if the ordinary fields of glory and conquest, rather than being despised, move from the state and economy to art and philosophy and the other nonserving spheres, will the tiresome history of wars be replaced by a more interesting history of the ambitious self. One condition for a peace that is not the peace of the churchyard is to use, rather than abandon, the passions of ambition for the defense of never-secure peace and liberty. Another is a social constitution that offers as broad a spectrum of value spheres as possible so everyone finds a constructive way to excel.

Value spheres would even solve Fukuyama's problem that liberal democracies give recognition to everyone only by recognizing their human rights but not the more vital recognition that comes from groups and is neither equal nor democratic.[11] Value spheres are the space for such vital recognition, as the recognition they grant is based on the degree of perfection attained by sphere-specific actions, and hence, is neither equal nor democratic. If there is a mission for the West, it is the institution of a state-independent and globalizable set of value spheres that hinge around the nonserving spheres.

[10]   Ibid. 47.
[11]   Fukuyama, *The End of History and the Last Man*, 334f.

Select Bibliography

Th. W. Adorno, *Prisms*, transl. S. and S. Weber, Cambridge, MA: MIT, 1967.

Hannah Arendt, *The Origins of Totalitarianism*, San Diego: Harvest, 1973 (1st ed. 1951).

Hannah Arendt, *The Human Condition*, University of Chicago Press, 1958.

Hannah Arendt, *Between Past and Future*, Ithaca, NY: Cornell University Press, 1954.

Hannah Arendt, *Eichmann in Jerusalem*, A Report on the Banality of Evil, New York: Penguin, 1963.

Hannah Arendt, *Crises of the Republic*, San Diego: Harcourt, 1972.

Hannah Arendt, *Men in Dark Times*, San Diego: Harcourt Brace, 1983.

Hannah Arendt, *Lectures on Kant's Political Philosophy*, ed. R. Beiner, University of Chicago Press, 1982.

Hannah Arendt, *The Promise of Politics*, New York: Schocken, 2005.

Aristotle, *Metaphysics, Text with introduction and commentary,* ed. D. Ross, 2 vols., Oxford: Clarendon, 1958.

Aristotle, *Nicomachean Ethics*, English transl. H. Rackham, Cambridge, MA: Harvard University Press (Loeb's Classical Library), 1934.

Aristotle, *Nicomachean Ethics*, transl. and ed. T. Irwin, Indianapolis: Hackett, 1999.

Aristotle, *Politics*, English transl. H. Rackham, Cambridge, MA: Harvard University Press (Loeb's Classical Library), 1944.

Muhammad Asad, *Islam at the Crossroads*, orig. New York 1934, Arab transl. 1941, Islamic Book Trust, 1982.

Peter Awn, *Satan's Tragedy and Redemption: Iblis in Sufi Psychology*, Leyden: Brill, 1983.

Jeremy Bentham, *Introduction to the Principles of Morals and Legislation* (1789), in J. St. Mill, *Utilitarianism*, ed. M. Warnock, Glasgow: Collins, 1962.

Harold Berman, *Law and Revolution*, Cambridge, MA: Harvard University Press, 1983.

Allan Bloom, *The Closing of the American Mind*, New York: Simon & Schuster, 1989.

Fernand Braudel, *A History of Civilizations*, New York: Lane, 1994 (orig. 1963).

Allen Buchanan, *Justice, Legitimacy, and Self-Determination. Moral Foundations for International Law*, Oxford University Press, 2004.

Giacomo Casanova, *History of My Life*, vol. 1, Baltimore, MD: John Hopkins University Press, 1966.

Shaohua Chen and Martin Ravallion, "How Have the World's Poorest Fared since the Early 1980s?" *World Bank Research Observer* 19(2), 2004.

Amy Chua, *World on Fire: How Exporting Free Market Democracy Breeds Ethnic Hatred and Global Instability*, New York: Anchor Books, 2004.

Cicero, *On Duties*, eds. M. T. Griffin and E. M. Atkins, Cambridge: Cambridge University Press, 1991.

Fred Dallmayr, "Sunyata East and West, Emptiness and Global Democracy," in F. Dallmayr, *Beyond Orientalism*, Albany, NY: State University of New York Press, 1996.

René Descartes, *Œuvres complètes publiés par Charles Adam et Paul Tannery*, 12 vols., Paris: Cerf, 1897.

René Descartes, *The Method, Meditations and Philosophy of Descartes*, transl. J. Veitch, Washington and London: Dunne, 1901.

Richard M. Dorson, "The Eclipse of Solar Mythology," *Journal of American Folklore* 68, 393–416, 1955.

Michael Doyle, *Empires*, Ithaca, NY: Cornell University Press, 1986.

Hal Draper, "The Death of the State in Marx and Engels," *Socialist Register* vol. 7, 281–307, 1970.

Peter F. Drucker, *The End of Economic Man. The Origins of Totalitarianism*, New Brunswick NJ: Transactions, 1995 (orig.1939).

Peter Drucker, *The Future of Industrial Man*, New Brunswick NJ: Transactions, 1995 (orig. 1942).

Peter F. Drucker, Isao Nakauchi, *Drucker on Asia*, Oxford: Butterworth, 1997.

Freeman Dyson, *Infinite in All Directions*, New York: Harper, 1988.

Freeman Dyson, *The Sun, the Genome, and the Internet*, New York: Oxford University Press, 1999.

Freeman Dyson, "Our Biotech Future," *New York Review of Books*, 2007.

Brian Ellis, *The Philosophy of Nature. A Guide to the New Essentialism*, Montreal: McGill-Queen's University Press, 2002.

Epicurus, *The Extant Remains*, ed. C. B. Bailey, Oxford: Clarendon, 1926.

Richard Feynman, *The Character of Physical Law*, Cambridge MA: MIT Press, 1967.

Johann Gottlob Fichte, *Die Staatslehre oder über das Verhältniss des Urstaates zum Vernunftreiche*, in Sämmtliche Werke, hg. J. H. Fichte, Bd. 4, Berlin: Veit und Co., 1845.

Norman Ford, *When Did I Begin?*, Cambridge: Cambridge University Press, 1989.

Sigmund Freud, "Vorlesungen zur Einführung in die Psychoanalyse." Neue Folge, in *Freud-Studienausgabe* Bd. 1, Frankfurt: Fischer, 1969.

Francis Fukuyama, "The End of History?" *The National Interest*, Summer 1989.

Francis Fukuyama, *The End of History and the Last Man*, New York: Free Press, 1992.

Francis Fukuyama, *After the Neocons*, London: Profile, 2007.

Jonathan Glover, *What Sort of People Should There Be?*, New York: Penguin, 1984.

Robert Goodin, "Globalising Justice," in D. Held and M. Koenig-Archibugi eds., *Taming Globalization*, Cambridge: Polity, 2003.

John Gray, "The Moving Target," *New York Review of Books*, 2006.

Jürgen Habermas, *Theorie des kommunikativen Handelns*, Frankfurt: Suhrkamp, 1981.

Jürgen Habermas, *Erkenntnis und Interesse*, Frankfurt: Suhrkamp, 1973.

Jürgen Habermas, *Die postnationale Konstellation*, Frankfurt: Suhrkamp, 1998.

Michael Hardt and Antonio Negri, *Empire*, Cambridge, MA: Harvard University Press, 2000.

L. E. Harrison and S. Huntington, eds., *Culture Matters*, New York: Basic Books, 2000.

Vaclav Havel, *Or Living in Truth*, Boston: Faber, 1987.

G. W. F. Hegel, "Grundlinien der Philosophie des Rechts," in Werke 7, eds. E. Moldenhauer and K. M. Michel, Frankfurt: Suhrkamp, 1970.

G. W. F. Hegel, *Phenomenology of Mind*, transl. J. B. Baillie, New York: Harper, 1967.

G. W. F. Hegel, *The Philosophy of History*, transl. J. Sibree, Kitchener, Ontario: Batoche Books, 2001.

Martin Heidegger, *Being and Time*, transl. J. Macquarrie and E. Robinson New York: Harper, 1962.

Gustav Hempel and Paul Oppenheim, "Studies in the Logic of Explanation," *Philosophy of Science* 15, 135–75, 1948. Reprinted in C. G. Hempel, *Aspects of Scientific Explanation and Other Essays in the Philosophy of Science*, New York: Free Press, 1965.

Edward Herman and Noam Chomsky, *Manufacturing Consent: The Political Economy of Mass Media*, New York: Pantheon, 1988.

Thomas Hobbes, *Leviathan*, ed. C. B. Macpherson, New York: Penguin, 1968.

Max Horkheimer and Theodor W. Adorno. *Dialectic of Enlightenment*, transl. J. Cumming, New York: Continuum, 1998 (orig. 1944).

David Hume, *A Treatise of Human Nature*, bk. 3, pt. 2, sec. 2, ed. Nidditch, Oxford: Clarendon, 1978.

Samuel Huntington, "The Clash of Civilizations?" *Foreign Affairs* 72(3), 22–49, 1993.

Samuel Huntington, "If Not Civilizations, What?" *Foreign Affairs* 72(5), 186–94, 1993.

Samuel Huntington, "The West: Unique, Not Universal," *Foreign Affairs* 75(6), 28–46, 1996.

Ronald Inglehart, *Culture and Democracy*, in L. E. Harrison and S. Huntington, eds., *Culture Matters*, New York: Basic Books, 2000.

John Paul II, Encyclical letter Fides et ratio, September 14, 1998.

Hans Jonas, *Organismus und Freiheit. Ansätze zu einer philosophischen Biologie*, Göttingen: Vandenhoeck, 1973.

Hans Jonas, "Der Gottesbegriff nach Auschwitz. Eine jüdische Stimme" (1984), in *Philosophische Untersuchungen und metaphysische Vermutungen*, Frankfurt: Suhrkamp, 1992.

Hans Jonas, *Technik, Medizin und Ethik. Zur Praxis des Prinzips Verantwortung*, Frankfurt: Suhrkamp, 1985.

Immanuel Kant, *Kritik der reinen Vernunft*, ed. R. Schmidt, Hamburg: Meiner, 1930.

Immanuel Kant, *Metaphysik der Sitten*, ed. Vorländer, Hamburg: Meiner, 1954.

Immanuel Kant, *Kritik der Urteilskraft*, ed. Vorländer, Hamburg: Meiner, 1959.

Immanuel Kant, *Critique of Judgment*, transl. J. H. Bernard, London: Macmillan, 1914.

Immanuel Kant, *Idea for a Universal History*, transl. L. W. Beck, in I. Kant, *On History*, Indianapolis: Bobbs-Merrill, 1963.

Immanuel Kant, *Grundlegung zur Metaphysik der Sitten*, ed. Vorländer, Hamburg: Meiner, 1962.

Rudyard Kipling, "The White Man's Burden," *McClure's Magazine* 12 (Feb.), 1899.

Alexandre Kojève, *Introduction to the Reading of Hegel*, Ithaca, NY, Cornell University Press, 1980.

David Landes, *The Wealth and Poverty of Nations*, London: Little, Brown, 1998.

G. W. Leibniz, *Die philosophischen Schriften*, ed. C. J. Gerhardt, vol. 5, Berlin: Schmidt, 1982.

Bernard Lewis, "The Roots of Muslim Rage," *Atlantic Monthly*, (Sept.), 47–60, 1990.

Benjamin Libet, "Do We Have Free Will?" *Journal of Consciousness Studies* 6 (8–9), 47–57, 1999.

Georg Christoph Lichtenberg, *Schriften und Briefe*, 2 vol., ed. W. Promies, Darmstadt: Wissenschaftliche Buchgesellschaft, 1968/1971.

John Locke, *An Essay Concerning Human Understanding*, ed. Nidditch, Oxford: Clarendon, 1975.

John Locke, *Two Treatises of Government* II, §§ 6 and 27, ed. P. Laslett, Cambridge: Cambridge University Press, 1960.

Bernard Mandeville, *The Fable of the Bees: Or, Private Vices, Publick Benefits*. ed. F. B. Kaye, 2 vols., Oxford: Oxford University Press, 1957 (orig 1924).

Hans-Peter Martin and Harald Schumann, *Die Globalisierungsfalle. Der Angriff auf Demokratie und Wohlstand*, Reinbek bei Hamburg: Rowohlt, 1998.

Karl Marx, *Capital*, vol. 1, transl. S. Moore and E. Aveling, Chicago: Kerr, 1906.

Karl Marx, "Formen die der kapitalistischen Produktion vorhergehn," in *Grundrisse der Kritik der politischen Ökonomie*, Berlin: Rohentwurf, 1974.

Karl Marx, *Grundrisse*, transl. M. Nicolaus, New York: Penguin, 1973.

Karl Marx and Friedrich Engels, *Werke*, Berlin: Dietz, 1956–1968 (often abbreviated as "MEW").

Karl Marx and Frederick Engels, *Selected Works*, Moscow: Progress Publishers, 1969.

Karl Marx and Frederick Engels, *Manifesto of the Communist Party*, transl. Samuel Moore in *Selected Works*, vol. 1, Moscow: Progress Publishers, 1969.

Jessica Tuchman Mathews, "Power Shift," *Foreign Affairs* 76, January/February 1997.

John Stuart Mill, "On Liberty," in *Utilitarianism*, ed. Mary Warnock, Glasgow: Collins, 1962.

Ludovicus de Molina, *Liberi Arbitrii cum Gratiae Donis, Divina Praescientia, Providentia, Praedestinatione, et Reprobatione, Concordia*, Antwerp: Trognaesius, 1595.

Herfried Münkler, *Empires*, Cambridge: Polity, 2007 (German ed., 2005).

V. S. Naipaul, *India. A Million Mutinies Now*, New York: Viking Penguin, 1990.

Friedrich Nietzsche, *On the Genealogy of Morals and Ecce Homo*, ed. W. Kaufman. New York: Vintage, 1989.

Friedrich Nietzsche, *Thus Spake Zarathustra*, transl. T. Common (1891), Radford: Wilder, 2008.

Friedrich Nietzsche, *Sämtliche Werke. Kritische Studienausgabe*, ed. G. Colli und M. Montinari, München: dtv, 1980.

Robert Nozick, *Anarchy, State, and Utopia*, New York: Basic Books, 1974.

Nussbaum, Martha, *Women and Human Development*, Cambridge: Cambridge University Press, 2000.

James Olds and Peter Milner, "Positive Reinforcement Produced by Electrical Stimulation of Septal Area and Other Regions of Rat Brain," *Journal of Comparative Physiological Psychology* 47, 419–27, 1954.

David Papineau, "The Rise of Physicalism," in C. Gillett and B. Loewer, *Physicalism and Its Discontents*, Cambridge: Cambridge University Press, 2001.

Philippe van Parijs, *Real Freedom for All*, Oxford: Oxford University Press, 1995.

Philip Pettit, "A Republican Right to Basic Income?" *Basic Income Studies* 2, 1–8, 2007.

Plato, *Republic*, transl. G. M. A. Grube, in *Plato, Republic*, Indianapolis: Hackett, 1992.

Thomas Pogge, *World Poverty and Human Rights*, Cambridge: Polity, 2002.

Karl Polanyi, *The Great Transformation*, New York: Farrar and Rinehart, 1944.

Karl Popper, *The Open Society*, London: Routledge (Jubilee ed.), 1995.

Karl Popper, *Objective Knowledge*, Oxford: Clarendon, 1979.

Sandra Pralong, "Minima Moralia. Is There an Ethics of the Open Society?" in I. Jarvie and S. Pralong, eds., *Popper's Open Society after Fifty Years*, London: Routledge, 1999.

W. Prinz, "Freiheit oder Wissenschaft," in M. v. Cranach und K. Foppa, eds., *Freiheit des Entscheidens und Handelns*, Heidelberg: Asanger, 86–103, 1996.

Sayyid Qutb, *Social Justice in Islam*, Islamic Publications International, 2001 (orig. 1949).

Seyyid Qutb, *Milestones*, Damascus: Dar al-Ilm, no date given (orig. 1965).

Tariq Ramadan, *Western Muslims and the Future of Islam*, New York: Oxford University Press, 2004.

John Rawls, *The Law of Peoples*, Cambridge, MA: Harvard University Press, 1999.

Martin Rees, *Our Final Hour, A Scientist's Warning: How Terror, Error, and Environmental Disaster Threaten Humankind's Future in This Century On Earth and Beyond*, New York: Basic Books, 2003.

Howard Robinson, *Perception*, London: Routledge, 1994.

Jacqueline de Romilly, *The Great Sophists in Periclean Athens*, Oxford: Clarendon, 1992.

Olivier Roy, *Globalized Islam*, New York: Columbia University Press, 2004.

Gilbert Ryle, *The Concept of Mind*, London, Hutchinson, 1949.

Max Scheler, *Die Stellung des Menschen im Kosmos*, Gesammelte Schriften Bd. 9: Bern: Francke, 1976.

Carl Schmitt, *The Concept of the Political*, ed. and transl. G. Schwab, University of Chicago Press, 2007.

Amartya Sen, *Development as Freedom*, Oxford: Oxford University Press, 1999.

Amartya Sen, *Commodities and Capabilities*, Delhi: Oxford University Press, 1999.

Anne-Marie Slaughter, *A New World Order*, Princeton: Princeton University Press, 2005.

Adam Smith, *The Wealth of Nations*, ed. A. Skinner, New York: Penguin, 1986 (orig. 1776).

George Soros, *The Alchemy of Finance*, New York: John Wiley, 1998.

George Soros, "Introduction to W. H. Newton-Smith," ed., *Popper in China*, London: Routledge, 1992.

Richard Stallman, *Free Software, Free Society*, Boston: GNU Press, 2002.

Hillel Steiner, *An Essay on Rights*, Oxford: Blackwell, 1994.

Hillel Steiner, "Liberty and Equality," *Political Studies* 29, 555–69, 1981.

Hillel Steiner, *Three Just Taxes*, in Ph. van Parijs, ed., *Arguing for Basic Income*, London: Verso, 1992.

Ulrich Steinvorth, *Freiheitstheorien der Philosophie der Neuzeit*, Darmstadt: Wissenschaftliche Buchgesellschaft, 1994.

Ulrich Steinvorth, *Kritik der Kritik des Klonens*, in J. S. Ach, G. Brudermüller, C. Runtenberg, Hg., *Hello Dolly?*, Frankfurt: Suhrkamp, 1998.

Ulrich Steinvorth, *Gleiche Freiheit*, Berlin: Akademie, 1999.

Ulrich Steinvorth, "Über den Anfang des menschlichen Individuums," *Jahrbuch für Wissenschaft und Ethik* 7, 165–78, 2002.

Ulrich Steinvorth, "Zur Legitimität des Klonens," in *Körper und Recht: anthropologische Dimensionen der Rechtsphilosophie.* ed. L. Schwarte, *München: Fink, 2003.*

Ulrich Steinvorth, "On Popper's Concept of an Open Society," in I. Jarvie, K. Milford, D. Miller eds., *Karl Popper: A Centenary Assessment*, vol. 1, London: Ashgate, 2006.

Ulrich Steinvorth, *IstdieEnzyklikaFidesetRatioeineHerausforderungandiePhilosophie,*in P. Koslowski, A. M. Hauk, eds., *Die Vernunft des Glaubens und der Glaube der Vernunft*, München: Fink, 2007.

Ulrich Steinvorth, *Wittgenstein über den Willen,* in Wilhelm Lütterfelds, ed., Das Sprachspiel der Freiheit, *Wittgenstein Studies* 16, 185–912, 2008.

Ulrich Steinvorth, *Zwei Wurzeln der Allmendebewegungen, eine Politik*, in S. Helfrich, ed., *Gene, Bytes und Emissionen*, München: Oekom, 2009.

Ulrich Steinvorth, *Reason and Will* in the *Idea for a Universal History and the Groundwork*, Festschrift für Volker Gerhardt (forthcoming).

Thomas Straubhaar, "Grundeinkommen: Nachhaltigkeit für den Sozialstaat Deutschland," *HWWI Update (*Mai), 2006.

Cass Sunstein, *republic.com*, Princeton: Princeton University Press, 2002.

Leonard Swidler, "Towards a Universal Declaration of a Global Ethic," *Dialogue and Humanism* 4 (4), 1993.

Charles Taylor, *Sources of the Self: The Making of Modern Identity*, Cambridge MA: Harvard University Press, 1989.

Ernst Tugendhat, *Vorlesungen zur Einführung in die sprachanalytische Philosophie*, Frankfurt: Suhrkamp, 1976.

Immanuel Wallerstein, *World Systems Analysis*, Durham and London: Duke University Press, 2004.

Max Weber, *Gesammelte Aufsätze zur Religionssoziologie*, 3 vols. Tübingen: Mohr, 1920–1921.

Max Weber, *Soziologie, universalgeschichtliche Analysen, Politik*, Stuttgart: Kröner, 1973.

Max Weber, "Parlament und Regierung im neugeordneten Deutschland," in *Gesammelte politische Schriften*, Tübingen: Mohr, 1958.

Steven Weinberg, *The First Three Minutes*, New York: Basic Books, 1977.

Steven Weinberg, *Dreams of a Final Theory*, New York: Vintage, 1994.

Bernard Williams, "The Macropoulos Case: Reflections on the Tedium of Immortality," in *Problems of the Self, Philosophical Papers 1956–1972*, Cambridge: Cambridge University Press, 1973.

Ludwig Wittgenstein, *Tractatus logico-philosophicus*, London: Kegan Paul, 1922.

Ludwig Wittgenstein, *Philosophical Investigations*, transl. G. E. M. Anscombe, Oxford: Blackwell, 1953.

Index